EVIL
Obsession

The Annie Cook Story

Nellie Snyder Yost

Copyright ©1991 by Nellie Snyder Yost. All rights reserved. No part of this publication may be reproduced, stored in a retrieval system, or transmitted in any form or by any means, electronic, mechanical, photocopying, recording, or otherwise, without the prior written permission of the author.

ISBN: 1-886225-28-1 (formerly 0-939644-84-3)

Library of Congress Catalog Number: 91-62601

Cover design: Noelle Kaplan, finedesign

Printed in the United States of America.

Acknowledgments

My sincere thanks to the workers at the Lincoln County courthouse, where I spent many days digging facts from voluminous records. Especially, I thank Anita Childerston and her staff, Clerk of the District Court; Betty Tatman and her staff, Register of Deeds; and Nadine Heath, County Clerk. They were always pleasant and helpful as they climbed ladders and hefted huge old tomes down to me, or searched long unused files (some of them charred from the great courthouse fire of 1923) for the documents I needed.

Wilma McFarland and her staff at the North Platte Public Library were equally helpful, as was Keith Blackledge of the North Platte *Telegraph*. I spent countless hours in both places, reading microfilmed newspapers of long ago, digging out everything that pertained to Annie Cook and her henchmen.

And there were the many folks, county officials and lay people, who supplied information and set me straight on technical details. County Judge Earl Morgan, the late Milton Murphy, attorney, and the late Samuel Diedrichs, were especially helpful. Many of the elderly people who shared their memories of Annie were only children when they knew the old woman, but not one had forgotten the fear he or she had felt for "the witch," as they called her. Mrs. Fred Anderson, Mrs. Harley Hood, Harvey Applegate and Claude Lindekugel were all of much assistance.

But most of all I appreciate the information given me by Joe Cook and Mary's daughter, Irene (Mrs. O. J.) Cotton. Without them I could not have written this book. The story that grew out of it all is hard to believe, though it is documented in every detail. It all happened.

Preface

This is a grim story, the tale of an insane woman's evil obsession that scarred and/or ruined the lives of many people, written in the hope that the facts set forth will awaken readers to their duty and obligation to report knowledge of any known abuse to the proper authorities and see that something is done to put an end to it. Do not "look the other way," and permit it to go on, as the people in this tale did.

At the time of Anna Cook's death, in the early '50s, and the probate of her estate, the local papers carried lurid stories of the goings on at the Cook Poor Farm. Soon afterward an acquaintance told me I should write a book about Annie, and introduced me to Joe Cook, the boy who grew up on the Poor Farm after Annie supposedly poisoned his mother, and who could tell me all about it.

Interested, I talked to Joe, and then went to call on Mary, Annie's niece. I shall never forget that afternoon. Mary, a sixtyish woman with a lined, care-worn face, came to the door of her modest northside home. I introduced myself and told her I wanted to talk about Annie Cook. A stricken expression came to her kindly face as she cried out, "Oh no, I can't talk about it. I don't even want to *think* about it." Her too evident pain made me regret that I had come. Apologizing, I turned away and started back to my car. Then she called me back. "Come in," she said, "I'll tell you what you want to know."

All that afternoon she poured out her memories of the years she had spent under her aunt's abusive hand and tongue, recalling the torture and starvation she had endured for sixteen years, telling me of the night she had run from Annie and her murderous butcher knife, to walk, barefoot, through the rain and darkness to town and help. The telling of it seemed to bring immense relief to the good woman, who had lived with it for so long.

But it took me days to recover from the horror of what I heard that afternoon. It was as if I had listened to a ghastly tale about medieval England or France. *I could not believe that such things had actually happened in western Nebraska, in my own Lincoln County, in the twentieth century in which I live.*

Over the years that followed, Joe told me more and more of what he remembered, and throughout the hours I spent with him I marvelled that his experiences had not turned him bitter, or emotionally twisted. Instead he seemed remarkably calm and composed, almost as if the unbelievable abuse he had undergone had happened to someone else.

In those early years of my initiation into Annie Cook's history, I realized that I could not write the story until the principle characters had all passed off the scene; all the county officials who had, actively or passively, aided and abetted Annie in her nefarious activities. However, I continued to question the people who had known her, and to collect information. Always, it seemed, they were eager to talk, to tell me what they knew.

As time went on and I finally prepared to write the book, I went to folks who had had a part in the story itself, such as the attorneys who had participated in the old woman's many court activities. Each time I approached such a person I feared being told he or she did not want to talk about it, that it was best kept quiet and forgotten. But this did not once happen. All the informants seemed willing, even eager, to tell me what they knew.

The result was a vast accumulation of notes and tapes, each helping to fill in the gaps, to complete the incredible tale of an evil woman and the hold she had on a county and its principle city for so many years. Of a woman who was not only greedy but who enjoyed hurting helpless people, whose insatiable ambition made her capable of alledgedly killing her own daughter, then using her insurance money to buy the farm she had long coveted.

Most of the people she so cruelly abused escaped her only by dying or running away; all but her gentle sister Lizzie. Though many knew of Annie's inhumane treatment of Liz, no one had the courage to oppose the powerful old woman and try to rescue the helpless sister. Only Annie's own death released the suffering Lizzie.

Much of the dialog in this story is taken directly from court transcripts, or quoted from informants I interviewed or the old newspapers I read. I have used the real names of the Cook family and of a few individuals who opposed Annie and her schemes. All other names have been changed to preserve the privacy, or avoid embarrassment, of the people involved.

Nellie Snyder Yost
North Platte, NE
June, 1991

Chapter 1

On the first day of June, 1923, an unseasonably cold, dreary, grey day, the Lincoln County commissioners moved their indigent wards to what would, for years thereafter, be known as the Cook Poor Farm. A pleasant place, with its big old farmhouse and barn shaded by tall cottonwoods and surrounded by orchards and gardens, it should have been a comfortable refuge for the county's unfortunate poor. That it was not—that it was, instead, to become a festering scandal in the community, was due to the woman, Annie Cook, who received the "patients" brought to the farm that day.

For the past half-century the facility responsible for the care of the county poor had been known as the County Hospital and Poorhouse, and the inmates as "patients." On the day of the move they numbered twelve: Two mothers, four children, and six men. The three members of the board of county commissioners arrived first in a little caravan, each bringing some of the patients in his car.

Annie Cook waited in the big, bare backyard between the house and the barn to receive them. A heavy, solidly built woman of about fifty, she wore a starched cotton dress over several petticoats and, due to the chill of the day, a shapeless, worn grey sweater. A baggy blue crocheted cap covered her head. With her loose-lipped mouth, sagging cheeks and slit eyes, she was quite unattractive, inspiring neither confidence nor admiration in the casual beholder. Yet two of the commissioners accorded her both deference and respect, tinged with a little fear.

The woman's money and power, *and* her eyes, commanded that attitude. Small, glinting, greenish eyes, their heavy lids drooped until they were mere slits. To the third commissioner, who had never seen her before, their narrow gaze seemed menacing and evil, even when she smiled her loose-lipped smile and spoke pleasantly.

Tall, lanky Harley Costin was the first member of the board to step out of his car and tip his hat to the woman, then nod, with a warm smile and a "Hi, Clara," to the round-faced, rather pleasant looking woman standing in the kitchen doorway. Gesturing toward the other two board members as they came up, he said, "Mrs. Cook, you already know Tom Cooper," nodding to a heavy-set man in a business suit (the other two wore denim pants and cotton work shirts), "but you ain't met Jess Evans, our new man on the board."

Evans nodded, and the woman narrowed her eyes even more as she squinted at the third commissioner, a lean man with keen, questioning blue eyes. Evans had voted against moving the county poor from the big old house in town where they had been comfortable and well-fed, and where the woman in charge had been kind to them. Now, as he looked at the woman in the yard, he was more convinced than ever that they were making a mistake. He didn't like her looks, nor the *feel* of her place.

Costin turned to his Ford roadster and motioned for the woman and child on its seat to get out. "This is Sarah Martin, the deaf and dumb woman I told you about, and her kid, little Joe," he explained to Annie. They all looked at the pair. The woman, about thirty, tall, slender and rather attractive, looked back at them with sad eyes. Her four-year-old son, with his dark eyes and mop of black hair, was a handsome, sturdy little fellow. Now, holding her child tightly by the hand, Sarah Martin stood uncertainly by the car, her worried eyes fastened on the older woman.

Costin went to the small carrier box on the back of his little car and lifted out a shabby old canvas telescope suitcase. Annie, turning toward the house, yelled, "Mary, Liz, get out here and help." Turning back to the commissioners, she jerked her head toward the woman in the doorway and introduced her to Cooper and Evans as "My daughter, Clara Cook." Clara smiled and nodded as two women slid past her through the door and hurried to the group in the yard.

One of the women, scarcely larger than a twelve-year-old child, looked old and bent; the other was younger and taller, both were thin and sharp-featured. The ill-clad pair wore men's heavy work shoes on their small feet; and both, it seemed to Jess Evans, had the manner of whipped dogs with their tails between their legs.

"My sister Liz and her daughter Mary," Annie introduced them, then ordered Liz to take Mrs. Martin's valise to her room. The older, smaller woman snatched the heavy case and headed for the house, followed by the woman and child.

Tom Cooper's five passenger Ford, second in the little caravan in the yard, carried another woman and three small children. "This is Mrs. Lucas and her family," Cooper told Annie. "Her husband's coming in the wagon." They all turned to look at the woman as she got out of the car. Probably twenty-five, she looked older. Her face, under straight, pale red hair, was care-worn and weathered. The year-old child she carried in her arms clung tightly to a dirty rag doll. A six-year-old boy came next, clutching the hand of a smaller sister. All of them looked as if they were about to cry. The commissioners helped them gather their sacks and bundles and Annie ordered Mary to see them to the house.

Next came the three walking patients in Evan's topless Ford touring car. A pathetic lot, one was thin and very lame; another was heavy and almost blind; the third, the youngest of the three, was so bent and crippled by rheumatism that he could barely get about. Annie waved them on to the woman in the doorway as Harley Costin announced, "Here comes Tim with the rest of 'em."

"Old Tim's made pretty good time on the road," he added. "We started him out early enough that he'd get here pretty soon after we did." He went on to explain to Annie that they had first considered hiring W. R. Munson's motor hearse, which also did duty as the city ambulance, but it was so narrow that it could accommodate only one person at a time. It would have had to make three trips to bring all the bedfast patients to the farm and, at ten cents a mile, would have cost the county $5.40. "Then old Tim Hannifin said he'd bring 'em all out at once for $2.50, so he got the job," the commissioner concluded as the city drayman turned into the lane and pulled his team to a stop at the end of the board walk leading to the kitchen door.

Wrapping his lines around the brake handle, the driver jumped down from his high seat and hurried to the back of his wagon. Annie and the commissioners followed him. "I'll get this here endgate right out," the little Irishman said. "Thought I'd best put it in so none of these poor buggers'd jolt out on the way here." He propped the endgate against a wheel and turned back to the wagon where three men lay on thin mattress pallets, their faces pinched and blue with cold and exhaustion.

"Well, let's get 'em unloaded," Costin said briskly. "Looks like they loaded this poor cuss in the casts last, so he'll have to come out first. Tim, you take one corner of his mattress and I'll take the other one and we'll ease him out. Tom and Jess, you catch the top end as we pull 'im out."

The red-haired woman came running out the door and joined the group at the wagon. "Charlie. How is he? Is he hurtin' bad?" she asked anxiously, and put out her hand to touch the man on the pallet. Annie pushed her back. "Just wait till we get 'im unloaded," she ordered. Then, noting the sympathetic glance Jess Evans gave the woman, she added, "The quicker we get these poor fellows to their beds, the better."

Charlie Lucas, in his early thirties, looked like a mummy in his casts and bandages. Horribly injured two weeks earlier in a runaway involving a county road drag and the six strong horses that pulled it, he had been without resources other than the job that had crippled him. The county, perforce obligated to care for him and his family until his many broken bones and lacerated muscles healed, had consigned him to the County Hospital and Poor Farm. Now the man gritted his teeth against the pain of every motion of the pallet as the four men carried him to his bed, his wife following helplessly, choking back her tears and watching Annie with frightened eyes.

The other two men in the wagon were merely old and ill, homeless and friendless. When the commissioners had gotten them into their beds, they made an inspection of the house. Costin, a friend of the Cooks, had been there often. The other two had never been on the place, but Costin's insistence that the move was a good one had persuaded Cooper to vote for it, though Evans had consistently voted against it.

The kitchen, a large room, was typical of farmhouse kitchens of the 1920s. Furnished with a long, oilcloth covered table, a Home Comfort cookstove, cupboards, and an iron sink with a pitcher pump at one end, it was lighted by a double width window in the west wall. Doubtless a cheerful enough place on a sunny day, it looked worn, dreary and forlorn that morning.

A square parlor and a bedroom opened off one side of the kitchen. On its other side were four bedrooms and a storeroom, divided by a narrow hallway down the middle. The small rooms were furnished only with paintless iron bedsteads and an old dresser or chest of drawers each. Not a chair or a table, or anything else to make them look comfortable or inviting.

Two of the bedfast men had been put into a double width bed, the injured man onto a cot beside it. To Evans there did not seem to be space enough around the beds to adequately care for the men in them. The room given the two mothers and their four children seemed equally crowded, with the women and the smallest child assigned the double bed and the other three children a narrow bed, two at the head and the other at the foot. In a third small room the three walking patients had a cot apiece. The fourth little bedroom belonged to Liz and Mary, Annie explained; and the front bedroom was her's and Clara's.

To Evans the place seemed impossibly crowded and depressing. All of the patients, especially the two mothers, looked worried, unhappy and frightened. "Yes," Evans thought, "there was certainly something baleful about that slit-eyed Annie Cook, though Costin and Cooper appeared to like her." And why, the third commissioner wondered, did those two poor, shabby woman in men's work shoes seem so scared, like whipped dogs with their tails between their legs?

Chapter 2

Annie had spent most of the long day on the train. For the first 100 miles her thoughts had been of the good time she'd had in Omaha; for the next 300 she had been busy with plans for the changes she meant to make when she reached home. Now, as the train neared the little town of Hershey, she had it pretty well figured out — she knew what she was going to do, and looked forward to it with relish.

All that fall she had felt quite unwell. When her nagging back pain defied the local doctors her husband, Frank, had insisted she go to Omaha to a specialist. Annie had held back, it would cost too much and they needed the money for other things. But Frank had gone to the bank for the money and told her to get ready.

She had met Jane in the waiting room on her first visit to the doctor, and Jane had changed everything. The doctor said she had a kidney dysfunction, prescribed some medicine and told her to come back in a week. "We can get a lot done in a week," Jane said, and proceeded to show her how.

Jane, thirtyish, slender, good looking and ambitious, had moved her from her cheap hotel to her own more pretentious establishment. There she met half a dozen other younger women who, like Jane, wore fashionable clothes and a great deal of makeup. That evening Jane introduced her to several men, mostly middle-aged, who seemed to have plenty of money.

Annie's new friend had quickly initiated her into the rites of rouge, lipstick, eyeshadow and mascara. The farm woman wasn't sure that she looked any better under all the cosmetics but she certainly looked different, more daring and — well, like the other girls at the hotel. Jane said she must have new clothes, too, something more in "style" than her twelve-year-old suit. Annie had admitted her need for new clothes but said she didn't have the money to buy them.

"You will have," Jane told her. "You take what you have and I'll loan you whatever more you need and we'll go shopping. You have a good figure. All it needs is dressing up." Jane selected the clothes, a new tan suit with a skirt that did not quite reach her ankles, a jacket with a smart flared peplum, and several blouses in bright colors.

The new clothes were in her suitcase now, back in the baggage car, but she would never dare wear them at home. That did not bother her, for she would be going back to Omaha again. Annie shifted her feet and made a little face at her floor-length grey wool skirt as she did so. The old fashioned thing had been a part of her wedding suit, twelve years ago, but it was still fashionable in Hershey, where she wore it only to church and to funerals.

Without a doubt the week—plus three more—she had spent in Omaha had been the most exciting and rewarding of her life. She'd made a fair amount of money, too, enough to pay Jane back and have a neat sum left over. The money made her feel good and she meant to have more, much more.

The train whistled for the Hershey stop and she put on her hat and gathered up her gloves and handbag. They were old, too, also a part of her wedding outfit, for she'd had little new since then. But things would be different now, even though she couldn't wear her fashionable new clothes at home because people would talk and Frank would wonder. But maybe it wouldn't matter now what Frank thought. She hadn't quite made up her mind what to do about him, or Clara, their eleven-year-old daughter.

The train ground to a stop and Annie moved forward with the two or three other passengers getting off in Hershey. On the top step she paused a moment, searching the little group of people awaiting the arrival of the evening local.

About five feet, four inches tall, she was slender and rather attractive, even in the old suit, for it set off her narrow, tightly corseted waist, straight shoulders and firmly rounded bust. Her head was well-poised on her slender neck and she had puffed her brown hair out around her face before she pinned it into its customary knot on the back of her head. In Omaha Jane had shown her how to crimp it with a curling iron and wear it in bangs across her forehead, a style entirely too daring for a thirty-one-year-old farm wife in Hershey, Nebraska, in the year of our Lord 1905.

Frank and Clara, anxious faces upturned, were watching for her. Frank Cook was a handsome man, six feet tall and well built. With his dark eyes and thick, dark hair and mustache, he was a man any woman could be proud of—and Annie sometimes wondered why he meant so little to her. Now she looked at him with actual distaste. He was dull, she thought. After the Omaha fellows, with their jokes, innuendos and laughter, he was just plain dull. And he had no ambition. Content with his fields and gardens, his Bible and his church, he wanted nothing more.

Annie's gaze shifted to Clara, a round-faced girl, rather large and well-developed for her eleven years. The child stirred little emotion in the mother, for she had never been really fond of her. But now, looking down at her daughter from the platform, she suddenly saw in her a new value — in two or three years she would be old enough to go to Omaha with her.

Annie descended the car steps to the depot platform, but when her husband and daughter would have embraced her she turned away, saying briskly, "Let's get started home. We're late enough as it is, with chores to do and supper to get."

On the two-mile drive home in the buggy Clara had many questions to ask and much to tell her mother. Then Frank broke in to say, "Annie, I'm afraid you didn't have enough money for such a long stay. I would've sent you more but you never sent me an address so I could."

"I had enough. I made it do," she told him.

"But did the doctor help you? How do you feel?" His face was anxious.

"I feel fine, but the doctor says it's a chronic thing, that I'll have to go back every now and then for more treatment."

Back at the farm Annie's sharp eyes saw nothing amiss. The poultry looked well cared for, the big garden had been plowed, the house seemed as clean and orderly as when she left it. Frank and Clara had done well, but she did not bother to tell them so.

It was well after dark by the time supper was over, the poultry fed and the cows milked. Clara still wanted to talk to her mother but Annie sent her to bed. "I've had a long day and I'm tired and want to go to bed myself," she told the disappointed little girl.

She undressed quickly, blew out the light and slid to the far side of the bed. When Frank came a little later, after he had read his Bible and made his last careful round of the barns and out-buildings, she lay rigid and quiet. It was as if she had raised a partition in the bed between them. She knew her husband felt it, and was hurt and puzzled by it, but she didn't care. It was going to be this way from now on and he'd just as well get used to it. If he wanted to stay where he was, satisfied with his little niche in life, let him, but he needn't expect her to stay there with him. She, Anna Cook, was going to be *somebody*, looked up to by the whole community.

In the still darkness her thoughts went back to when she had first seen Frank, at her home in Denver. Her parents were Russian Jews and she was one of several sons and daughters. Her father owned a large livery stable business in the city and everybody in the family worked, and worked hard.

She hadn't minded the work but she *had* resented the fact that she and her younger sister, Liz, never saw any of the money they helped earn. Their brothers were paid but they were not, and she had early felt a strong desire to possess money of her own. Liz, poor spineless thing, hadn't cared about the money. All she cared about was animals, especially horses. From early childhood she had liked working at the stables. Annie worked wherever she was told to, helping her mother in the big house, or her father and brothers in the stables. Work was work.

Twelve years ago, when she was nineteen, Frank Cook had made a trip to Denver to haul home supplies for the farm he had lately bought in the Platte Valley. When he pulled in at the big barn to stable his fine team for the night, her father and brothers had taken a liking to the tall farmer from Nebraska and invited him home to eat supper and stay all night, a privilege reserved for favored customers.

The young man had talked with her a good deal that evening, and the next, after spending the day buying and loading his supplies. She had learned that he owned a fine eighty-acre farm in the big valley, and the water right that went with it. The irrigation ditch crossed his farm, he said, and with water guaranteed he could be sure of a good crop, even in a dry year. He seemed to have a sort of reverence for the land, she noted, and for all a man could do with land if he took care of it.

So, when Frank came back and asked her to marry him, she had consented. She saw in him her means of getting away from her man dominated family, a means of owning something of her own; for she knew she'd be the dominant member of the family if Frank Cook was the other partner. They were married in Denver and she returned to Hershey with him, late in the winter of 1893. She was twenty years old.

Snug in her new husband's top buggy, under a lined horsehide lap robe, she had watched eagerly as the good looking trotter turned into the home lane of his own accord. The short lane led into a wide, bare back yard, where she had her first view of her new home, a long, narrow farmhouse, flanked by a sturdy horse barn, under tall, leafless cottonwoods.

Frank halted the buggy at the end of a neat board walk leading to the kitchen door and cramped the front wheels so he could help her out without fouling her long skirts on the wheel rims.

Most farmhouses of the period had front doors that were seldom used, and Frank's was no exception. The back door, handiest to the road, was the one to which he brought his bride. The house was a large one, a big kitchen, a parlor, five bedrooms and a storeroom. Her husband had bought the farm from a man who had a wife and ten children.

Annie had liked the place at first sight; under the proper management it would be a money maker. That summer she talked Frank into taking out a $1,500 mortgage. Hating debt, he had resisted. They could make a good living on the farm the way it was, he said. She had refused to give up. She wanted far more than a "good living," and she meant to have it.

With the money they built chicken houses and a cow barn, and bought laying hens and milk cows to fill them. That winter Annie bought books on raising poultry and studied them religiously.

Clara was born the following February. She had hated her months of pregnancy, especially the last three when she had been so awkward and heavy. Her labor had been long and difficult and Frank had been beside himself, first with fear, and then with joy when his plump little daughter finally arrived. She had been disgusted with him both ways, and she saw nothing remarkable in the fat red baby. She had hoped for a boy, another strong hand on the farm. A girl, however, would do almost as well; hadn't she always done as much work as her brothers?

She had made up her mind then that there would be no more children, and by the time she had gotten Clara past infancy she was doubly sure of it. The baby had been colicky for weeks, but it was Frank who walked the floor with her night after night. Neither had she bothered to change the infant's wet diapers often enough, or do anything about the severe rash that developed as a result. It was Frank who had gone to town for a can of baby talcum, and applied it to the suffering child every time he came to the house.

She did not remember that her husband had ever blamed her for any of the baby's problems. She was working as hard as he was, he said, what with caring for her growing poultry flocks—the several hundred baby chicks with which she'd twice filled the new brooder houses that spring, and the hundred turkey poults she'd bought. And always there was the milking, and then the churning; for she had worked up a good business in town with her superior butter and fresh cream and egg route.

They had made money that year. Their crops had been good and she had helped pick the corn, saving the price of a hired man. They had put the baby in the front end of the high wagon box, under the seat, where she napped and played while her parents kept up a steady tatoo of corn ears on the bangboard above her.

They had paid off a third of the mortgage when they sold the corn and holiday turkeys. She and Frank had worked far into the nights, dressing out those turkeys, but the check had been most satisfactory.

Mindful of the pond in the edge of the cow pasture south of the new barn, she had added ducklings to her poultry order the next spring, and some guinea hens. The guineas wouldn't help any financially, but the noisy, useless birds fascinated her. All had gone well until late July, when a savage hailstorm had wiped out their garden and most of their corn and potato crops. There was no payment on the mortgage that fall.

The next spring they had set out the orchard, nearly an acre of apple and cherry trees; and Frank had set out a row of lilac seedlings along the east yard fence. She told him they were a waste of time, but he said his mother had had lilacs in the yard of his old home in Ohio.

That year, and the next one, had been good, and in the fall of '98 they had paid off the mortgage.

"Now we can begin to plan to buy the Eighty across the road from us," she had told Frank as they left the bank.

"Yes, if that's what you want," he had answered in his quiet way.

Chapter 3

Annie's parents and Liz had come to visit, that fall of '98, just before corn picking. Annie hadn't seen them since her marriage, five years earlier, and they had never seen Clara. She had never felt close to her parents, and for Liz she had only contempt, but on this occasion she was pleased to see them and to catch up on family news.

The livery and dray business was still good, her father said, but a few of the new fangled gas buggies were now seen on Denver's streets. "They'll get bigger and better," he predicted, "and one of these days we won't be using so many horses." Annie's oldest brother and his half-grown sons were doing most of the stable work now, since the two younger brothers had gone into the ministry. Annie was astonished at that. Her brothers? In the ministry? But her parents seemed rather pleased; in the old country ministers were looked up to.

Liz was as quiet and shy as ever, but she was healthy, and strong in spite of her small size, and it crossed Annie's mind that she'd be good help to have around. She could milk cows, carry feed and water to the poultry houses, weed the gardens and pick turkeys. She might even be a good corn picker. The thought would bear looking into.

After supper Liz, always daft about babies, carried four-year-old Clara off to her room to put her to bed. The rest of them sat visiting around the kitchen table, and presently Annie's father said, "Frank and Annie, we want to talk to you about Liz. She don't care for men, outside the family, that is, and it don't look like she'd ever marry. Mother and I have been thinking about what we should do with her. Do you think you could give her a good home here?"

Before Annie could answer, he added, "It's not as if she won't have something. Emil, of course, will get the business, but he has his own home. So Liz will get the big house and whatever else is left. Everything but the business will be hers when Mother and I are gone."

"Of course," Annie said, trying to sound matter of fact about it. She had never expected it to be so easy. But her father was looking at Frank, awaiting his approval.

"Of course," he echoed his wife, "we'll be glad to give her a home as long as she...."

"In fact," Annie cut him off, "I've been thinking all evening that it would be nice to have Liz around. She can stay now, if you like, and you can send her things down after you get home."

But her father shook his head. They needed Liz to help her mother in the big house, he said, and to help Emil at the stables in rush times. He spoke in his old tone of dictatorial finality, the old-country tone of a man to his women folk that Annie hated. Even so, she was well pleased. One of these days she would have Liz — and Liz's inheritance. The prospect brought ownership of the second Eighty closer.

Liz came to Frank and Annie in the summer of 1900. Besides her clothes she brought with her only the old dark wood parlor clock her mother had brought from Russia a half-century ago, and her own little patented platform rocking chair.

She was still small, quiet and shy, although she had filled out a little and was quick and strong. Her short, curly dark hair framed a rather pretty little face and she wore small, sparkly earrings in her pretty ears. They were her one vanity, those twinkling ear bangles, though Annie would not let her wear them except on Sunday, when they all went to church.

Frank, who had helped organize the Methodist church in Hershey when he first came to the community, never missed a Sunday morning service. On Annie's first Sunday on the farm he had put on his wedding suit, hitched his trotter to the buggy and brought it to the end of the board walk. So Annie, although she didn't care for church and considered it a waste of time, put on her wedding clothes, hat and gloves, and accompanied him.

Practically everyone in the community except a few bachelors, she learned, went either to the Methodist church, or to the Catholic church in the other end of town. Frank had been proud to introduce her to his friends that day, the local banker, the postmaster, the storekeeper and several farmers and their wives. They were still going to church in the buggy, with Clara sitting on a folding "third seat" between them, when Liz came.

Since there wasn't room in the buggy for the four of them, the next Sunday morning Frank hitched a team to the wagon and they went in that. Most of the other farm families drove wagons to church, but Annie made up her mind that day to get a two-seated carriage as soon as she could manage it. The banker and his family came to church in a carriage as did the Cook's neighbors, Sam Russell and his family, from their prosperous dairy farm a half-mile up the road.

Life on the farm had not been too bad for Liz at first. Annie had put her in charge of the poultry houses, with six-year-old Clara to help, and the city girl had found the chickens, turkeys, ducks and guinea hens interesting and amusing. Then Annie said she must learn to milk, and that Clara was old enough to learn, too, and they could learn together. After that Frank and the girls did the milking and Annie quit helping in the barn.

Again Liz hadn't minded, for she liked all animals; and cows, she found, were almost as fascinating as horses. There were gentle cows and cross cows, smart cows and dumb cows. Liz made friends with them all.

Soon after her arrival Liz had started bringing in the mail from the rural mail box at the end of the lane. Annie had seen no reason to object, so Liz was always the first to see the day's mail. This was important to the girl, for she had brought a secret with her to the farm.

The previous spring a new customer, a tall man in boots and a wide-brimmed hat, had shown up at the stable one busy evening when Liz was helping out. She had shown him where to put his wagon in the stable yard and helped him unhook his teams. When she told him she'd care for the horses he had replied, smiling, that he'd help her. The horses fed and bedded, she took him to the office and introduced him to her father as "Joe Knox, from Nebraska."

The cowboy explained that he was from Hyannis, in the Sandhill ranch country, that his parents ran a hotel and livery stable in the little cow town and that they could buy their supplies in Denver, and freight them home, cheaper than they could buy them locally. He'd be loading up the next day and pulling out the following morning, he said, and Liz's father had then invited him to the big house for supper and lodging.

Joe Knox had made a second freighting trip to Denver before Liz went to Annie's, and she had told him that she'd be going to Nebraska soon. He'd been pleased. "Hershey is only about seventy-five miles from Hyannis," he said. "I'll be seeing you there."

Liz's parents had told Annie none of this. So used to thinking of Liz as their dependent little daughter who would never marry, they had paid no attention to her quiet friendship with the tall cowboy. Neither had Liz mentioned it to her sister — and with good reason. She remembered too well how, when they were girls at home, Annie had betrayed her little confidences, tattling to her parents, or her brothers, and getting her into trouble.

Now she feared that, if she told Annie about Joe Knox and their "understanding," she would again tell their father and he would put a stop to her seeing him again. She knew that their parent, with his old-country ways, had made up his mind that she was to live with Annie the rest of her life; and that in the homeland the men of the family disposed of their women folks futures as seemed best to them. So she told no one.

Now and then the mail brought a card or a letter from Joe. He told her he missed her and that he planned to see her before Christmas. She wondered fearfully if she could manage to see him without Annie knowing about it, or if she'd be able to see him at all. If he came while she was at work in the cornfield Annie would send him away and she wouldn't even know that he had been there.

Joe came on the Saturday before Christmas, and by then they had picked the corn and dressed the holiday birds. Those had been grueling days. Up well before dawn to milk the cows, care for the poultry and eat breakfast. With the grey light of day barely revealing the corn rows, they were in the field, their corn ears beating a rapid tatoo on the bangboards. At first Annie had gone to the field with them for a little while before going back to the house to get their noon and evening meals. After a few days she didn't go out with them any more.

By the time the corn was in the cribs it was time to dress the turkeys and ducks for the holidays. They had worked well into the nights, right up to Thanksgiving, and again until the week before Christmas. Hard, disagreeable work it was, and cold; for Frank and Liz picked and drew the birds in an open shed at the end of the barn, then carried them to the house where Annie went over them inch by inch, removing every tiny pinfeather. She meant that her holiday birds should be the best sold in North Platte.

Frank and Annie were in town, delivering butter, cream, eggs, and dressed poultry to Annie's customers when Joe came. Clara had gone with them. Her father was buying her a new pair of shoes and a hair ribbon for Christmas, and letting her pick them out.

Joe brought Liz a Christmas present, a pair of small, glittering earrings, and told her she looked "peaked." The weary girl cried over her gift, confessed that she had never worked so hard in her life, and told him what she had been doing.

The young man had whistled in astonishment. Such work would have been backbreaking for a man, he allowed, let alone a slip of a girl like Liz. Then he told her that he would come for her as soon as he could in the spring and they would be married. They would live in Hyannis and help his parents run the hotel and stable and she'd never have to work hard like that again. It was her cowboy's promise, and his letters, that kept Liz going the rest of that hard winter.

Chapter 4

The milk cows had freshened, the fields and gardens were planted and most of Annie's chicks, turkey poults and ducklings were well feathered out by the time Joe came for Liz. The girl could scarcely remember when she had had a good night's sleep, or when she hadn't been bone tired. Frank and Annie worked just as hard, and even Clara turned off a lot of work for a girl of seven. It was just that Annie's insatiable desire to get ahead, to own more land, drove them all to the limit of their strength.

When Joe had written that he'd be in North Platte on the evening of May 28, and that he'd meet her at the courthouse the next morning, he had been sure that she would find a way to be there. And she did—simply by walking away from her set task of cleaning the big chicken house while Annie was busy in the kitchen, working up the week's churning into neat moulds of butter for the Saturday deliveries.

Though the sun had not yet cleared the tops of the trees ahead of her as she hurried down the road toward town, the milking was done, the poultry tended, breakfast over and Clara doing the dishes. Meadow larks whistled from the tops of fence posts beside the road and the new green of corn tinged the fields, but Liz saw and heard nothing.

Excitement and fear raced through her veins—everything depended on her meeting Joe this morning.

Liz knew that she did not look like a bride on her way to meet her groom, but there was nothing she could do about it. There had been no chance to change into her Sunday dress and shoes, hidden in the haymow the night before; for Frank had decided to clean the barn that morning. Frank was her good friend and would probably have helped her get away from Annie, but she hadn't dared chance telling him. So her only preparation had been to slip her few pairs of precious earrings into her apron pocket before she left her room.

But it didn't matter, she told herself as she began to run. Nothing mattered but getting away. Joe would buy her new clothes and take care of everything if she could only make it to the courthouse. Looking over her shoulder often, she ran until a stitch in her side slowed her to a fast walk. One could never tell about Annie. She should be busy with the butter for the next two hours, but at any moment she was apt to take a notion to check outside to make sure Frank and Liz were not dawdling.

The girl had covered more than two miles when a farmer came along and offered her a ride in his wagon. When he tried to question her she retreated into her usual shyness and gave him no answer, until he asked her where she was going.

"To the courthouse," she said, and he nodded and replied, "Fine, I'm going there, too."

Joe was waiting in front of the tall old cupolaed building and Liz's heart lurched in relief. "I knew you'd make it," he said as he helped her out of the wagon. In spite of her worn, shabby dress and broken shoes, he thought she looked very pretty that morning, her dark eyes sparkling with excitement and her short brown curls framing her eager little face.

When she told him she'd had no chance to change into her good clothes, he had offered at once to buy her a new outfit to be married in, but Liz said no.

"Let's get married first," she insisted, "no matter how awful I look. If Annie get's here before we're married she'll stop us."

"Oh no she won't. I wouldn't let her," Joe said.

"You couldn't stop her," Liz told him, shivering. "No one could."

So they went into the courthouse, bought their license to wed, went across the hall to the office of the Justice of the Peace and were married. The day was May 29, 1901.

From the courthouse they went to a store and bought Liz some clothes, and when she had everything she thought she needed, Joe bought her a blue velvet bonnet. Back at the wagon, Joe pointed out the new canvas cover he'd put on it, just for this trip. They'd have to camp out a couple of nights on the way to Hyannis, he told her, and the covered wagon would be better than a tent. Liz admired the clean new cover, and then Joe proposed that they go to a restaurant to eat their wedding dinner before they started home.

Liz wouldn't hear to it. "We can eat something as we ride along," she said. The most important thing in the world, just now, was to put as much distance as possible between themselves and Annie. Joe chuckled indulgently and untied his team. As soon as they started Liz took her new bonnet out of its wrappings and put it on.

They ate cheese and crackers and a bag of peppermints as they rode along, but Liz was uneasy and looked over her shoulder often, even though she could see little of the road behind them through the small rear opening in the canvas wagon cover.

The North Platte River was near its spring high when they crossed it, its grey waters rolling dangerously close to the floor of the long,

Joseph and Lizzie Knox. Their wedding picture, 1901.

narrow wooden bridge, but Liz laughed with pleasure. She would feel safer with the wide, angry river behind them — between her and Annie.

They were soon in the sandhills, where Joe let his team trot on all the down slopes, making better time. Liz gazed with wonder at the green hills rolling endlessly away to where the blue sky met their tops. Their bareness astonished her. Denver and its surrounding mountains had been full of trees, and there were trees on every farm in the Platte Valley. Here there were none, just miles and miles of low hills sweeping away to the skyline.

They passed only one or two habitations, set far back from the road, and Joe told her this was ranch country, with many miles between the houses. Now and then they saw grazing cattle and once he pointed out a herd of antelope, flowing over a far hilltop in fluid motion. "These hills was full of antelope, only a few years back," he told her, "but now you don't see many. They've been hunted down to a few little bunches."

Joe had put a bedspring and mattress on the wagon overjet, and made up the bed with new blankets. Under the tight canvas cover, he said, they'd be warm in the chilly spring nights, and dry in case of a nighttime shower. As they ate their supper Liz said she had decided not to put on her new clothes until the day they would get to Hyannis.

"You've already seen me in these old things," she told her husband, "so I'll keep the new ones nice for when we get to the hotel and I meet your folks, but I'll wear my bonnet all the way." Joe was pleased, for her little face was pert and pretty beneath its sheltering velvet brim.

When they pulled into the little town of Hyannis on the third day, Joe turned to grin at Liz, all decked out in her new clothes. "Well, honey, we're here, and Annie hasn't caught us yet."

"But she will," Liz said with grim conviction. "Annie will come soon."

Annie came a few days later and Liz, nervous and uneasy, introduced her to Joe and his parents. Looking injured and aggrieved, the woman told them all how frightened and worried they had been when they couldn't find Liz. It was not until the next day she said, that the neighbor who had given her a ride to town came over to tell her he had let her sister off at the courthouse, where a cowboy took charge of her.

Then, asking to talk with Liz alone, she had demanded bluntly where she had met Joe Knox. Liz told her, and then admitted to the letters that had passed between them, and to Joe's visit just before Christmas.

"Where did you get the stamps to mail letters? You didn't have any money."

"Joe sent them to me."

"Damn him. Well, I guess you've found out by now that all he wanted was a free hired girl to help his mother with this hotel. I guess scrubbing floors and emptying chamber pots and cleaning spittoons isn't much fun, is it?"

"It's not as hard as picking corn and turkeys and milking cows," Liz said stoutly.

"Maybe I did put more onto you than I should've," Annie conceded, narrowing her eyes calculatingly, "but you come home with me now, Liz, and you won't have to work so hard any more."

But Liz, screwing up her courage, stood firm in her refusal. "Joe and his folks are good to me and I like it here. I'll never come back to your place," she managed to tell her sister.

In the end Annie lost patience and began to shout. When they were girls at home she had always been able to browbeat her timid little sister into submission, but this time her scolding, threats and curses didn't seem to work.

"Damn it," she yelled finally, "bring that Joe back in here. Maybe I can talk some sense into *him*."

Joe stood with his arm around his shaking wife while Annie threatened to have the law on him for kidnapping, fraud, and other infractions of the law. Joe told her there was no way she could make her crazy charges stick, that Liz was of age and they had married fair and square and that she, Annie, would just have to make the best of it.

Annie yelled back that Liz was not very bright, that their parents had given her into her care for that very reason, and made her promise to care for her as long as she lived. "They will testify to that in court," she shouted, "and I'll prove that she's incompetent and that you used fraud to get her to marry you so's you could get a free hired girl to work for your damned old lady."

At that Joe ordered Annie off the premises. "You'd better get going or I'll get my gun and see that you do." She left then, still swearing that she'd sue and that she'd use Joe's threat against him in court.

Chapter 5

Annie was genuinely worried over Liz's defection. She had not only lost a valuable free farm hand, she might even lose the money that came with Liz. Upon her return from Hyannis she made a quick trip to Denver to see what she could find out. Her mother seemed very frail, but both parents were happy to see her and eager to learn how Liz was doing. Annie told them Liz was well and happy, and asked her father about Joe Knox.

"He seems to have taken a fancy to Liz and they are talking about getting married," she told her parents. "But I think, next time he comes to see Liz, I'd better tell him she isn't real bright and he'd probably have some idiot kids if her married her." Her father agreed.

"You've got the money to take care of her," he said. "She don't need a man, and he might not be good to her anyway. You just keep her and look after her."

Annie's mother died that fall and she returned to Denver for the funeral, and to see what should be done about her father and the big house. When he and her brothers asked why Liz didn't come, she replied, "Well, you know how she is. She's always been afraid of death and she didn't want to see Mama dead, so she stayed home to help with the chores and to look after Clara." When one of the brothers said he didn't remember that Liz had ever been afraid of dead people, Annie said shortly, "Well, she is now."

After the funeral, the brother who lived in Nunn, Colorado, asked his father to come and live with him. He seemed to be rather permanently located in the little town, and to have a parsonage large enough to accommodate another family member. It probably wouldn't be for long, anyway, Annie and her brothers agreed, for the old man seemed pretty feeble. Annie put the big house up for sale and went home.

With Liz gone, Annie had had to go back to work in the fields and helping with the chores. Clara milked her cow night and morning and helped with the poultry, but she was hardly big enough to pick corn or help with the field work. Annie needed Liz. So that fall she went to Hyannis again to see about bringing her back. Maybe she had had enough of the hotel drudgery.

She found Liz cheerful and happy, seemingly well satisfied with life at the hotel. "Joe and Pa and Ma Knox are good to me," she said, "and

I'm going to stay with them." Annie's promises that she wouldn't have to pick corn, milk cows or dress poultry, and that she would buy her pretty clothes and earrings, had no effect on her sister. "Joe buys me plenty of clothes and earrings," she said. "I'm staying here."

Liz's little girl was born in July, 1902, and when Annie heard the news she gave up trying to get her sister back, for the present, at least. Burdened with a small baby, she would be of little use on the farm, anyway; and Clara was growing fast. At eight, she was a large, strong girl.

The orchard had come into bearing by then and, barring the spring they had the late freeze, the cherry and apple crops had been heavy. They had handled the harvest by inviting all who wanted fruit to pick it themselves, at a nominal cost. There were few orchards in the county and the fruit hungry people came by the scores, especially from North Platte.

By the second year fruit picking at the Cook farm had turned into driving out on pleasant Sunday afternoons, bringing their families and well-filled lunch hampers. The McDonalds, long-time bankers, came; and young Charlie Temple, real estate; and the Birges, wealthy lumber dealers; and the Wilcoxes, owners of the town's largest department store; and old C. J. Pass, town florist. Several lawyers were among the regulars, J. G. Beeler, old John Grant and the Hoagland brothers; and two or three doctors, Nicholas McCabe, J. S. Twinem, and Marie Ames, the town's only woman doctor, all with their families. From the courthouse came Ray Landers, county treasurer, and dignified Judge Elder.

The orchard rang with laughter, those afternoons, and tall Frank Cook moved among the crowd, quiet and friendly, setting up ladders and advising as to the best apples for eating, for pies, or for long keeping. Everybody liked Frank.

In the late afternoons, their carriages and buggies loaded with apples, the visitors spread their picnic lunches in the shade of the trees, and Annie, bringing platters of fried chicken to the feast, joined them. She enjoyed associating with these people, and she picked up new customers for her delivery route from among them. Some day she would be one of them, and it did not bother her that, as of now, she was their butter and egg lady. As a girl in Denver, Annie remembered her mother buying fish at the back door from a young man who, by the time she was grown up, was the wealthy owner of a huge meat market.

Some day these people picnicking in her orchard would mention the name of Annie Cook with respect as they recalled that they used to buy their good country butter and eggs from her.

On her visit to Omaha, that spring of 1905, Annie heard an interesting bit of news at Jane's hotel. A ranchman, coming in from the

Sandhill cattle country with several carloads of dry cows, had mentioned loading out at Hyannis, and that the town had been upset over the sudden death, the night before, of the old lady who ran the hotel there.

The news could mean that she'd get Liz back. Before she slept that night she had composed the letter she would write to Liz in the morning.

In the letter she asked Liz to bring her little girl and come to the farm for a visit. "Ma and Pa left me a little money to take care of you," she wrote, "and if you'll come we will have a good time. Tell Joe I will buy you and your girl new clothes, whatever you need. Let me know if you can come and I will send you a ticket from Hyannis to Kearney on the train. I will meet you there and we will come back to Hershey on the afternoon train."

In Hyannis Liz read the letter over several times. Her few years with Joe and his parents had been the happiest of her life. She had worked hard at the hotel, more from choice than necessity, for she liked being busy. Making beds, cleaning rooms, helping cook and do the laundry hadn't really been such hard work, not when compared with the backbreaking sixteen hour days she had put in at Annie's.

The Knox family had made little more than a good living, those years they ran the hotel and livery business, and without the old lady, their mainstay, Joe and his father knew they would have to give it up. They would go back to working as ranch hands, but what would they do with Liz and two-year-old Mary until they could make better arrangements?

Liz showed the letter to Joe and asked what she should do about it.

"What do you want to do?" he asked her. "Do you want to go to Annie's?"

"Oh, Joe, I don't know. Maybe she's changed. It sounds like it, and it has been a long time since I left her."

They decided that she should go, just for a visit. Then, as soon as he could get things squared away, Joe said, he would come for her and little Mary.

Annie sent the ticket and Liz and Mary rode the train to Kearney on the day Annie set. She met them there and they boarded the next westbound train an hour later. Long before they reached Hershey Liz knew that she had made a terrible mistake.

It was as if she had never been away, except that it was winter when she returned, and cold, with snow on the ground. In obedience to Annie's gruff orders, she helped with the milking and separating that evening of her return, and every morning and evening afterward, and with caring for the poultry and cleaning chicken houses and cow barns.

Annie scolded her constantly, and kept little Mary frightened and crying.

Joe had tucked some government postal cards and a little money into Liz's hand satchel, "so you can let me know how you're doing," he had told her. But Annie didn't let Liz bring in the mail any more, or even go near the mail box. Even so she managed to mail her husband a card, begging him to come after them. "Don't write, just come."

Joe came and Annie swore at him and ordered him off the place. When he said he wouldn't leave without his family, she went to the wall and took down the shotgun from its pegs. With the gun pointed at his chest and Annie's slit eyes glaring at him above it; and with Liz in the corner, shaking with fear, the screaming baby in her arms, Joe had stumbled away. "Don't worry. I'll be back for you," he yelled at Liz as he climbed into his wagon and turned into the lane. But Liz had little hope. Annie was too strong for any of them, too strong for them all.

Annie had gone through Liz's things then, taking the cards and the money. "I'll just keep these so you can't make any more trouble," she said, walking out of the room with the cards and the few small bills.

A few days later Liz saw Annie packing little Mary's clothes into a bag. "What are you doing?" she asked fearfully.

"I'm sending this bawling brat up to brother Sam in Nunn," Annie told her. "All she does is squall and sniffle, but Sam wants her. Him and Em don't have any brats of their own, and now that Pa's dead they want this one."

"No," Liz screamed. "No, No." But Annie sent the little girl up to her brother in Colorado.

Joe came again, and yet again. The first time Annie ran him off with the gun again. The second time he came he brought a lawyer with him, an old man whose fees weren't very high. When he told Annie he had come prepared to force her, by law, to let his wife and child go, she had laughed at him. The law, she told him, was on her side. She could always give Liz and her child a better home than he ever could, and she would be glad to prove it in court. And then she picked up the gun again. Joe did not come back.

Chapter 6

The sale of her parents' Denver home had not brought as much as Annie had hoped for, not nearly enough to buy the second Eighty, and there hadn't been much else for Liz to inherit. Annie put the money in the Cook bank account at the First National, and considered their needs. She thought briefly of the new carriage she had wanted ever since Liz came to live with them. Lately Clara too, had been urging her parents to buy a carriage. Most of her friends now rode in carriages, she said, and she hated bouncing along in an old lumber wagon.

In the end Annie decided in favor of a new "entryway" she had long needed at the back door. "Entryways" were the utility rooms of their day. A small leanto-type room sheltering the back door, it provided storage room for the family washtubs and clothes boiler, for the milk pails, egg buckets, and extra baskets of corncobs and scuttles of coal; a place to hang winter work jackets and to take off overshoes.

Annie had Frank build hers to the right of the kitchen door and the board walk, and had him cut a new doorway from the entryway into the kitchen; so that farm visitors would not have to come through the always cluttered little room to her kitchen.

Clara was much on her mother's mind, that year of 1907. She had finished the eighth grade at the district school that spring and, at thirteen, was taller than her mother, a well-rounded budding young woman. In September Annie's "kidney trouble" necessitated another trip to Omaha. She took Clara with her.

On the way down on the train she told the girl of her pleasant visits to the city the past four years, of the nightly parties and sleeping late in the mornings, of a way of life that appealed to the girl, who had known little but long days of hard work on the farm.

With the help of Jane, who seemed always to be in need of new girls, she outfitted her daughter with new clothes and took her to a beauty parlor to have her hair trimmed and marcelled, her eyebrows plucked and shaped. When finished, she was no Clara Bow, but her clean, wholesome youth was attractive and Jane said she'd do very well. When the girl learned all that was expected of her she had been frightened and reluctant; but with her mother and Jane advising and encouraging her she had managed to please all concerned.

When, in early October, Annie said they must be getting home, Clara had begged to stay longer. The exciting and comparatively easy life at the hotel was far more inviting than the long hours in the cornfield that the girl knew awaited her. But her mother said they must get the corn out before a heavy snowstorm made picking impossible. Because of an early storm two years ago they had had to leave half of the corn in the field until spring, and she didn't want that to happen again.

On the train, on the way home, Annie told her daughter something of her plans for the future. "We're just small farmers now. We don't amount to much yet, but we're going to. We'll keep building and improving and people will look up to us someday. Your father doesn't have any ambition. All he wants is to pay his bills and give to the church. But that's not enough, not near enough.

"I want you to go to high school. You can start in January, the second semester. We'll buy a house in town and you and I will live there while you go to school. I can keep an eye on your pa and Liz, and we'll work up a little business in town, on the side. I want you to have an education, especially in bookkeeping, for we're going to have to keep books pretty soon. Records on income and expenses, so I'll know where we stand, what's paying and what isn't."

Clara listened to the long speech and agreed. Now that she had had a taste of city life, she hated the farm more than ever.

Back at the farm Annie hustled Frank, Liz and Clara into the cornfield while she made a quick trip to Nunn, Colorado. She knew that her brother and his wife had become very fond of little Mary and meant to keep and rear her as their own. Their letters to Liz told her how bright and good the little girl was, and that, for one so young, she had an exceptional singing voice and had memorized many songs and loved to sing them, especially in church. Liz always cried over the letters and begged Annie to bring her little girl back.

But Mary was five now, old enough and big enough to work. Annie walked the few blocks from the depot to her brother's house. He was gone for the day, his wife said, but he'd be home by evening and she knew he'd be glad to see his sister. But Annie told her briskly that she couldn't stay. Liz, she explained, was very sick, pneumonia, and begging to see Mary. "That's why I've come. But we are picking corn and I'm needed at home. It's a bad time to be gone, but Liz might not get well and she wants to see her baby. If we can pack her things right away, we can catch the afternoon train and be home yet tonight."

Mary, Annie noted with satisfaction, had grown a lot—enough to do most of the poultry work, all but cleaning the chicken houses. The child, excited at the prospect of seeing her mother, flew around, helping get her things together. On the train she tried to talk to Annie about her "sick mama," but her aunt cut her off with a gruff, "Your mama's not sick, I told Nettie that so she wouldn't make a fuss about me taking you. Now shut up and let me think."

It was nearly midnight when the train pulled into Hershey, where Frank, Liz and Clara waited beside the tracks, their breaths steaming in the frosty air. When Annie and Mary came out on the train platform, Liz rushed forward, screaming, "My baby, my baby," with tears running down her cheeks. Frank reached up to take the child off the platform and put her in her mother's arms. Even Clara was touched by the reunion of the mother and child, but Annie cut in roughly, "Now cut out the squalling and let's get home. It's late."

Even though it was well after midnight when they got to bed, Annie got them all up at four in the morning, the usual time, all except Mary, still asleep in her mother's bed when Liz bundled up and went out to milk. Annie routed the child out and ordered her to set the table.

After breakfast, when the others headed for the barn to hitch the teams and go to the field, Annie ordered the little girl to take off her good shoes and stockings and put on her old shoes and coat. "You'll have to keep your good clothes for church," she said.

"But I didn't bring my ever' day shoes," Mary said. "Aunt Nettie said I wouldn't need 'em, that I wouldn't be here long."

"Then go barefoot. You're not wearing your good ones to the chicken house."

Frightened, the child did as she was told, and Annie handed her a pail of hot water, picked up two more steaming pails and led the way to the chicken houses. The thick coat of hoar frost on the ground made her cry out in pain, but her aunt told her to hush her bawling and hurry up. She showed her how to feed and water the two houses full of laying hens, then took her to the pond to break the ice for the ducks and scatter buckets of corn for them. All the while Mary was silently crying from the pain in her freezing feet.

Back in the kitchen again, her feet were numb and white and she no longer felt any pain. Annie, fearful then that she had gone too far, filled a pan with warm water and told Mary to put her feet in it. When color and feeling returned to her feet and she cried out with pain, the woman slapped her and told her to shut up. "Now remember what we did this morning," she said. "Every morning it will be your job to take care of the poultry, and I want it done right."

Mary, frightened and bewildered by the sudden change in her life, and by the cruelty of this woman who was her gentle mother's sister, had already learned instant obedience. All forenoon she was busy, fetching and carrying, running to keep up. When the corn pickers came in for their noon meal, all three noted her tear-reddened eyes and the way she cringed every time Annie looked at her or spoke to her. When Liz tried to take the child in her arms and comfort her,

Annie slapped both of them and ordered them to eat their dinners and get back to work.

Frank looked sadly at his wife and asked if she couldn't go a trifle easy on the little girl. Annie didn't bother to answer him.

When the dishes were done Annie went to the parlor to sit in her rocking chair, rest her feet a while and work on an everyday wool cap she was crocheting for herself.

Mary, desperate after her morning experience, went resolutely to work to better her situation. From a heap of castoffs in a corner of the entryway, she sorted out a nearly worn out pair of shoes, probably Annie's, and stuffed them with some rags from the pile. Pushing her little feet into the cracked old shoes and fastening the broken laces as best she could, she looked at her grotesque footwear with satisfaction. They would keep her bare feet off the frosty ground, and off the filthy floors of the hen houses.

She had barely finished when her aunt came to show her where to look for eggs in the nests in the chicken houses, and in the feed boxes and other hide-away nests the hens found for themselves in the barn and sheds. Gathering the eggs, cleaning the soiled ones, and putting them all into the cases, ready for the store on Saturdays, took a long time. Afraid she'd break an egg and be punished for it, Mary was stiff with tension while she worked, and exhausted when she had finished.

Chapter 7

The corn was picked by Thanksgiving, the poultry dressed, and Annie had promised Clara that they'd go to North Platte the following Monday to look for a house and see about enrolling her in high school.

On the Sunday after the holiday the family went to church as usual. The day was cloudy and cold, with a harsh wind sweeping across the winter-brown valley. As Annie climbed into the wagon and settled herself in the spring seat beside Frank, he said they ought to get a carriage soon, one with side-curtains, that it was getting too cold to ride in an open wagon, especially for little Mary.

But Annie replied shortly that a little cold never hurt anybody and they had more important needs. Disappointed and disgusted, Clara said, "Oh, Ma, it wouldn't hurt to spend a dollar now and then for something nice."

To herself, Annie agreed with them that the carriage was a good idea. She had wanted one ever since Liz came to live with them, but there had always been something else they needed more. Turning part way around in her seat, she looked at the three in the back seat. Clara was a young lady now, and she looked very nice in the new clothes they had bought in Omaha. Liz didn't look so bad, either, though her dress, coat and hat were old and faded now, but no one paid any attention to Liz anyway. Her narrow, calculating eyes slid to Mary, sitting between her mother and Clara.

Mary was a pretty little girl. She had to admit that. The ladies at church had made quite a fuss over her when she first came, her dimples, her pretty, dark hair and lively, sparkling eyes. She looked quite fetching, that cold Sunday morning, in her little fur hat and muff, and the new plush coat her aunt and uncle had bought her just before Annie came for her. But she had one defect, a dark mole on her right cheek. It was not large, and some might even have thought it attractive, a "beauty spot," prized by the women of some countries and some professions.

When she had first brought Mary back, Annie had explained to their neighbors and church friends that she had had to take the child in, since her father had deserted her and her mother. They had all thought it very kind and generous of her.

Now, as Frank headed the team down the lane and she turned back in her seat, she was still thinking of the carriage, but first things first. She must see about the house in town this coming week; the house could help pay for the carriage.

After dinner that day Frank, saying something about going over to see Orson Covell, left the house. When Liz and Mary finished the dishes they started for their room, to enjoy this little while on Sunday afternoons that was the only time they could spend together. But Annie stopped them before they reached the door.

"Come here," she commanded the little girl. Mary started hesitantly toward her and Annie raised her voice. "Come here, I said, and don't be all day about it." Then, seizing the child by the arm, she turned her so that the light from the west kitchen window fell on her face.

"That big, ugly mole looks like the devil," she said, "but Aunt Annie can take it off for you."

She had often made fun of the mole, bringing both Mary and her mother to tears, and now they tensed in fear as Annie picked up the stove poker, lifted the stove lid and thrust the end of the poker into the coals.

"Oh, no, Annie. Please, please," Liz implored.

"All right for you," her sister said as she seized her by the arms, thrust her into her room and locked the door. "You'd only yell and blubber anyway," she shouted at her, "so you can just stay in there until I'm done." Then she turned to her daughter. "Clara, you hold Mary and we'll soon get rid of that damn mole." Clara only stared at her.

"Come on, you can do it. Sit down and I'll show you." She pushed the girl down onto a kitchen chair, then grasped the screaming child and plopped her down on Clara's lap. She put the older girl's arms around Mary, pinning her arms firmly to her sides, and put Clara's legs over Mary's so that the child was immobilized.

"Now," she growled, "if you'll hold her like that, tighter'n hell, I can do the job."

She stood back and looked at her work. Clara looked frightened but determined. Mary's little face was paper white with fright and the black mole stood out with startling distinctness. Annie nodded her satisfaction and reached for the poker.

"Don't you worry, Mary. When Auntie's done that ugly mole will be gone." But there was neither comfort nor tenderness in her voice, only a malicious pleasure. She narrowed her eyes and inspected the glowing end of the poker. "Yes, this'll do," she smiled.

Mary screamed, and kept on screaming, one long, desperate shriek after another. From behind the bedroom door the mother's despairing wails joined the child's screams. Clara, terrorized, sat frozen in immobility, her arms and legs holding the child as firmly as straps and chains could have done.

The stench of burning flesh filled the kitchen. Clara caught her breath and would have turned her face away but for her mother's gritted command to "hold still." The thing was over in a few seconds—but not before Mary had fainted from the pain, and Clara was retching from the odor. Sliding from under the child and letting her crumple to the floor, she dashed outside to be sick.

Dropping the poker into the coal scuttle, Annie unlocked the bedroom door. "Now stop that screeching and come look after your brat," she ordered her sister.

Liz gathered her unconscious child into her arms and gave one last, hoarse wail as she looked at the horrible, blistered wound on the little girl's cheek. Putting her down on the old kitchen couch, she ran to the wash stand, dipped a towel in the water bucket and ran back to bathe the little face with the wet cloth and dribble cooling water onto the burned flesh.

Annie and Clara went to North Platte the next day to look for a house. Of the several they looked at, a large white frame house on Main Street, two blocks north of the tracks, seemed the most suitable. It had a large parlor, five bedrooms, electric lights in every room, and was within walking distance of the high school. Annie told the owner she'd take it and arranged to close the deal later in the week.

Then she took Clara to the superintendent's office at the high school to enroll her for the second semester. The superintendent was reluctant. Clara should wait until the following September and start at the beginning of the year, he said. Annie said no, she wanted her to start now. It was a battle of wills—and she won. Her victory felt good. If a woman had the grit to stand up to a man he'd back down. Hereafter she intended to do it whenever she had to, or wanted to.

She thought again of Frank, and of how angry he had been yesterday when he came home and saw what she had done to little Mary. He had actually turned on her and raised his fist as if to strike her, his face working with rage and disgust. She had never seen him so upset, so furious, but she had stood her ground and glared him down until, regaining control of himself, he turned and almost ran from the house.

But it had not been fear of Annie, nor her reptilian stare, that had turned her husband away from her, there in the kitchen where the stench of burned flesh was still strong. It had been his own strict upbringing in the old school, under the rigid code that a man does not strike a woman, nor use profanity in her presence.

Had he been present when she was about to burn little Mary with the red-hot poker, he would have used force, if necessary, to stop her. But to raise his hand and strike her, no matter how richly she deserved it, he could not do it. The very thought of doing it sickened him.

All week Annie made sure that no one outside the family saw the child and her terribly burned face. On Sunday she ordered Liz to stay home with Mary, while she and Clara wedged themselves into the buggy seat with Frank and drove in to Hershey to church.

Frank had not spoken to her since the evening he had raised his hand against her, and he did not speak to her now, so it was a silent threesome that drove to church, that cold December morning. In the churchyard Clara and Annie climbed out of the buggy and went inside to their pew. Frank, after tying his old trotter to the hitch rack, went in alone and sat at the back of the room, away from his wife.

Annie, however, was all smiles and affability as usual. To questions about Liz and little Mary she replied that the poor child was sick, and her mother, naturally, would not leave her. No, she didn't think it was anything serious, as far as she knew the child hadn't been exposed to anything. The following Sunday was too stormy for any of them to go to church, and so, by one means or another, she kept the pair from showing up in church until the winter was nearly over. By then the burn had healed, although the scar was deep, and puckered at the edges.

Annie stayed close to Liz and Mary, that first Sunday back in church. When anyone asked what had happened, she explained that the little girl had been running with a hot curling iron in her hand, and had tripped and fallen on the end of it.

Chapter 8

By the first of the year Annie and Clara were moved into the town house and Annie had secured a "boarder." A good looking single young woman who occupied one of the bedrooms upstairs and fixed her own meals in the kitchen. Her name was Abbie, and Annie had hired her away from the foremost bordello in town.

To the neighbors Annie explained that Abbie was a young widow who needed a nice place to live, and that she had been an answer to prayer, as she could not leave her fourteen-year-old daughter alone in the house on the nights she had to stay out at the farm.

Business was good and Annie soon installed another boarder in a second upstairs bedroom, and then a third. Still desirous of maintaining a respectable reputation for herself and Clara, she laid down a few rules for her house. If there were several callers in the parlor, the girls were not to take their visitors upstairs by the open front stairway. Instead, they were to invite them to the kitchen for a friendly cup of coffee, then take them up the backstairs.

That way, Annie believed, it would look as if the young women really *were* boarders. Sometimes, too, an evening caller was a respectable family man, come to see Annie on farm business, and she did not want him to get any other ideas about her house. It would have been easier, all in all, if she could just run a hotel like Jane's in Omaha. As it was, she didn't want it known, while Clara was still in high school, that her mother ran a "place." Later on, when she had money and prestige, it wouldn't matter.

Meanwhile she was giving Clara all the exposure possible. If all went well she should make a good marriage, which could be of considerable help to her mother. She installed a piano in the parlor, where she and the girls met the men who came of an evening, and kept Clara, fresh and pretty in one of her new dresses, playing until bedtime.

The girl had always liked music. From babyhood her father had taught her songs and sung them with her, and now that they were in town her mother was giving her piano lessons. She had taken to the instrument with unexpected eagerness and ability and learned quickly. The nightly "practicing" at the piano was no hardship.

Liz and Mary, too, had a part in it all. Once a week Annie took them into town with her, as soon as their farm chores were finished, and put them to cleaning the big house, with special attention to the bedrooms and parlor. The house had no bathroom, only the usual facility out back, and a part of their work consisted of carrying out and emptying the slop jars from the bedrooms—the task Annie had once used as a good reason for Liz to leave the hotel in Hyannis.

Sometimes Liz thought of that, and remembered she had not minded such chores there; for then Joe and his mother had helped her when they could, and there had been kind words and loving pats to make the work easier. Here there were only harsh words and curses from Annie's tongue, and sharp slaps from the hard palm of her stubby hand.

In February Annie placed her usual orders for baby chicks, turkeys and ducks, and this year she added one hundred goslings to the list. Grass in the orchard had been a problem the past year, and Frank had several times had to stop his field work to disc it down. Annie's poultry magazines said geese were great grass eaters, so she ordered the goslings and had Frank build a small brooder house for them. Not only would they keep the orchard grass grazed down but, come winter, they'd be saleable as choice dressed poultry.

With affairs going so well, both at the town house and on the farm, Annie bought the new carriage just before Easter. A phaeton style, two-seated rig with a fringed canopy top, it cost her nearly $200, but it had side curtains that could be buttoned on to break the wind and keep it dry inside, and elliptic springs for comfortable, easy riding. Expensive though it was, it was now a necessity for after school was out, they would be driving into town two or three times a week to clean the big house, to take Clara for her piano lesson, and to make the Saturday deliveries. Spinning along in the light rig, they could make the trip in half the time it took them in the lumber wagon.

Frank, as pleased with the new carriage as the rest of them, built a shingled shed beside the barn to shelter its fine, polished body and upholstery from the weather. It would look quite elegant, sitting there, when the folks came out from town to pick cherries and apples, Annie thought, and load their own rigs with the garden stuff she gave them.

Shortly before the last day of school Annie put a fourth "boarder" into Clara's room and moved the girl in with her in the downstairs bedroom. Clara protested, but her mother told her it would be only for the summer, and that they couldn't afford to let the room stand empty for three months when it could be bringing in a good income.

"We can use the money to buy your new clothes for school this fall," she said, narrowing her eyes calculatingly, and Ciara was mollified. She had always liked pretty clothes.

The goslings had grown into geese by midsummer, and the task of heading them in the orchard fell to Mary, and for that she was thankful. Even though she had to carry a stick to ward off the biggest young gander, who considered the orchard his personal domain and came at her, neck outstretched, wings flailing, and hissing wickedly.

Those wings could hurt like blows from a two-by-four, but the child delighted in the peaceful hours spent under the trees with the always interesting birds. And while herding the geese she didn't have to go to town with Liz and Clara to clean the big house.

In mid-August Sam Russell gave his son, Scott, a new red-wheeled buggy for his seventeenth birthday. He would need it, the father said, to drive himself and his sister into town to high school. But young Scott didn't wait for school to start to break in his new rig. He drove a spirited team, and when he came down the road past the Cook place he scattered the turkeys, chickens and guineas scratching in the gravel there.

The first time she saw her birds running, flapping and squawking, from the flying rig, Annie shook her fist at the driver and damned him to hell. When, the third time he sped by, a spinning red wheel caught and killed a hen that didn't move fast enough, she put Liz to dressing the hen for dinner, then drove up to Russell's in her carriage.

Furious though she was, Annie was civil as she told the dairy farmer what had happened and asked him to pay for the hen. But Russell reminded her that the law required owners to keep their livestock off public roads—or bear the consequences. He refused to pay for the hen, but agreed to caution his son about fast driving past the Cook farm.

Annie went home fuming, gave Mary a good shaking and ordered her to keep the poultry off the road from now on. After that the girl was on the run most of the time, keeping the geese *in* the orchard and the rest of the poultry *off* the road.

Chapter 9

Shortly before school started that fall, neighbor Orson Covell, director of the local school board, stopped in. He was making the rounds of the Nichols district, he said, to see how many children would be enrolling in school in September. He put Mary's name on his list, visited awhile with Annie, accepted a sack of early apples, and went on his way.

Annie grudgingly allowed Mary to go, that first day, after she had done all her chores. Liz wanted Mary to have a new dress for school, but Annie said no, that those she brought from Colorado were still good enough, since she never wore them except on Sundays. That they were too short and tight didn't matter.

Mary ran most of the half-mile to school, that first morning, and every morning that her aunt permitted her to go, dashing into the school yard, panting and breathless, just as the last bell rang.

Annie took Clara back to the town house, and school, on Monday, settled up with her girls and visited awhile. She was a hard "Madame," but she paid well and she was fair. The turnover in girls at her place was small.

On Friday she kept Mary out of school and took her to town to help clean the big house. When Clara came from school they all drove back to the farm. Clara hadn't wanted to go but her mother was firm. "Later on you can stay in town over Sunday, but now we have apples to pick."

The next week she kept Mary home three days to catch up on her work and help pick apples. Tears trickled down the little girl's face as she worked. She not only loved school and her teacher but, for those few hours each day she was out from under Annie's heavy, punishing hand and harsh voice. Since leaving Colorado she had seen no other children, except at church when her aunt was always beside her.

At school she could be with girls her own age and she hadn't minded, much, when they asked her, first thing, what made the bad scar on her cheek. Now that the burn didn't hurt anymore, except when her face was cold, she seldom thought of it. She explained simply that she had a mole taken off her cheek, and after that no one said anymore about it.

After school, those warm September days, the other children lingered in the school yard, visiting and playing, before breaking into groups and heading for their homes, still loitering along the road. Mary longed to join the group going her way but, mindful of Annie's order to "get home as fast as you can. There's work to do," she snatched her lunch pail and hurried out the door, to run most of the way home.

The third week of school, when the teacher questioned her as to why she was absent so much, Mary told her simply that she had to stay home to work. The teacher called Orson Covell, and a day or two later he called on Annie to remind her that the state required that a child be in school until age sixteen.

Annie explained that it was their busy time of year, what with apples to pick and all, but that she'd see to it that Mary did better from now on. Then she gave the director a bushel of choice apples. Pulling at a little blue lump that had lately appeared on her lower lip, she watched him drive away. Maybe he'd let her alone now. Stop butting into her private affairs.

Mary was back in school on Monday, a warm, sunny day. All afternoon, through the window beside her desk, she watched for Annie to come down the road from town. She hadn't seen the carriage yet when school let out. Unless she had missed it when her class was at the teacher's desk, reciting their lesson, Annie was still in town or on the way home.

As the children poured out of the school house, Mary joined her best friends, Mona Scott and Jessie Able, classmates going her way. She had made up her mind to walk with them, and at the same time keep a sharp lookout over her shoulder. If she saw a rig coming she could take off, running, for home. But no one showed up behind them and she loitered happily, she and Jessie scuffing their bare feet in the dust of the road. Mona never came to school barefooted, she said her mother wouldn't let her.

At the home lane Mary turned in, and began to run. She could see the carriage in its shed. Growling curses, Annie met her, buggy whip in hand, and whipped her legs until the blood ran.

By mid-November the girl was missing as much school as ever — and the teacher was complaining to the director again. On the Monday before Thanksgiving Covell called at the Cook farm to see about it. Frank, Liz, Annie and Mary were dressing poultry, a task that had kept them busy for a week.

"We'll be finished by tonight and I'll have Mary back in school in the morning," Annie promised smoothly. The director was studying Liz and Mary, a frown on his weathered face. Both looked ready to drop in their tracks.

"Be sure you do," Covell said. "That little girl should be in school every day."

"Of course," Annie agreed. Frank was piling finished birds into a tub, ready to be carried to the shed where already frozen carcasses awaited delivery the next day. The woman plucked a fat, trussed goose out of the tub and followed the director to his wagon. "Here, I want you to have this bird for your Thanksgiving dinner."

The man hesitated. The goose looked too much like a bribe and he wanted to refuse it, but Annie was insistent. "We're neighbors, ain't we?"

"Well, thanks. It's mighty nice of you." He took the goose, tipped his hat and climbed into his wagon.

Annie watched him go, her eyes mere slits. He had bothered her three times now, and three times she had given him gifts. If he came again there would be no more gifts.

All day Tuesday Annie delivered her Thanksgiving orders. Frank, who usually helped, had to stay home with a milk cow that was trying to calve and having trouble. So she took Liz along to hold the horses while she carried the baskets in to her customers. The day was cold and overcast, with a sharp wind sweeping down from the north. Now and then gusts of sleet splattered like birdshot against the top and side curtains of the carriage.

At each house Annie went into a warm kitchen, emptied her basket onto the kitchen table, collected her money and visited awhile. Every now and then she accepted a cup of hot coffee. Outside Liz huddled in the carriage, growing colder and colder.

At noon they stopped for a little while at the town house. The girls were still in bed, but Abbie got up and trailed sleepily into the kitchen. Clara did not come home. Doubtless she'd rather skip lunch than face the bitter wind home from school, her mother decided. Well, no matter. The girl was a bit plump anyway.

Liz was so cold she could scarce swallow the food Annie set out for them, but her sister ordered her to hurry up anyway; they had a lot of stops to make yet.

Annie drove the carriage back to town on Wednesday, after laying down a long list of tasks for Liz and Mary. She would be staying in town with Clara until Saturday afternoon, she said.

Frank, Liz and Mary spent a quietly happy three days together at the farm. It was difficult, at first, for Liz and Mary to realize that they were free from the lash of Annie's buggy whip and her strident tongue. That they could talk with each other and with Frank, and even laugh a little when they felt like it.

They roasted a turkey for their dinner, a crippled bird that was not fat enough for the market. Frank, a good cook (a skill he had learned in his bachelor days), made the dressing and stuffed the bird. Mary and Liz scurried about excitedly, peeling potatoes, and apples for a pie. Frank made the crusts and the flaky biscuits, and the three of them ate a leisurely meal, relaxed and at ease—until they heard something at the door.

Liz seemed suddenly to shrink in size, and Mary gasped and choked on her pie. Frank hurried to the door. It was only his old dog, Shep, and he laughed, trying to ease the tension that had gripped the child and her mother. What, he wondered for the thousandth time, could make one human being treat others, especially one's own kin, as Annie treated these two.

Though he tried in every way he could to make their hard lot easier, Frank had learned long ago that it was best not to interfere with Annie's treatment of her sister and niece. Any remonstrance he made, any kindness he showed them, or any aid he tried to give them, only resulted in more work and punishment for the ill-stared pair.

At first, when he saw his wife's cruelty to the little girl, he had considered writing to her preacher brother at Nunn, telling him what was going on. But knowing Annie's shrewdness and determination, he gave up the idea. He had met the brother, a mild, good-natured man, and knew he was no match for his sister. If it came to a custody battle in the courts, Annie could doubtless prove that her parents had given Liz and her inheritance into her keeping, and that she, Annie Cook, a prosperous farm owner, could do more for her sister and her child than the preacher ever could.

He could see Annie in the court room, smiling and explaining, in her "vanilla voice," (as one of the girls in the town house called it—a soft, pleasant tone that contrasted markedly with the harsh voice she habitually used to her family) just how it was. She would keep Liz and Mary in the background and run the whole show herself—and after she won the case she would be twice as hard on her victims as before. He had not dared risk it.

None of them, however, neglected the work Annie had laid out for them. Her sharp eyes would detect the least thing undone when she came home. The milk and cream must be cared for, the churning done, the eggs gathered, cleaned and cased, the big pile of apples in the cellar sorted and bagged, ready for the store in town that took all they could spare. There was little time to rest, but the freedom from her unrelenting supervision was enough.

Chapter 10

On Thanksgiving Annie roasted a fat turkey for herself, Clara and the girls, and that evening they sat in the parlor while Clara played the piano for the girls and their callers. One of the men who came that evening was new, a slim, well-dressed, polite little Japanese. Abbie introduced him as Mr. Watanabe, owner of the new Manor House on Front Street, across from the Union Pacific depot. Annie had heard about the new place, an elegant hostelry with genuine Japanese paintings and wall hangings in every room; a gift bazaar filled with Japanese art; and a dining room with stained glass chandeliers, and silk embroidered wall panels in the booths.

Japanese people were late comers to North Platte and the city directory did not yet recognize them by name, listing only their house numbers, followed by the designation "Japs." It was the same with Greeks, i.e., "418 West Front—Japs, 1014 West Eighth—Greeks." There was no doubt, however, that this Japanese had money, nor that he was lonely and trying to make a place for himself in the town. He spoke English quite well, though with a strong oriental intonation. During the hour or so that he spent in the parlor he kept his eyes on Clara, and Annie pulled at the blue lump on her lip and made plans for the morrow.

At noon the next day she and Clara dropped in at the Manor House Cafe for lunch. The dining room was, indeed, elegant, and Mr. Watanabe came from behind his desk to greet them, bowing and smiling, and to lead them to a corner booth where the silk embroidered panel on one wall was a magnificent tiger, poised to spring. A cherry branch in full bloom covered the other wall. The mother and daughter were impressed.

Their host brought them menus and invited them to order the best that his poor house could provide, as he was most honored to have them as his guests. He seldom took his eyes off Clara. The menu, Annie noted, featured duck prepared in various ways. When the proper opening offered, she told him that she raised ducks on her farm and, if he should need another supplier, she could probably help him out. Still gazing at Clara, he placed a generous weekly order. As they left the cafe, Annie invited the polite little man to visit her house whenever he could spare the time. He assured her he would do so.

As they walked back to the house Annie said, "Clara, that little Jap is stuck on you." The girl shrugged indifferently. He was twice her age—and a "Jap."

Mr. Watanabe rang the Cook doorbell at eight that evening. The girls and their callers had already gone upstairs. Clara was in the room she still shared with her mother, finishing a Mary J. Holmes novel one of the girls had loaned her.

Bowing low in the doorway, Mr. Watanabe told Annie he wished to talk to her privately. Smiling warmly, she showed him in. He got down to business at once. He wanted Clara and he was prepared to pay for her. The bargaining took awhile. In Nebraska there was a law against Amerasian marriages, the same as against black-white marriages, but Mr. Watanabe was not seeking marriage. Some day he would marry, a woman of his own people, but just now he found Miss Clara most attractive and he wanted to buy her.

By the time he had bowed his way out of the door they had closed the deal, for $500, and Annie had the money. She had insisted on one condition, however; Clara was to live in the big house and Mr. Watanabe was to come there to see her. This had to be, she said, because the girl would be in school for two and a half years yet, and she didn't want her reputation harmed.

Annie went to her room and explained the arrangement to Clara, who was not enthused. Her mother told her it wouldn't be so bad, the man was not to come oftener than three times a week, and tomorrow she could move back into her old room upstairs. The $500 would almost pay off the remaining debt on the big house—and it was all for *her* anyway. "Someday" Annie told her daughter, "you will be a very rich woman."

On Monday Annie let one of her girls go and put Clara back in her old room. Mr. Watanabe settled into a regular pattern of visitation and on Saturdays Annie brought Liz and Mary in to clean the house while she made her deliveries. At the Manor House the Japanese, beaming his satisfaction, both with the poultry she brought him and with his other bargain in flesh, had tea with her in the corner booth where the tiger was about to spring and one could almost smell the cherry blossoms.

On Sundays they all went to church in the carriage. Everyone smiled and spoke to Clara, fresh and pretty in her fashionable school clothes, and to Annie, tightly corseted and wearing the good suit she had bought in Omaha. Frank, who still sat in the back of the church with some of the other men, always looked well in his dark blue serge wedding suit, even though it was getting shiny along the seams and in the seat of the pants.

Only Liz, in her faded dress and coat, shapeless hat and high-topped, cracked leather shoes; and Mary in her too short dress and coat, looked worn and shabby, like poor relations. Which was what they were, as Annie had told them so often that she had come to believe it herself. Poor Lizzie, who had never understood about the money her parents had left her, believed it, too.

Chapter 11

As a bride on the farm, Annie had bought a washing machine, a Quick and Easy, ordered from Sears, Roebuck and costing $1.93, plus freight from Kansas City. Few other women in the valley had yet risen above the drudgery of the washboard and Annie's machine was a marvel. It's oval tub, with its cleated metal bottom, stood on legs and its washboard like "rubber" with its upright cross-arm, enabled the laundress to stand erect as she pushed the rubber back and forth.

Liz had put in countless hours at the washer, while Annie scolded and slapped her because she didn't push the rubber faster. But Mary was too short to reach the cross-arm, so Annie decided that the old Quick and Easy was worn out and bought a new machine. One with a flywheel on the side that Mary could turn, and a "dolly" instead of a rubber to swish the clothes in the hot suds.

Both Liz and Mary dreaded wash day for, whichever of them was at the wheel, she made a handy target for Annie's tongue, "Turn that damn wheel faster, you lazy bastard," and for her cutting buggy whip.

One hot July day in her seventh summer, after a hard forenoon at the washing machine, Mary thankfully escaped to the orchard with the geese. She was fond of the waddling honkers and had made friends and pets of many of them. Some she had named: Satan, the gander that chased her, Millie, Suzy and Snowball, Kinky, a goose with a wry neck.

Late in the afternoon she brought the gaggle into the barnyard and scattered corn for the birds while Annie counted them. The count was one short. "Damn it, you must've left one in the orchard," her aunt scolded, and ordered her to go back and look for it.

"What the hell have you done with it?" Annie demanded when she came back without the goose. "Nothing," Mary defended herself. "I don't know where it is."

"You're lying," the woman gritted between her teeth, and lashed her legs until she danced with the pain.

The next day Frank came in with a dead goose. "Here it is," he told his wife. "It flew into a crotch in an apple tree and got caught, and died there. It was beginning to smell and that's how I found it. It wasn't Mary's fault."

"See, Aunt Annie. I told you I didn't do anything to it," the child said.

"Sass me, will you, you damn bastard," the woman shouted, catching up her whip and slashing at her niece's legs.

Saturday morning, after chores, Annie, Liz and Clara drove off to town in the carriage, leaving Mary to watch the poultry and weed the garden. That afternoon, as she bent over the vegetable rows under a scorching sun, the Gypsies came.

A few wagon loads of Gypsies came every summer, but Annie would never let them pull off the road or come into the yard. Mary had never seen any of them up close, though she heard many stories about them, how they'd steal you blind if you let them come on the place, and steal white children every chance they had. According to Annie they were all "lazy good-for-nothings" and the women "fat, thieving slobs."

The rig had already turned into the lane before Mary looked up from her work and saw it, a creaky old covered wagon and a bony team, headed for the water tank. Dropping her hoe, she ran for the yard, meaning to order the outfit back to the road. A woman held the spliced old leather lines in her brown hands, and several small, dark faces peered out from behind her.

Whether the woman was old or young, Mary could not tell, but she was slender and her eyes were black, deep and black and filled with a strange brilliance. The child sensed a curious pity in their gaze. Before she could give her order to turn back, the woman leaned out of the wagon, smiled, and asked to water her horses. That was all she wanted, just a little drink for her poor thirsty horses.

Mary looked at the tired animals, drooping under the broiling sun, and could not tell the woman no. While the horses drank the Gypsy studied the child with her pitying dark gaze. Her wise eyes noted the skinny little figure, ragged and barefooted, the scabby legs and the long, tangled hair hanging loose about the sweaty little face, where an old burn scar stood out against the sunburned skin.

Then the woman smiled at her and said softly, "I like you. You nice little girl. I tell you nice things. You put out your hand and I tell you good things. Then you get chicken for me."

Mary knew she was doing a dangerous thing but she couldn't seem to help herself. The Gypsy woman's eyes compelled her. She climbed upon the wheel hub and held out her hand, palm up. The woman bent over it for a little space, then looked up at the girl. Her black eyes glittered.

"Stormy," she said in a husky voice. "All stormy. Black clouds over you. You work hard and it's all stormy, but someday you have nice life. You leave this place and have good life, easy times." She smiled again and patted the callused, scratched little hand. "Now you get chicken for me."

Mary jumped down from the wheel, went into the chicken house and caught a fat hen. The woman tied its legs together, handed it to a child behind her and drove away. The girl stood in the barnyard a long time, looking down the road after the wagon. Her life was stormy now, that was for sure, but some day she was to have a good life, an easy life, *not on this place*. Hope rose within her. For the first time it seemed sure that she would some day get away. Then she saw the chickens and guineas on the road and ran to chase them back into the yard.

Later that summer Annie found out about the Gypsies and the chicken. How, Mary never knew, or maybe she only guessed, but she punished the girl cruelly, not only with the buggy whip but with a blow to the mouth with the wooden spoon she had in her hand. Because of her cut and swollen lips, Mary missed church the following Sunday.

Chapter 12

By the beginning of her junior year in high school, her mother had twice taken Clara to see Dr. Myra Ally, specialist in women's diseases. A highly qualified physician, Dr. Myra had a thriving practice in both "back stair" customers and those who came openly up the front stairs. All doctors of the period established their offices above the shops and stores on main street, and Dr. Myra's back stairs, used by the girls from the "houses," was often busier than her front stairs, climbed by the respectable women of the town.

As the citizens of North Platte ignored their town's prospering illegal gambling establishments and "houses," so too, they ignored Dr. Myra's flourishing back stairs business. But, like Annie, everyone knew where to go when the need arose.

All through Clara's year and a half in high school her mother had been strict with her, seeing to it that she came straight home from school, that she had no dates during the school week, and that she spent most of her weekends on the farm. By discouraging all intimacy, Annie hoped to keep her daughter from stupidly, or unwittingly, confiding her Omaha experiences to her school friends, or letting slip any mention of Mr. Watanabe. It was important that the girl's classmates and their families believe that Clara Cook was the innocent, inexperienced sixteen-year-old she looked to be.

Although she had occasionally rebelled against her mother's rules in the end the girl submitted to her will. Overall, Annie had been pleased. She enjoyed her reputation as the strict and loving mother of the pretty girl from the Cook farm.

For reasons not too plain in her own mind, Annie had determined that Clara was to graduate from high school. Perhaps it was that, in a time when many boys and girls did not go on to high school, or became early drop outs, there was a definite importance and prestige attached to those who went on to graduation. At any rate she planned and worked for the day when Clara would sit with the other graduates of the class of 1911, and resolved to buy her the prettiest and most expensive dress of any in the class.

But her grandiose plans crumpled into nothingness on that October day in 1910 that Clara married Bill Van Lue, delivery boy (he was 26) for McDonald's grocery store. Clara met the young man soon after she and her mother moved back to town in September, when he stopped his delivery wagon at the back door and brought in the groceries Annie had ordered. Their furtive courtship had been difficult, and when they talked of marriage they found they had a problem. Clara, only sixteen, would have to have the consent of a parent to marry. "Don't worry," she told her suitor, "I can manage it, just so we don't let Ma find out about it."

She had gone to her father, who had never refused her anything within his power to give her; and shortly afterward they had driven into town to meet the bridegroom at the courthouse. There Frank gave his signed consent to the marriage, and drove the couple to the Presbyterian manse for the ceremony, after which they faced the greatest hazard of all—telling Annie.

That she took the news calmly, seeming only a little hurt that they hadn't told her in the beginning, was the one reaction they were not prepared for. "Well, you'll have to quit school now," she told her daughter, "but you'll live here, of course, and we'll give Bill a steady job. To start with he can help finish picking the corn."

As smoothly as that, she took over their lives. Within a year she had destroyed the marriage and Bill had fled the farm, thankful to be rid of the "old woman." And not until it was all over; and Clara, at her mother's insistence, had applied for her divorce, did Annie let herself go, pouring out the wrath and vituperation pent up within her since the hour she had learned of the marriage.

How Clara's stupid action had ruined her mother's plans for her graduation, and her own chance to be somebody. By marrying that no account bastard of a nobody, she had wasted a year of her life, and had left to her poor mother the difficult task of settling with poor Mr. Watanabe. But now, she damn well hoped, Clara had learned her lesson and would show a little sense when she picked her next man. The tirade had been long and bitter.

It was Annie who selected Clara's second husband, Joseph Possa, a handsome young Hungarian.

By the autumn of 1912, with the heavy work of the summer done and the harvest in, Clara and Annie were spending most of their time at the town house, and it was there that they met Joseph. Charlie Hemphill, a prominent realtor and respectable business man, brought him to the house and introduced him, with the admonition to "be good to this young fellow, he's a special friend of mine," before he went upstairs with Annie's newest girl.

Well-dressed and sleek, Joe Possa looked like a "comer" to Annie and she welcomed him warmly. In the three weeks that followed he several times took Clara out for dinner, and brought flowers and gifts to the house for her and her mother. When her daughter told her that he had proposed marriage, Annie was delighted. "Joe Possa will be a big man in this town," she predicted, and bought Clara a new suit for the wedding.

They were married in the Judge's office at the court house, with Annie as one of their witnesses. After the ceremony, while Annie visited with the judge and invited him to the farm any time he could come, Possa took his bride aside and asked her to borrow $500 from her mother for their expenses for the next few days.

Clara stood dumb-struck at his request. "You're fooling," she finally said. "Not a bit of it. I'm broke, and I was counting on your old lady to help me out." He seemed not the least embarrassed by his admission. When Clara drew back and told him flatly that she would never ask her mother for money for him, he gave her a long, searching look, tipped his hat and said, "Well then, good day to you," and walked out. She never saw him again.

Chapter 13

The next spring Annie noticed a Union Pacific engine shunting a half dozen bunk cars and a dining car onto a seldom used sidetrack a little over a mile south of the Cook Eighty. In former years the extra gang had been sidetracked on the west edge of Hershey. This time it was almost next door to her. That evening she hitched a horse to the old buggy and, in the early dusk, drove down the road at the side of the field to the siding.

Extra gang crews, sent out by the railroad company to repair and maintain the grades and tracks, ate and slept in the cars provided for them. The crews, made up of Mexicans, Greeks or Indians, would be located there for a month or more, Annie knew, and would have two or three pay days before they moved on.

Most of the men were already in the cars when she pulled up beside the tracks, but she hailed one who came hurrying by and told him she wanted to see his boss. Presently a man came lounging out of one of the cars and strolled up to her buggy. In the dim light from the lamps in the nearest car, she could see that he was very dark, probably a Greek, and when she spoke to him he answered with a strong foreign accent.

They were able to understand each other well enough, however, and she was quite satisfied with the results of her call when she turned her horse and drove home. Back at the house, Clara was not pleased with her mother's proposition. They argued and quarreled for an hour, but Annie was determined, and in the end the daughter agreed. She was beginning to have almost as powerful an appetite for money as her mother; but she was a little more particular how she came by it.

When Mary, Liz and Frank, wearied by their long day's work, were in bed and asleep the next night, and all was dark and quiet at the farmhouse, two shadowy figures made their way down the road at the side of the field, crossed the yard and approached the house. From the kitchen door Annie called to them softly and they followed her inside. When they left a little later, two other shadows, squatting at the end of the field road, stood up and crossed the yard to meet them. They exchanged a word or two and the newcomers went on to the kitchen door. All that night the parade went on, and the next night and the next, but by daylight each morning the road was empty.

During the weeks that the extra gang cars stood on the siding Annie and Clara took daytime naps, affording Liz and Mary a little respite from the older woman's biting tongue and stinging whip, and more time to spend with Frank. Both of them loved the kindly, soft-spoken man but whenever Annie saw either of them with him she flew into a frenzy and ordered them to work elsewhere.

Frank had a good baritone voice and liked to use it, and when Liz or Mary were with him he taught them songs that they sang together, hymns, ballads, and catchy little verses set to music. Liz's voice was thin and tinny, but Mary's was strong and sweet and the man encouraged her to use it, to sing at her work as much as she could. "It will take your mind off your troubles, make things easier," he told her.

Frank taught them Bible verses, too, whole psalms and other passages. Liz had trouble remembering them, word for word, but Mary memorized easily and accurately. When there was time they asked him to tell them Bible stories, the splendid narratives of the hard times of the Israelites, and of Joseph and Daniel and Job. Especially Job. The tale of his troubles made their own seem a little easier to bear. At least they had never had boils, although Mary's fingers went instinctively to the scar on her cheek.

Frank knew a great deal about many things: the names of the wild flowers and birds of the valley; the names and habits of the little things that lived in the grass, and in the waters of the pond. There was never time enough to hear it all, and if they forgot to watch and Annie caught them together it meant extra punishment and hard work for Liz and Mary. Though she included her husband in her cursing and tongue lashing, he had long ago learned to shut his ears to her words, and she dared not lift her whip against him.

Sometimes the man wondered why he did not, or could not, make any determined attempt to stop the woman's abuse of Liz and her little girl. Although he tried to avoid provoking her and rousing her anger, he was not afraid of his wife. Her sharp tongue and the bitter things she said had hurt him deeply until he had conditioned himself not to hear them. A man of quiet ways, he was most at peace among his trees and plants and growing crops, or with his gentle, willing horses. In the end he always hurried back to his fields and gardens, there to work off his accusing, self-debasing thoughts.

By the time an engine pulled the extra gang cars back onto the main tracks and steamed off with them, the ruts at the side of the field were worn deep, and Annie's bank account was several hundred dollars fatter. In the account book she and Clara kept the money was listed as "miscellaneous income." Studying the figures, Clara demanded that her name be added to the checking account, or that she be given an account of her own.

Annie said that was unnecessary; she could have money any time she wanted it for anything she really needed. When Clara persisted, her mother finally promised to give her an account of her own when she turned twenty-one, two years later.

Shortly after the extra gang left Annie bought another house in town. Similar to the first, it housed the same kind of business, except that she hired a woman to run it for her, a woman known to her friends and customers as "Rannie." A tall, thin female, she dyed her hair a violent, brassy red and used, and sold, morphine. She had a good business going in the drug and would be willing to give Annie a cut in that, too, in exchange for an option to buy the house and its business as soon as she could afford it.

Rannie had long wanted a house of her own, and had several times saved up nearly enough to buy it, but something always seemed to happen to the money before she could make the deal. Annie knew what happened, and figured she'd be getting her cut for as long as she wanted—for the red-headed woman was a compulsive gambler. Each time she managed to save a sizable sum of money she set out to double it, after which she started all over again. But she was honest and bet only her own money, never that of her girls or her landlady.

The following week Annie took Clara to Dr. Myra again. Though they went up the front stairs, as before, she did not care anymore what the gossips might say. She no longer had any hope for a respectable marriage for her daughter, and it no longer mattered very much. She was on her way to wealth now, and she was tired of all the bother of keeping up a respectable front.

Leaving Clara in her consulting room to undress, Dr. Myra came back into her office to talk with Annie. Presently, as the doctor turned to go, Annie drew some bills from her handbag and asked, "Ain't there something lasting you can do?" The woman's eyes slid to the bills, and back to the mother's face. "I'll see what I can do," she replied.

Chapter 14

Upon turning twenty-one in February, 1915, Clara reminded her mother of her promise to give her her own checking account. They spent the next week arguing and quarreling over a fair settlement figure. In the end the amount was a little more than Annie wanted to give, and a little less than Clara had meant to take.

The first check Clara wrote on her new account paid for a piano of her own. Her one real love was her music, and now that she and her mother spent more time on the farm than they did in town, she missed her piano. Until spring work began, when they worked until bedtime, she played it of an evening and asked her father and Mary to sing with her. If Annie wasn't in a bad mood she sat back and enjoyed the music; if she was she quickly put an end to the "caterwauling."

That spring, too, the Cooks planted the thirty-five acres just south of the farmstead to sugar beets. A good many valley farmers had found beets to be better money makers than corn, although considerably more work. But beet workers could be hired very cheaply and, with half their farm in beets, Annie figured, Frank, Mary and Liz could handily pick the corn off the other half before snow flew.

With the establishment of beet raising in the valley a tall elevator or "dump" reared its spidery iron supports beside the railroad tracks in Hershey, and every fall long lines of beet wagons pulled alongside it, waiting their turns to unload the big, sweet tubers.

Each spring wagon loads of dirt-poor itinerant "Nationals" came into the valley, looking for beet work, and the farmers hired them by families and put them into beet shacks to tend the crops through the summer. Stooping from daylight till dark over the rows, thinning the crowded plants with short-handled hoes, then chopping out weeds and irrigating until the crop was grown and harvested, the patient Nationals labored for the meager wages with which to feed themselves the coming winter.

The laborers were mostly Mexican. Some were Russian, a few were Japanese. Parents, grandparents, uncles, cousins, and many children made up a "family." Each family could tend thirty to forty acres of beets, and each was housed in a beet shack. No one ever called the structures "houses," and it seemed not to matter if the shack leaked, or the wind blew through it. The occupants, who spoke little or no English, never complained.

Some farmers had old granaries or sheds that served as beet shacks. The Cooks had no such building available, so Annie bought a pile of old lumber from a neighbor and put Frank and Liz to building the shack. Frank, a good carpenter, did his best with the rotted boards but the finished structure was little better than those on neighboring farms. Annie located the shack in the edge of the field, just beyond the orchard, a long block from their own windmill. That way, the beet workers could carry their water and she didn't have to put down a well for them.

The Mexican family Annie hired the first year, half a dozen adults and many children, moved into the shack as soon as the beets were ready to thin. The mother carried her nursing baby to the field with her and left it on a ragged blanket at the end of the rows, where three or four of its older siblings looked after it while the others worked.

Mary and Liz worked quite as hard as their fellow slaves. They had to have the cows milked, the separating done, the separator washed, and the poultry feeders and water troughs filled, all before breakfast at sunup. By then the ducks and geese were taking their morning swim on the pond and it was time to turn the chickens out. After that Mary had to keep all the fowl off the road and help with the churning, garden weeding, and cleaning chicken houses or turning the washing machine, her spindly legs flying most of the day. Liz, between morning and evening chores, worked in the beet field, too, except for her day in town cleaning the big house.

By 1916 Annie had decided to fence the barnyard off from the road with a chicken-tight fence, thus freeing Mary from herding poultry off the roadway. The girl, almost fourteen now, was worth more to her aunt in the beet field than chasing chickens off the road.

That year a Russian family tended the beets, and Annie, grim-faced and slit-eyed, buggy whip in hand, tramped the field most of the day, making sure everyone was working at top speed and doing a proper job. There was soon to be an addition to the already large family, she noted, but the mother still did her daylight to dark stint in the field. The five oldest children thinned beets, too. A sixth, a six-year-old, had started with the rest but her work did not suit Annie — she chopped out too many plants — and she ordered her out of the field.

On a hot forenoon, as she tramped down a beet row, swinging her whip and checking her crew, Annie scanned the brassy sky. The feel of the air, and some low clouds, just rising above the far horizon, foretold rain by night. Enough rain to keep them out of the field for a day or two meant trouble, for the inch high beets would keep right on growing and much of the field remained to be thinned.

With cracks and pops of her whip, she urged her cowed workers to a faster pace. As she neared the pregnant woman she saw her straighten up and clutch her sides. "Missus," the woman gasped, her face twisting in pain as she tried to tell Annie, with her few English words, that she needed to go to the shack, her baby was coming.

"No," Annie shouted. "You're not stopping work. You lazy bitches sluff on the job every chance you get, but you damn well won't get away with it in my fields. Get to choppin', damn you," and she swung the whip at the woman. With a look of despair, she bent to her task again.

Annie kept a close watch on the woman. Half an hour later, when she straightened up, took off her coarse sacking apron and clumsily lay down between the beet rows, Annie knew what was happening. She looked across the field to where Mary and Liz were thinning. Mary was nearest and Annie yelled at her to come, and be quick about it. By the time they reached her, the birthing was over and a *pair* of boy babies were wriggling on the apron.

"Mary, take these brats to the shack," Annie ordered, cursing that the woman had chosen such an inconvenient time to have her babies. "Now get back to work," she ordered the mother. "You've wasted enough time, what with a rain coming up and this field a long way from done." The whip snapped twice, once on Mary's bare legs as she knelt on the ground to wrap the babies in the apron, and once on the mother's as she struggled to her feet.

Swaying, the woman bent and began chopping, while Mary gathered the bloody, squirming newborns in her arms and sped away toward the shack. "And don't fool around," Annie yelled after her. "You get right back here and get to work."

At the shack the four older children pushed in to look at their new brothers, while Mary took a few minutes to help the six-year-old put some water in a pan and find a rag to wash the babies. Then, mindful of Annie and her whip, she ran back to her place in the field. If only she could have stayed at the shack to help that little girl and make sure she got those babies clean.

After the noon stop to eat, when the Russians hurried back to the field, the twins went with them in an old basket with the other children in attendance. The mother stopped twice that afternoon to nurse the little things — and that night it rained. Enough to keep the workers out of the muddy field, and give the mother a day to stay at the shack with her babies. Every day thereafter the twins went to the field in their basket — and by the end of the season, when the family loaded into their old wagon and drove away, they were fat, healthy, sunburned little fellows.

The beet yield was good, that year, but when the harvest was in, Annie looked out across the field, figuring. Beets were hard on the land. Soon they would have to plant the field to alfalfa or corn, but the remaining forty acres of the farm was not level enough for beets, and a row of old cottonwoods along the south fence would have to come out. They sapped the ground of too much moisture. But it would be expensive to take out the trees and level the ground, damned expensive. She'd have to think about it. Damn! If she only owned that north Eighty she'd have land enough to switch crops and really make the place pay.

The Cooks made good money on the beets, and on the corn Frank and Liz picked, with Mary helping on the days Annie kept her out of school. The orchard had paid well, too, and the holiday poultry, not to mention the houses in town. When the money was all in, and the Cook bank account considerably fatter, Annie decided to take it all out of the First National and bring it home. Banks could go broke or be robbed, or someone in the bank could embezzle the money, she said, and it would be safer at home where they could look after it.

Frank hadn't wanted her to withdraw the money, and Clara had objected violently. She liked having her own bank account and the measure of independence it gave her. The two women argued and quarreled about it for days — until Annie went to town and brought the money home.

After the others were in bed that night, she and Clara cleared the kitchen table and spread the money out in piles of one hundred dollars each, nearly ninety of them. "It looks pretty," Clara said. "I never knew what that much money looked like."

"It will all be yours someday," her mother replied, "and more than that, but first I've got to buy that north Eighty."

They wrote the total amount on a piece of paper, with the date, then stacked the bills into a bundle and tied it with a string. Annie pulled two brown paper bags from the space behind the cupboard where she kept them, fitted them together, one inside the other, then added a third bag for good measure and put the money inside. She slept with the money bag that night and every night thereafter, and Clara helped her hide it by day.

Of their several hiding places they considered the fruit cellar the best. The cellar entrance was at the side of the house, beside the kitchen door, and Annie had Frank put an extra heavy padlock and hasp on the stout plank door. A thief would practically have to pry the whole door off its cement base to get into the cellar now, she thought, as she put the key in her pocket. Down in the dusky underground room they tucked the money sack into a hole behind a row of canned tomatoes on a middle shelf. Each evening Annie pulled it from its hiding place and took it to bed with her.

As an added precaution, now that they had the money at home, Annie got a watchdog. Frank had had a dog when she first came to the farm, a gentle old animal, but Annie had never cared for dogs and when old Shep died she had refused to have another on the place. But now she "asked around" until she found a dog that suited her, a big, bad tempered animal she named Brute. It pleased her when he growled and lifted his upper lip at almost everyone that came on the place; and pleased her even more when the neighbors and Sunday visitors assured her they wouldn't want to meet that dog if *she* wasn't around.

Still unsatisfied with her security measures, she next went to Derryberry's Hardware and bought a gun, a high-powered Winchester self-loading, repeating rifle. Bullets fired from the gun, Sam Derryberry told her, would penetrate quarter-inch steel plates, or planks an inch thick. It was the best gun in his store, and even at $19.98 she regarded it as low-cost insurance.

She learned to use the gun by shooting out across the empty beet field, her target a small black circle nailed to a fence post. With a good eye and a steady hand, she was soon hitting the circle with almost every shot. She knew, too, that the neighbors saw her practicing. Two or three of them came over to see how she was doing—and the word would get around.

As a final safeguard she bought stout new locks and had Frank put them on all the outer doors. Now, with the doors locked at night, the geese to honk and the dog to bark and snarl if a stranger came on the place, and the gun at hand beside her bed and the money sack beneath her pillow, her money was safe. Safer than in a bank, anyway.

On Saturday nights, after making the weekly deliveries and collecting from the houses, the two women waited until they were alone in the kitchen to bring out the money sack. Each time they added the new money they sorted it all into those neat hundred dollar piles, then added the new total and the date into their account book. It became a sort of ritual they both looked forward to. A ritual performed weekly, year after year.

Chapter 15

There was a mystery about the Cook farm, a strangeness, an awareness that things were different there, that both attracted and repelled the neighbors, and caused townspeople to drive out on summer Sunday afternoons to see for themselves—a score or more of buggies, carriages and automobiles.

Annie, in her long, full skirts, well corseted, and smiling her loose-lipped smile, with the surly dog behind her, greeted them all, loaded their rigs with the largesse of the Cook gardens and orchards and urged them to come back. Clara, neat and pleasant, was there helping, but always in the background, in her mother's shadow.

There were important people in those Sunday parades, Asa Morse, a prominent druggist who was also a city councilman; A. E. Timmerman, owner of the big Front Street saloon, and his family; Charley Hemphill, real estate and insurance, and his pretty wife; even the mayor, Dr. Nicholas McCabe, one Sunday; and Annie's former banker, Riley Landers, never missing an opportunity to urge her to bring her money back to his bank.

As the visitors took the dusty road home they wondered aloud why Frank Cook, the husband and father, was almost never seen. And what about that strange, shabby little woman, Annie's sister, wasn't she, and her little girl? Shadowy figures, flitting about on the edge of the scene, fetching and carrying. And that dog? A dangerous brute for sure. Someone usually mentioned the gun, the high-powered rifle it was said she used so expertly, seldom missing anything she aimed at. Yes, she was a strange woman, that Annie Cook, but pleasant and friendly, *and* generous, no one could deny that. Driving out to the Cook farm was a pleasant and profitable way to spend a Sunday afternoon.

On a weekday morning in early July, Jennie Hemphill came back to the farm, driving her new sports roadster, a wide veil tied over her pretty face and her stiff-brimmed sailor hat, her long tan duster coat swishing about her ankles as she climbed out of the car. She and Charlie were having company tomorrow, she told Annie, and she needed a couple of her good dressed fryers and enough cherries for two pies.

Mary, on hands and knees, weeding a long row of young carrots, froze suddenly as her aunt's voice came to her, "Mary, oh Mary, come here dear, I need you."

Annie was calling in her "vanilla voice, " as one of the girls at the town house called it; the light, soft voice she used for visitors and important people, so different from the harsh tone she reserved for her family. Why? the girl wondered.

Then, mindful of Annie's whip when she didn't move fast enough, she sprang to her feet and came running. "Mary, Mrs. Hemphill wants a gallon of cherries. Will you pick them for her?" Annie handed her a pail, and as the barefoot girl hurried away she heard her aunt telling the visitor, apologetically, "Mary has better clothes, but for every day she'd rather wear those raggy old things."

For a long time now Annie had made her wear Clara's old dresses, even as she made Liz wear her own cast-offs. Much too large, the faded, ragged garments drooped on their slight figures like slipping feathers on moulting chickens. Ashamed, they kept out of sight of visitors as much as they could—and now Annie was blaming *them* for the way they looked.

Inviting her caller in for a glass of lemonade, Annie sent Clara to tell Liz to kill and dress a couple of fryers. And when the order was filled and the lady driving away, the woman turned to Mary, her eyes glittering between her scowling, slit lids, and said. "I want to tell you something, you maggoty bitch, and I don't want you to forget it. When I call you 'Mary' and 'dear,' like I had to today in front of Mrs. Hemphill, I don't mean anything nice. What I'm *really* calling you is a slut, you dirty little bastard. Now, get back to work. Get, I tell you."

Crouched over her row of carrots and shaking inside, Mary wondered, as she had many times before, why her aunt hated her so much. She worked hard, she was obedient, she did her best. Why wasn't it enough? As long as she lived she would see Annie as she had looked that morning, the bitter glare in her little eyes, and hear the venomous spite in her rasping voice, spitting out those bruising words.

By fall the apple trees bent under the weight of their fruit and Mary was missing school again to help Frank and Liz pick and store the winter apples. Annie had given most of the summer fruit to her Sunday visitors, but the winter varieties brought a good price in the stores in town. Then, with over half the orchard yet to be picked, there came a violent wind in the night. By morning apples were inches deep under the trees. Bruised by the fall, they'd soon spoil.

Annie cursed their bad luck. Frank said the fallen apples would make good cider. While the rest of the family piled the apples, Annie hurried into town, bought a double-tub cider press and trotted the team home again. All the rest of the day Liz and Mary turned the crank on the side of the mill and the sweet apple juice flowed into the jugs and jars Clara brought from the house. Frank carried apples to the press and hauled away the jugged cider.

In town that morning Annie had told numerous people that there would be fresh cider on the farm that day. By mid-afternoon rigs were turning into the lane and Annie was selling jugs of fresh cider by the dozen.

Turning the cider press, like turning the washing machine, anchored Mary and Liz to the spot, where Annie could best get at them with her tongue and whip, urging them to "turn that damn wheel faster," enforcing her words with the flat of her hand to their ears and the sting of the buggy whip to their legs. By dusk, when she called a halt and sent them to their chores, they trembled with exhaustion. But Annie made good money on the cider, even after deducting the $12 she had paid for the press.

That winter, on the advice of Charlie Hemphill, she began buying tax delinquent properties. There were always good deals awaiting anyone with ready cash, Charlie said. At the courthouse she studied the delinquent property tax lists, then drove around inspecting the houses or business buildings and buying the ones she liked by paying the back taxes. Selling them later for their appraised value, or more, she found the profits quite satisfactory.

If only that north Eighty would come up for taxes, but Glenn Lay was a good farmer and there was little chance of that. She would just have to wait until the money sack was fatter, buy and sell a few more houses, get her own south Forty leveled and planted to beets, work a little harder.

Through her visits to the courthouse that winter she came to know a good many county officials, the commissioners, the county clerk, treasurer, judge and attorney, and the sheriff, Bart Sayman. Annie and the sheriff became good friends.

First elected to his office in 1912, Bart Sayman, basically an honest man, had not been able to stand against the tide of graft and easy money he found rampant in the county. The kickbacks and "deals" inherent to his office had already made him a man of considerable means, although some of the things he had to do bothered his sleep. But once involved there seemed no way out, short of giving up his office. In her new enterprise Annie every now and then needed his help.

Generous and kindly to the townspeople who drove out to the farm on Sunday afternoons, Annie had no mercy on the hard-up families who had fallen into arrears on their taxes, often through no fault of their own. To her it was a simple legal matter; they owed all the back taxes the county would allow, and so forfeited their homes. It was their hard luck, not hers, and if she could turn an honest dollar by paying the delinquent taxes and reselling the property—so be it. And if the families she put out, or called on Sheriff Sayman to put out, had no place else to go, she couldn't help that. Let the county take care of them, if it came to that.

On her more frequent trips to North Platte, that spring and summer of 1916, Annie noted a new house going up on the Bostwick place on the west edge of town, a large white frame bungalow, a new style in houses. With each trip past it she admired it more, and on an afternoon in late summer, after the house was finished, she stopped and asked to see inside it.

Carefully, she noted the built-in cupboards in the kitchen, the colonnaded archway between the living room and dining room, making them almost one large room. The "front bedroom" opened off the dining room, another off the kitchen. Upstairs, she admired the two bedrooms, each with a roomy closet under the steep slope of the roof. As she took her leave, Annie told the owner she was going to have a house exactly like it built on her farm in the spring.

"I have a daughter, you know, and my sister and her little girl live with us. A house like this one will be so nice for us all." Smiling and rubbing the blue mole on her lip, she tramped down the porch steps and across the yard to her carriage.

On her next trip to town she hunted up Jake Plaugher, the carpenter who built the Bostwick house, and told him she wanted one just like it. "As soon as the weather warms up in the spring, I want you to be ready to start on it."

By spring the United States had gone to war with Germany and building materials were unavailable to civilians. Sugar prices, however, had gone skyward. So Annie, forced to put off building her new house, put her mind on sugar. Raising all the sugar beets she could was the least she could do for her country in war time, she said.

She found another way to help, too. With a thousand posters and newspaper articles urging patriotic Americans to save on food, especially sugar, meat and grains, Annie was glad to do her part. She observed all the meatless days and used very little sugar in her cooking or on the table. She enthusiastically used the potato flour and other wheat substitutes in her baking, though her family, like the others in the valley, found the breads, biscuits and pancakes heavy and unappetizing.

At meal time she ordered her family to "go light" on the food they put on their plates. "You all eat too much, anyway," she grumbled; but when the war was over and all restrictions lifted, she still complained that they ate too much and refused Liz and Mary second helpings. For them, too, she found other ways of cutting down on what they ate. She could always accuse them of "gobbling" or "slurping " at the table, or could call up some fault of the day, a vegetable row not weeded cleanly enough, or the egg Mary dropped and broke when Brute growled at her. Whatever it was it was grounds for ordering the culprit to put her plate down for the dog and leave the table. Liz and Mary missed many meals that way.

Frank took care of these occasions as best he could by keeping a supply of nickel candy bars hidden where he could dole them out to the always hungry pair. Even so, if it hadn't been for the milk Mary and Liz would have fared poorly indeed. Annie never bothered to oversee the milking and they drank their fill there. Later, when Mary became the faster milker of the two, Annie took Liz off the milking crew and put her to feeding and caring for the poultry, night and morning.

After that Mary managed, at each milking, to fill a tin can and leave it behind the privy as she carried her pails of milk to the house. Even Annie would not be suspicious when Liz had to go to the privy.

One summer during the war, on a day that Annie had made her give her dinner to the dog, Mary found another way to relieve her gnawing pains of hunger. Annie finished her own meal, then told Mary and Liz that she and Clara were going to town, and laid out a long list of tasks for them to do that afternoon.

The girl was wiping dishes as her mother washed, when the two women came through the kitchen on their way to the waiting carriage. As she passed the big oak icebox, Annie opened it and took a small steak from the little pile awaiting supper. Holding it up, she said, "Mary, wouldn't you like to have this?" Mary could feel her empty stomach heave against her ribs. She nodded. Was her aunt actually feeling sorry for her because she'd had no dinner?

"I thought so," Annie sneered, then walked to the door and tossed the meat to Brute as she went out. "There goes your supper, too." she told the hungry girl.

Tears trickled down Mary's thin cheeks as she went to the storeroom to wash and case the baskets and pails of eggs waiting beside the crates. As she scrubbed a dirty egg she thought again, as she often did, of the Gypsy fortune-teller's words, "Someday you have nice, easy life." A nice, easy life would surely mean all she wanted to eat every day, all the steak and pie and pancakes — pancakes! Why not some pancakes right now?

She flew to the kitchen, stuffed some sticks into the nearly dead fire in the range, snatched a bowl, an egg, flour and milk, and began to mix, her hands trembling with eagerness and fear. Would Annie find out, someway, and punish her? It didn't matter. Right now she was going to eat. When the griddle was hot she ran to the door and called her mother from the garden. They wolfed down the cakes, with cream and sugar, washed up the dishes and did away with all signs of the stolen meal, then worked faster than ever all afternoon to make up for the time they had stolen from Annie. How good it felt, having their stomachs full for once. They would do it again, the next time they were left alone.

The next time they tried it Annie caught them. They were just ready to eat their stack of cakes when the carriage came clattering back into the yard and Annie climbed out and hurried into the house for something she had forgotten. Annie, who seldom forgot anything, was already angry with herself for wasting time in having to come back. Cursing furiously, she made Mary feed the cakes to the dog and lashed their legs until they bled. That evening, as soon as they had taken their places at the supper table, she ordered them to their room, then sent them, supperless, to finish their chores. Frank, with his little hoard of candy bars and chewing gum, helped them through that bad time, too.

But Mary, in her hungry desperation, did not give up. The next time the two women left in the carriage, she climbed the windmill tower and watched until the carriage went out of sight, two miles away—and then a little while longer—and it was well that she did. For, a little way past the two-mile corner, Annie, suspicious now, turned around and came spinning back. Finding Liz and Mary hard at work, she was satisfied that they had learned their lesson.

When she was out of sight that second time, Mary went to the house and mixed up her pancakes. After that she and Liz usually managed a good fill of pancakes when Annie and Clara went to town without them—but never until after Mary had climbed the windmill and made sure the coast was clear.

Chapter 16

By the summer of 1919 building materials were again in fairly good supply and Annie set her carpenter to building her a house exactly like the Bostwick bungalow. But first she stopped in again at the Bostwick's to look at the house, even counting the narrow boards in the hardwood floors of the living and dining rooms, so that she could see to it that Plaugher used at least as many in hers. She then bought the best of everything, but haggled and bargained over the price of every keg of nails, bundle of lath, or sack of plaster that went into the house, and over the wages of her carpenter and his helper.

As the house neared completion, Annie and Clara set to buying furniture at W. R. Munson's Furniture and Undertaking. W. R. himself, his broad Irish face beaming, showed them over his well-stocked floors and helped them select his best Queen Anne period parlor set; a davenport and two big chairs, fatly upholstered in maroon velvet, a mahogany finished library table, and an ornate lamp with fringed rose silk poplin shade.

The golden oak drop-leaf dining table they chose could be extended to seat twelve. The heavy mirrored oak buffet, the china cabinet and the leather upholstered chairs matched the table. For the windows they bought Nottingham lace curtains in bird patterns, peacocks for the parlor and doves for the dining room. For the floors, Wilton velvet seamless flowered rugs, and tasseled tapestry portieres for the archway between the rooms. As a final elegant touch, they bought an art glass pull-down lamp with glass bead fringe to hang above the dining room table.

His heavy brass and enamel bedsteads were the latest style, Munson assured them, and the gleaming satin bedspreads and pillow shams the newest items in his store. They bought them, and tapestry Brussels rugs for the floors, and scalloped, ruffled lace curtains for the windows.

The kitchen, with its built-in cabinets, needed only the blue enamel front, colonial style Windsor range with shining nickel trim to complete its furnishings.

Munson smacked his full Irish lips over the bills Annie counted out to him, and she, too, was satisfied. Her bungalow was furnished more elegantly by far than Lena Bostwick's, and probably as well as any fine house in town. And, given a little time, it would all pay for itself.

Compelling as was her desire to own the finest house in the valley, there were two improvements Annie refused to put into her new house: a furnace and a well. The bungalow had a full basement and she had had a heat grating set into the floor in the center of the archway, but when she priced furnaces at Derryberry' s Hardware she decided immediately that they cost too much. Instead, she bought a double-burner kerosene parlor heater.

It was the same with the well. Although the house was fully plumbed, she would not pay the price of putting down a well. Someday, she said, she'd put in the furnace and put down the well. In the meantime the bathroom went unfurnished and Liz and Mary carried water to the house in five gallon cream cans.

Clara fumed and grumbled at the omissions but Annie had her way.

Her next need was a woman who could set up good meals for a dozen or more people. "Asking around" led her to Mrs. Earl Comstock in Hershey; a pleasant, friendly young woman whose husband was the town handy man. Lela Comstock was an excellent cook, but there was little outlet for her talent in the farming community of Hershey, where every housewife of necessity did her own cooking, unless she was sick or having a baby. Lela helped out at such times, but the pay was small and the occasions few.

When Annie came to her with her proposition she was interested. Cooking and serving big meals in the fine new house once a week or so. Yes, she could handle that. "You won't need to do no ridding up, afterward," Annie said. "Mary and Liz'll do all that. There'll be jobs for Earl, too, off and on."

"What will the pay be?" Lela finally asked.

After more discussion, Annie mentioned a figure that seemed generous to Lela — until she said, "But I don't plan on paying you in cash. I can't afford that right now. So here's what I will do, and it will pay you a lot better in the long run; I'll make out a deed to you and Earl, a deed to my whole farm. When I'm done it will be yours, all free and clear. I'll have the deed, all made out, to give to you at the first dinner you cook for me. But keep it quiet. This is just between you and me and the gatepost. *Don't tell anybody*."

Lela and Earl talked it over. "You'd think she'd want to leave her farm to Clara," Earl said. "I know, but she talks about Clara making a good marriage. Maybe she figures she won't need it; and she said she'd bring the deed, all made out, to the first dinner I cook. It looks like a sure thing."

All that autumn Annie complained bitterly of the pain in her feet, they hurt like the very devil most of the time, she said. Clara said it was because she was getting fat, too much to carry around. She denied it, all the more angrily because she knew there was some truth to the accusation. They hurt, she said, because she had to be on them so much, making sure that Mary and Liz and the dumb beet field workers didn't loaf all day on the job. The pair took to quarreling often about their weight, for Clara had always been a little on the plump side.

With the harvest in and the new house almost ready for occupancy, Annie began spending the evenings in the parlor, in her old wicker rocking chair, her stockinged feet on a worn footstool, her hands busy with her crocheting. They would need tidies to protect the arms and backs of the fine velour furniture in the new house, so she'd just as well turn out a few while she rested.

Those evenings Liz sat, wearily humped over, in her little rocker behind the heating stove, ready to put in another stick of wood or lump of coal when Annie told her to. Clara played the piano, losing herself in her music. Frank sat by the lamp on the little library table, reading his Bible, or one of his few treasured books: *4000 Questions and Answers on the Old and New Testament*, *Ridpath's History of the United States*, or his book on the building of the Panama Canal. Mary, on the other side of the table, was reading, too. She loved to read, and found so little time for it.

One evening Annie suddenly demanded that Mary read aloud, so she could see if she was "learning anything at that damn school Covell was so hell-bent on making her go to." Startled, Mary began, hesitantly at first, then with smoothness and expression. "Hmph," Annie grunted, when the girl finished, "You don't do so bad."

Nearly every evening after that she ordered Mary to read to her, and while the girl read an almost benign expression settled on her face, erasing its usual grimness, and Mary began to hope that things might be a little better. At last there seemed to be something she could do that pleased her aunt.

On another evening soon afterward, when her feet hurt her more than usual, Annie ordered Liz to "get over here and rub these damn stumps." Liz came quickly, knelt before her sister and began to rub her puffy feet. Her scowl deepened. "Liz, you're no good. You're all thumbs," she barked. "Mary, you get over here and try it."

Mary took her mother's place and began to rub gently. "Oh, Mary, that feels so damn good. Keep it up." She was almost purring. Pleased, Mary went on rubbing the thick, stubby feet. Even though it meant giving up her treasured reading time, she had found one more thing she could do to please her aunt.

And while she rubbed, Mary watched her aunt's flying fingers, the crochet hook glinting in the lamp light as the delicate "tidy" took shape in her thick hands. Someday, when she came to the "nice, easy" part of her life, she too would sit in her rocking chair and crochet.

For another brief winter or two those evenings, spent around the heating stove in the parlor of the old farmhouse, were the nearest thing to normal family life the little group was ever to know.

Chapter 17

By early December the big bungalow was finished. Imposing in its pristine whiteness, it stood back against the orchard, a definite sign of improvement. To Annie it signified her standing in the community, her progress and importance. Clara was proud of it, too, but to a much lesser degree; for she was never driven by the unflagging ambition that so relentlessly urged her mother on. To Frank Cook the new house had little meaning in any way. He had never set foot inside it and had no desire to do so.

To Liz and Mary the new house meant only more hard work. Annie had put them over every inch of it, scrubbing and waxing the hardwood floors, ready for the fine rugs, and cleaning and polishing the many windows until they sparkled. Under the sting of the buggy whip, they ran the Bissels carpet sweeper over the rugs, and made up the beds with new sheets and the satin spreads and shams.

As they dusted and polished the new furniture, Liz had gasped with pleasure when she spied the stereoptican and its basket of views on the library table. They had had one like it in her Denver home, and she longed now to gaze one more time into the awesome depths of the Grand Canyon, or to look again at the view of Niagara, where the water seemed to be actually moving over the brink of the fall in its mighty plunge into the chasm below. But Annie's little eyes were on her and she dared not take the time.

Annie and Clara held their first dinner party in the new house in mid-month. In preparation for it they brought the piano out from the town house and installed it in the parlor, where Clara could play it for after dinner entertainment. They didn't need it in town anyway, Annie said, since they seldom spent a night there anymore.

While Lela Comstock, with Liz and Mary's help, made the dinner, Annie and her daughter dressed in their room in the old house, then hurried across the yard in the cold December dusk to the bungalow to see what they had wrought. The dining room table, made out to its full length, sparkled under the new white linen tablecloth, set with the china, silver and glass ware that Munson had selected for them. A silver napkin ring held a stiff linen napkin at each place and the whole looked warmly inviting under the amber light of the hanging art glass lamp.

Lela, trimly neat in her brown gingham dress and long white apron, came in from the kitchen to tell them it was the most elegant looking table she had ever seen. Annie smiled. From occasional service in some of North Platte's finer homes, Lela knew about these things.

The parlor looked quite as fine in the rosy glow of the poplin shaded lamp, and Clara had never looked better, her mother decided. That new navy wool tricotine, with its heavy embroidery above the waist and its straight-line, ankle length skirt had been a good buy. It made her hips look slimmer.

For Annie still hoped for an advantageous marriage for her daughter—and one of the county officials invited for that evening was a bachelor. Pudgy and balding, but an eligible bachelor. After all, Clara, though twice married, was only twenty-five, still a desirable young woman.

Annie, her thickening body stuffed firmly into her corset and her best wool suit, was not overly concerned about her own appearance. She didn't need to be, now that she had something better to depend on—money and influence. Not as much as she meant to have, but enough to command the respect of her guests that evening.

For this party was for her county friends, the officials she had met in her dealings for tax delinquent properties: Emmet Sodman and Tom Cooper, two of the three county commissioners; Arlie Aden, county clerk, and Sylvester Sellers, the ambitious young county treasurer, and his assistant, Ed Bader. To balance her table she invited four of her best looking and most popular girls from her town houses.

When she invited Sheriff Charlie Sayman she asked him if he knew where she could get a little good liquor to liven things up a bit. What with prohibition and all, one couldn't just walk into a saloon and buy it nowadays. The sheriff's attention had quickened at once. A tall, well-built man, he liked his whiskey on occasion. "You bet I do," he told her. "I've raided some good stills lately and I have plenty on hand. Have to keep it for evidence, but I'll bring a jug or two along to your party."

The food was surpassingly good, that evening. The roast goose done to a turn, Lela's dressing spicy, her mashed potatoes light and flaky, her suet pudding rich and tangy. The guests were loud in their praise and Annie was pleased. As soon as she had led them back into the parlor and Clara had taken her seat at the piano, she excused herself and went to the kitchen.

"You did a fine job tonight, Lela," she smiled, "and now you can go. Liz and Mary will clean up here. I'll want you again next week. But remember, you help me out now and this house and this farm will all be yours someday. Here's the deed that says so." She took a folded paper from the top shelf of one of the built-in cupboards. "See, it's made out to you and Earl, all straight and legal. If anything happens to me all you have to do is take it to the courthouse and record it. Now you look it over, then put it back in the cupboard and go on home." Rubbing the blue lump on her lip, she smiled as she went back to the parlor.

Getting Lela out of the way before the next phase of her party was needful. A religiously strait-laced woman, she would not approve of the whiskey, illegal or not, that Annie would soon be serving. Churchy as she was, she might even walk out on the whole deal, deed and all, if she knew what was going on. She had dared include the girls from town only because she knew that Lela would not know who they were or where they came from.

Back in the parlor Clara was finishing a spirited rendition of "How You Gonna Keep 'Em Down On The Farm." As soon as Lela left Annie returned to the kitchen and filled a tray of her new long-stemmed wine glasses with the sheriff's bootleg whiskey and served it to her guests.

Clara, busy at the piano, took only an occasional sip from her glass, and Annie, though tipping hers often, barely wet her lips. She didn't like the stuff, never had, but the idea was to get her visitors loosened up and talking freely. No telling what useful bits of information she might pick up.

The sheriff was soon telling off-color stories, while the county clerk, Arlie Aden, dropped into a morose alcoholic silence and paid no attention to Clara or anyone else. Commissioner Tom Cooper, glowing with generosity, came to sit beside Annie and tell her that, if they had any bad snow storms that winter, he would see that the road to her place was the first to be plowed open, and that, come spring, if she needed any land leveled or any stumps pulled, all she needed to do was call on him. "We've got the machinery and we'll be glad to help you out," he assured her, "and it won't cost you a cent, you being a good taxpayer and all."

Back in her bedroom in the old house after the party, Annie went over the whole evening. It had cost her very little, what with most of the food grown right there on the farm with non-paid labor, and cooked and served by more non-paid labor, and even the whiskey donated by the sheriff. On the plus side she had cemented some contacts with officials who could be very useful to her, especially commissioner Tom Cooper. She would be taking him up on his offer to put the county's heavy machinery at her disposal.

Yes, she had done well this evening, but before she was done she would have some really important people eating her good food and enjoying her hospitality. Some state senators and congressmen, maybe even a governor or two.

Chapter 18

By 1920 far more automobiles than horse-drawn rigs were seen in the towns and on the country roads, and most of the vehicles in the Sunday parades to the Cook farm were cars. It was high time, the Cook women decided, that they, too, bought an automobile. With all the trips they had to make into town to handle their business there, a machine would save a lot of time, and speed up their Saturday deliveries, too.

They bought their Ford touring car early that spring. Although Clara did all the driving, from the beginning it was Annie's car. Frank never drove it, or even got behind its steering wheel, though he patched its tires and tinkered away its minor ailments. And without waiting to be asked, he drove the carriage, now faded with age, out behind the barn and enclosed the old shed, making it into a weather-tight little garage for the Ford.

On Sundays they all drove in to Hershey to church, Clara proud behind the wheel, Annie, stiffly upright in her tight corset, beside her, Frank in the back with Mary and Liz. Annie didn't go regularly to church anymore. She figured she had already established her standing as a Christian and regular attendance could be dispensed with if she had more important business to attend to on the Lord's day. She kept Mary and Liz home, too, if she needed their services. But, knowing Frank would go whether anyone else did or not, she encouraged Clara to go and take him. It would look better that way. Even so, there were occasional Sundays when Frank went alone, driving a work mare to the ancient buggy, a settled sadness in his lined, kindly face.

The election of that fall of 1920 brought a new commissioner into the county government, Harley Costin, of Sutherland. Since he represented Annie's district, as soon as he threw his hat into the ring she invited him to a dinner party and looked him over. A tall, weathered man in his mid-fifties, he was married and the father of a large family, mostly grown children, and was involved in half a dozen different enterprises. Likable and well respected in the community, he struck her as a man she could do business with.

Clara, quite pretty that evening in a new rose crepe de Chine beaded gown, immediately attracted the new guest's attention. Annie was not surprised; any well-dressed girl in her mid-twenties would probably be attractive to a man of Costin's age; but Clara's reciprocation did. Except for her infatuation with her first husband, nearly a decade ago, Clara had not seemed to care for any man. But that evening she had warmed at once to the greying candidate for county office and had changed her mother's seating arrangements at the table so she could sit beside him.

All evening she had listened attentively to everything he said. In the parlor, after dinner, when the long-stemmed glasses were passed around, she saw to the refilling of his glass. And Costin, who had come to the county in his teens and "sort of grew up with it," held the young woman's hand at parting and assured her he hadn't had such a good time since "the day the hawgs ate my little brother."

Afterward Clara said little about the dinner, or the man, except that she wanted him invited to their next party. Annie was pleased, although she couldn't tell as yet how helpful this conquest of Clara's might be.

Costin won the election handily and Clara and Annie held a big party to celebrate the victory, with most of the "courthouse ring" on hand to help. As of that autumn, Annie felt that she could count most of the elected county officials as her friends.

During the two years of Costin's term as county commissioner his Ford roadster was seen often in the Cook yard and he was present at most of the parties in the new house. By 1922 he was campaigning for re-election in the fall, and Clara and Annie were helping all they could, helping him buy space in the newspapers and pay for posters to put up on country telephone poles.

In October Costin came to the Cook farm with a proposition he thought might interest the women. It had to do with the county's care of its indigent poor, he said. For nearly twenty-five years the paupers of the county had been cared for by Mrs. Emma Pulver in her big town house near the railroad tracks. The number of inmates had ranged from four to fourteen, mostly old men, or fellows who didn't have all their marbles.

The contract for the care of the poor was awarded annually, on bids submitted by qualified county residents and, although the rates seemed low, there were always several bidders. One reason for this, Costin said, was that usually some of the "patients" were able to work: Fellows not bright enough to hold down self-supporting jobs, but who could still turn off a good deal of work under supervision; or old ladies who had no home and were no longer able to handle the work of a two-dollar-a-week hired girl. With the help of people such as these, whoever got the contract could pretty well run the outfit without hiring extra help, and so make money on the rates, low as they were.

Although there had been few complaints on old lady Pulver's care of the poor, Costin said, people thought she'd had the job long enough and someone else should be given a chance at it. A year ago the commissioners had given the contract to a Mrs. Bertha Dean, of Hershey, after she underbid Emma Pulver. But her next door neighbor, J. Abbot, had objected to having the poor house next door to his property, or even in the town of Hershey. When the commissioners stood by their decision he had gathered signatures on a petition against the poor house and presented it, along with his previous protests, to the commissioners.

All this had taken time and the matter was still in limbo, but if the Cooks wanted the contract he was sure he could swing it for them — and get the whole mess settled at the same time.

Anyway, since they raised their meat, fruit and vegetables right there on the farm, and since there were usually some "patients" able to turn out a pretty fair day's work, they should be able to make more than most folks out of the deal, Costin pointed out. Besides, the county paid for all towels, bed linens and such that they'd need for the poor, and for any clothes they had to have. "But you won't need much in that line. The last time I was to see Mrs. Pulver, she showed me a lot of stuff, clothes, shoes, and things people had brought in. Some of it pretty good, too."

The commissioner handed Annie a list of the rates charged the county the past year: she scowled over it, figuring in her head.

Regular paupers	.75 per day.
Sick, injured, etc.	1.00 per day, 6.50 per week.
Insane, constant care	1.25 per day of 24 hours.
Transients	.25 per meal, .25 per night.

"Mrs. Pulver used to do it cheaper than that, but since the war everything costs more. I think you could even charge a little more than that, if you want to make a bid."

Annie looked up. "You sure you can get this contract for us?" she asked. Costin said he was. That Tom Cooper would vote with him, though Jess Evans would vote to give it to Mrs. Pulver again. With "two to one" the Cooks would get it.

"We'll take it," Annie said.

Costin grinned. He had counted on Annie to see the advantages inherent in the deal, but there was one condition. "I want Clara to make the bid and sign the contract," he said.

All bids must be in by the first of the year, he told them, although the contract wouldn't be awarded until May, and the "patients" transferred until June.

The institution had long been officially known as "The Lincoln County Hospital," (the reason the inmates were called "patients" rather than "paupers"), and, with Annie's and Costin's approval, Clara submitted her bid before the deadline.

Regular paupers	1.00 per day.
Sick, injured, etc.	1.25 per day, 8.00 per week.
Insane, constant care	1.50 per 24 hours.

A few weeks later Costin turned his roadster into the Cook yard to tell the women they could count on the winning bid. There had been several others, but he had held out for Clara's as the best. It was safe, he said, for them to go ahead and get ready for the patients on June 1.

Shortly afterward, Annie picked one of her one-sided fights with Frank. Most of the time she ignored him, not even speaking to him for days at a time, then breaking her silences by accusing him of something, some duty neglected, some fancied mistake. She liked to bring these things up at meal time, when they were all at the table. Frank's answer was always the same—he simply got up from his place and left the house. Sometimes Clara tried to defend her father, resulting in a sizzling quarrel between the two women.

This time Annie chose an evening when Clara was entertaining Harley Costin in the bungalow. The four of them had no more than settled themselves at the table than Annie turned her malignant, slit gaze on her husband—and accused him of sneaking into Liz's room and having himself a piece with her.

Frank's jaw literally dropped as his face went white with sick amazement and strangling anger. Letting his fork clatter to his plate, he stood up and stumbled from the room. Annie's little eyes glinted with satisfaction.

Frank did not come back to the house that night. Early the next morning he went to his room, gathered a few things and carried them to the empty beet shack, where he spent the day cleaning the room and settling in. Thereafter he cooked his meals there, on the tiny topsy stove, except in the busy seasons when he came to the house to eat with the family, silently, finishing quickly and leaving the house. In the spring, when the beet workers returned to the shack, he moved his blankets to the haymow. Not until the last month of his life, years later, did he sleep in the house again.

Annie seemed well pleased with the result of her evening's work. The following week she put Mary and Liz to cleaning out his room. By moving three cots into it, she said, they could take care of the three bedfast men Harley had said would be coming—if they all lived that long. By the time she had finished her preparations for receiving the county poor she had moved Mary and Liz into the storeroom. Their old room would be fine for the other men on the poor house list, she said.

There were still "white sales" going on in town and Annie had Clara drive her in and help her stock up on sheets, pillow slips and towels. The county commissioners needn't know that all the new linens went over to the bungalow, or to the houses in town. Her old sheets and towels were plenty good enough for the county patients.

Then, in the early morning of April 30, 1923, the Lincoln County courthouse burned down. A two-story brick structure with several chimneys and a tall cupola, it had stood on its specious square in the center of town since 1876. Beginning in 1914, there had been periods of furious agitation for voting a special tax to build a new courthouse. Finally, at a special election held in 1919, the proposition passed and the tax was levied. By the spring of the next year the elaborate new structure had been designed and construction started. The old courthouse had cost a little less than $20,000, but Lincoln County had come a long way since then and the new building was to cost a cool $100,000.

In the spring of 1923 the brick walls of the fine new courthouse overshadowed its dingy old predecessor, but by then the funds had all been spent and, amid howls of protest and mismanagement, bonds voted to raise another $100,000 to roof and complete the structure. At that point the flames that blackened the reputations of several highly respected county officials blasted out of the old courthouse windows, soon after midnight, on that fateful Monday morning.

Chapter 19

About one o'clock that morning, as druggist Earnest Rincker and a friend drove by the courthouse they were startled by flames blazing up inside the front windows of the old building, upstairs and down. Whipping his car into the garage across the street from the courthouse, where a late-working mechanic's light still burned, Rincker ran for the telephone.

The alarm given, the druggist ran back across the street to the Macabe Hotel to rouse the court reporter, Frank Smith, who lived there. With the additional help of the hotel night clerk, the men ran back to the burning building and hurled themselves against the big front door. Not even locked, it opened readily and they dashed inside just as the city fire truck clattered up.

The building was already hot and full of smoke, but Smith's office was near the door and the men filled their arms with papers and books and ran outside. By then the whole building seemed to be ablaze, and half-dressed townspeople were coming from every direction. Two hours later the fire was under control and beginning to smoulder out, leaving the old courthouse a blackened, roofless shell. Fortunately, the light breeze blowing that spring morning had been from the north and the fine Indiana Bedford stone walls and columns of the new building were not even blackened.

Excitement ran high, that Monday morning, as hordes of angry citizens gathered to look at the remains of their old courthouse. Many said they weren't surprised, that they'd been looking for something to happen, and now it looked like the crooked old courthouse ring had finally smoked itself out into the open.

Annie and Clara heard the news at breakfast, when "Central" put out the "general ring," twelve short jingles on the party line. They left a cloud of dust behind the hurrying wheels of their car as they drove to town to join the upset citizens milling about on the town square. Annie's little eyes glinted as she listened to the angry conversation swirling about her, and both women welcomed Harley Costin when he pushed his way to them through the crowd.

The commissioner assured them the courthouse fire wouldn't make any difference in their deal. The contract had been let and signed and they would get the county poor on June 1.

On his way home to Sutherland, that evening, Costin stopped in at the Cook's with a copy of the *Telegraph*, just off the press. Under the biggest, blackest headline it had used in years, the paper reported that the big county safe, open and empty, had been looted of $60,000 in bonds and securities and thousands of dollars worth of county irrigation coupons; and that the warrant books from the offices of Arlie Aden, county clerk, and Steven Sellers, county treasurer, were missing. "Robbery was undoubtedly the motive for the fire," the report concluded.

It looked like Bill Shuman was about to bust things wide open, Costin told the women, and went on to explain. When, the previous summer, it became clear that the $100,000 raised by the 1919 bond issue was no more than half enough to complete the new courthouse, the county officials, amid bitter accusations of wild extravagance and squandering of county funds, had managed to pass a second bond issue for another $100,000.

Shuman, an attorney who had opposed the fund raisers all the way, had then organized a Tax Payers League for the purpose of investigating affairs at the courthouse. A large number of unhappy taxpayers had joined his league and promoted and passed a $17,000 bond issue for the purpose of running a complete twenty-year audit of the county's books.

The battle between the league and the county officials had raged on until Shuman, snooping in all the dark crannies of the county's business, had uncovered a $4,000 shortage in county clerk Aden's accounts with an Omaha printer. The League was jubilant—until the county clerk showed that the shortage was only a bookkeeping error. But Shuman, hanging on like grim death to a sick sodbuster, a day or two later found that Aden had corrected the "error" by transferring the missing $4,000 from "fees received" to the Omaha account. At that point the "Courthouse Ring" had given in to the League's demand for an audit.

"The League hired a Minnesota outfit to go through the county's books. The auditors got into town Saturday and was all set to go to work this morning. But I hear they're going ahead with the audit anyway, auditing everything that didn't burn up last night. Now Shuman and his crowd are looking for the fellas that set the fire, and I wouldn't wonder but what Sellers and Aden are doing some heavy sweating right about now," he finished.

By mid-week the name of Steven Sellers topped the list of suspects; and to many honest citizens that was the cruelest blow of all. "Not Steve Sellers," they declared. "Why, he's lived here all his life. He's a good man with a fine young family. He's been county treasurer for the last six years and he's done a darned good job. It's got to be somebody else." Some even called attention to his biographical sketch in the *Lincoln County History*, published only three years before, and naming him as "a man of tried and trusted integrity."

But there were others who said they'd been wondering for quite awhile how a former school teacher, not yet 40 years old, had been able to buy a town house *and* a farm in the last half dozen years; *and* to stock the farm with a stable of Kentucky Thoroughbreds, which his family and friends rode in parades and at horse shows.

When Sellers and Emmet Bader, his deputy, were arrested later in the week several prominent people, outspokenly angry at such a manifest mistake, quickly came to the treasurer's aid and put up the $4,000 bond required for his appearance at the hearing on May 28.

Every issue of the *Telegraph* brought more news from the courthouse, and Harley Costin filled Annie and Clara in on details the paper missed, or did not know. The League had hired three Pinkerton detectives and set them ferreting out evidence in the tangled case. The newly appointed county clerk, Thaddeus Long, replacing Arlie Aden, now charged with embezzlement, announced that the audit would be a long one. Practically all of the tax records for the year 1922 had burned, he said, and it would take a year and $5,000 just to make up a new set of record books.

When the *Telegraph* published the notice that "All persons who have paid their 1922 taxes will either have to show a tax receipt or pay them again," a howl heard in high places went up from property owners. Many tax payers, not yet liable under the new Federal Income Tax law, hadn't bothered to keep the receipts, others could not find them. Many Lincoln Countians would be forced to pay their 1922 taxes twice.

So far, the county commissioners were not being investigated for anything and Annie could enjoy the furor. Her tax receipts were safe, but there were property owners who would not be able to pay a second time. There would be some good properties for sale for unpaid taxes in the near future.

The Pinkerton men were finding plenty of evidence of arson, such as the 17 five-gallon oil cans, still half full, found in the fire-gutted building. Had the oil-splashed rooms had even a few minutes more to burn, the cans would have exploded with terrific force, spraying fire and fuel in all directions, and totally destroying the courthouse and its contents. One of the oil cans, it turned out, had been sold to Sellers on Sunday by the service station across the street.

At that point Sellers' bondsmen changed their minds about his "trusted integrity" and asked to be released from their bonds, resulting in the arrest and jailing of the former county treasurer. On May 22 his relatives signed the bond, now raised to $30,000, that released him from jail. At the grand jury hearing on May 28 Annie rubbed her mole and watched as Sellers' four attorneys faced County Attorney W. C. Jones, and special prosecutors George Gibbs and Bill Shuman, head of the Tax Payers League, to argue the 28 charges brought against the accused. Steven Sellers, his deputy, Emmet Bader, and former County Clerk Arlie Aden, were indicted and bound over for the November term of district court.

The hearing over, Steven Sellers quietly disappeared, and Annie and Clara went home to make ready to receive the county poor.

Annie soon had her establishment whipped into shape.

Clara was in charge of the kitchen. Especially good with bread and cakes, her offerings were always the first sold at the annual church bazaars in Hershey. Mary, Liz, Sarah Martin and Alice Lucas cleaned, washed dishes and cared for the bedfast patients, the old men and the children. They changed the beds once a week, carried trays and fed the men, Lucas and Tibbles, who could not feed themselves. In their "free" time they worked in the gardens and poultry houses.

Though her gardens, cellars, orchards and poultry provided an abundance of raw materials, with the coming of the county poor Annie seemed to tighten up even more on the rations allowed: thin oatmeal gruel for breakfast; watery soup, only one slice of Clara's good bread, or one small roll to a person at each of the other meals; and her household, except for herself and Clara, was always hungry.

When the children cried for something to eat Annie scolded the "damn sniveling brats" and swished her buggy whip. So the little ones hushed, and kept out of her sight as much as they could. Again it was Frank who made their lives bearable, doling out candy bars, apples and carrots to the hungry tots.

Annie never actually touched one of the patients with her whip, that first summer. It would have been useless to whip the men too old or crippled to work; and the status of the Lucas family was up in the air for the time being. Negotiations were going on between the county commissioners and some California relatives. Eventually, no doubt, the family would be sent there, so Annie only threatened with the whip. She didn't intend that they, or their relatives, should come back on her with a law suit for abuse.

Neither did she use the lash on Sarah Martin or her child. Instead she made use of Sarah to shame and abuse Mary and Liz. The deaf and dumb woman was a fast and competent worker and Annie took pleasure in bawling, "Why can't you work as fast as Sarah does, you damn, lazy sluts? She works circles around you every day and all you do is loaf and dawdle. And she's a poor dumb brute besides. You should be ashamed of yourselves, you lazy bastards."

Chapter 20

Busy though she was that summer, Annie made it a point to keep up with the news from the courthouse. Costin helped by dropping in often to talk it over. By late June the county had recovered $9,000 in insurance, with which it rough finished some rooms in the roofless new building and carried on its business.

In July the Grand Jury, still digging into old county deals and examining more than one hundred witnesses, returned an indictment against Commissioner Tom Cooper on six counts of embezzlement, a charge of receiving "pecuniary benefits" from the contractors building the new courthouse, and for using county men, teams and wagons to build a private road to the home of a friend.

These charges, too, were to be tried in the November term of district court. Annie didn't sleep too well, that fall, for fear that her deal with Cooper for leveling her west 40 and pulling down the trees that bordered it would come to the attention of the investigators.

In September the *Telegraph* startled its readers with the announcement that Sheriff Berthe had arrested Steve Sellers in Florida for the attempted sale of Lincoln County irrigation coupons, and that he was now lodged in the county jail, awaiting trial in November.

Over coffee and cake, Clara and Annie sat long at the kitchen table with Harley Costin, talking over this latest development. It didn't look too good for the new courthouse either, he told them. All that summer and fall work had gone ahead on the new building, but the second hundred thousand was now about to run out, with the structure yet unfinished. "The taxpayers are spittin' mad and the talk is that they'll not vote another dime to finish the damn courthouse. Can't say as I blame them either." Costin paused a moment, then added, "there'll be a general house cleaning at the election this fall and I'm afraid I'll damn well be turned out in the cold with the rest of 'em."

As he stood up to leave, the tall commissioner turned to Clara, "Oh yes, before I forget I'd better tell you that old Dr. Soper'll be out Thursday to inspect your place. It's a county ordinance and has to be done, but you're not supposed to know it ahead of time, so act surprised when he shows up. It wouldn't hurt anything either," he added, turning to Annie, "if you was to give him a little present for his trouble. The county don't pay much."

Annie smiled lopsidedly and went to that day's hiding place for the money sack. She came back with a fifty-dollar bill and Costin smiled his approval as he tucked it into his pocket.

She worked her four women hard the next two days, changing filthy beds, scrubbing floors, even bathing the bed patients as best they could and putting clean nightshirts on them the morning the inspector was due. By mid-forenoon, when the doctor arrived, she had the women busy in the kitchen, putting together a really substantial meal.

A pot-bellied little man in a soiled white shirt, he didn't seem to notice the foul odor in the men's rooms, intermixed as it was with the fresh fumes of lysol and ammonia, nor the emaciated appearance of all the patients, even the one who had come to the farm forty pounds overweight. With Annie at his side, he talked briefly with the patients, who darted frightened glances at their landlady as they told him "Yes, everything's all right." In the kitchen, filled with savory smells from the bubbling kettles, he talked a little longer with Annie and Clara, then tipped his hat to them and headed his car back to town.

The result of his visit was published in the "County Commissioners Proceedings," in the *Telegraph* the following week.

October 2, 1923

To Board of County Commissioners, North Platte.

At the request of Commissioner Costin, I today examined the inmates of the County Poor Farm under the care of Clara Cook for the purpose of classification as a basis for pay for their care under the present contract, and submit the following

Patients

Levi Brown	day treatment	$8.00
Chas Lucas	bedfast	15.00
Jake Doty	day treatment	8.00
George Kidder	bedfast	15.00
Edgar Miller	day treatment	8.00
F. W. Tibbles	bedfast	15.00

Boarders

Sarah Martin	deaf and dumb	$4.00
Joe Martin	age 3	4.00
Mrs. Chas Lucas		4.00
Glenn Lucas	" 6	4.00
Mary Lucas	" 4	4.00
Rose Lucas	" 1	4.00

In my opinion the care given the patients is very satisfactory and they seem contented. The rates charged for patients is low for the services and supplies rendered.

Respectfully: John S. Soper.

Annie smiled and rubbed her mole vigorously. Her fifty dollars had been well spent. She must remember to handle all future inspections in the same efficient manner.

That evening she gathered her family about her in the parlor, where a cheerful fire blazed in the big heating stove. Except for Sarah and little Joe, none of the county poor were allowed in the parlor. The rules were strict. The patients had their own rooms, where they could go whenever they liked. They had their places at the common dining table for their meals, and they could go where they pleased outside. So, after the weather turned chilly, they went to bed in their unheated rooms immediately after supper, the warmest place left to them. Those who slept on army cots still spent miserable nights, for Annie was also stingy with the blankets.

That winter Frank was not at his place by the table, reading his beloved books, and Mary's heart ached for him, alone in the little beet shack on the edge of the field.

Annie's feet hurt her even more this winter than last. Settling her keg-like body in her chair and picking up her crocheting, she kicked off her felt slippers, hoisted her aching feet to her footstool and put Mary to rubbing them. Clara went to her piano and began to play. Liz and Sarah sat, silent and weary, in their places near the stove. The little boy crouched beside his mother, his big, wary black eyes never leaving Annie's face.

Feeling a need to signalize her satisfaction with the inspector's report, she glanced about the room. Her slit gaze falling upon little Joe, she laid aside her crocheting and, in her best vanilla voice, called the child to her. Hauling him onto her lap, she took a handful of the cheap hard candy she liked to suck on from her apron pocket and said, "Joe, honey, if you will go slap Sarah's face, hard, I'll give you all this candy."

And little Joe, afraid of Annie and always hungry, did her bidding. Climbing up on his mother's lap, he slapped her face. "Again," Annie commanded, "Slap her again, harder." When he had done it she said, "Now clap your hands and laugh." And when that was done she told him to come and get his candy.

The mother, hearing none of the exchange, sat dumbly on her chair, tears sliding slowly down her cheeks, while Annie's little eyes gleamed her satisfaction. Clara, absorbed in her music, seemed unaware of her mother's little game. Liz, hunched on her chair back of the stove, and

Mary, vigorously rubbing her aunt's feet, carefully hid the pity they felt for their deaf friend.

The trial opened as scheduled on November 5, with Arlie Aden surprising everybody by promptly pleading guilty to the charge of embezzlement. The charge against Sellers, "approximately 150 counts of forgery, embezzlement, arson and falsification of public records," next came before the court. The defense tried hard to have W. E. Shuman, counsel for the state, put off the case due to bias and prejudice. During the noon adjournment of the court, County Attorney Jones and Defense Attorney Joe Hoagland, engaging in a brief bout of fisticuffs, were pulled apart by bystanders before they damaged each other. The trial then settled down to a month long series of technicalities and delays. On December 7 the defense finally succeeded in getting state's attorney Shuman not only ousted from the prosecution team but barred from the court room while the Sellers' case was before the court.

Annie, busy with her many affairs, depended on Costin to keep her up-to-date on the progress of the trial. Both Sellers and Bader were convicted before the court recessed for Christmas. Both filed appeals. Among the minor cases quickly disposed of before the holidays, was that of Tom Cooper, suspended and dismissed from office back in September.

Annie and Clara were present in court for that one, Annie nervously rubbing her mole. There was always the possibility that one of the snooping Leaguers might stumble onto the fact that Cooper had done that gratis work for her, or that someone would turn snitch. Not the neighbors—they would be afraid to tell on her—but maybe one of the men who had worked the grader or the stump puller.

When it was over, with Cooper fuming over his heavy fine, Annie went home relieved. Her name had not come up and all was well.

Sellers, Bader and Aden served their time in the state penitentiary at Lincoln. And there were few to mourn their fate among the citizens who, for the next ten years, transacted their county business in the unfinished unpainted rooms and offices of the new courthouse. Or looked upon its unsightly exterior, its stately facade marred by the rough bridge planks that boarded up its tall Grecian Doric windows.

Chapter 21

Sarah and Mary had become close friends, for, in addition to Annie, they had much in common. And each had a cross to bear—Sarah in her total deafness, Mary in the burn scar on her cheek. No longer so puckered and disfiguring, it still made her wince every time she looked in the scratched old mirror above the wash stand.

The deaf woman carried a pad and pencil in her apron pocket, and it was to Mary that she told her story, her flying pencil inscribing her words almost as fast as Mary talked. She had been deaf, she wrote, for as long as she could remember, but her parents had sent her to a good school for the deaf. There she had not only learned sign language but also to read and write, and to cook and sew.

Orphaned before she had quite finished her schooling, she had gone into domestic service to support herself. She had done well enough until the war with Germany, when she had been engaged as housekeeper in the home of a well-to-do Omaha business man. Then the man's wife had been called away to help care for a sick relative—and there the flying pencil stopped.

When she picked it up again she wrote that she had been sent to a home for unwed mothers, where little Joe was born. In time the checks that paid for her care and keep, and that of her child, had stopped and she and little Joe had been sent to North Platte, to the County Hospital and Poor House.

She had been happy there, helping Mrs. Pulver, who doted on the black-haired, black-eyed little Joe. Mother Pulver took good care of the old people and fed us all well, not like here, Sarah wrote on, then quickly scratched out the last three words. When Mrs. Pulver learned that her contract was not to be renewed she had tried to keep little Joe and his mother. She had even gone before the county commissioners at their weekly meeting and offered to keep the pair for free, but two of the commissioners had voted to refuse her offer. So here she was, she and little Joe.

In return Mary wrote her own story on the pad for Sarah to read, and sharing their troubled lives seemed to help, to make their hard days a little easier.

When Costin next stopped in at the farm, Annie told him it looked like "that old bastard, Kidder, is on his last legs."

"Maybe you better call Doc Dunkin out tomorrow to have a look at him," the commissioner advised.

Annie called the county physician the next morning, and put Mary and Liz to changing the old man's bed linens and cleaning him up. The portly, florid faced Dr. Duncan, arriving a little later, satchel in hand, immediately struck Annie as a man she could do business with.

The physician looked gravely at the emaciated man on the bed. "He's pretty thin," he said, slanting a measuring glance at Annie. She nodded. "Yes, these old folks don't eat much, hardly anything."

"I see," the doctor said. "Well, it's only a matter of time now, a day or two at the most."

In the kitchen he accepted a cup of coffee and a slice of chocolate layer cake. "When the old fellow dies," he told Clara, "you'll have to have the county coroner sign his death certificate. That's Wells' job, but he is county attorney, too, and too busy lately to be bothered. So Munson has been doing it for him. He might as well. He's the county mortician, too, and has to come after the body anyway."

The patient died in his sleep two days later. In the morning Annie called her old friend, W. R. Munson. She did not bother to have the patient or his bed cleaned up for Munson. She considered him already somewhat under obligation to her for the house full of furniture she had bought from him and, agreeably, he signed the death certificate, listing "old age and heart failure" as the cause of death, ignoring the all too plain evidence that starvation had caused, or contributed to, the death of the unfortunate pauper.

Late that fall two new patients arrived at the farm, an elderly woman and a severely retarded man. Annie judged that the woman, a Mrs. Baker, would still be able to turn off a good deal of useful work: peeling vegetables, picking chickens and making beds. The man, Cabe, though young, strong and able, would need supervision most of the time. No one knew where he came from, the commissioners told Clara. He had found work on local farms during the summer, but was so unpleasant to have in a home or at the table that, after a few days, farm wives refused to have him on their premises. Now, with corn picking about over and winter coming on, the county had to take him in.

Clara and Annie found him objectionable, too, but handled the matter by making him eat by himself in the entryway. Wherever he ate he made a mess but, with Mary, Liz or Sarah to clean up after him, there was no problem. Otherwise, Cabe, the first able-bodied man to be sent to the farm, was most welcome. He would not only bring in his weekly $4.00 boarding fee, but he could milk cows, feed pigs, clean stables and poultry houses and pick holiday birds.

And Annie needed him, for the Lucas case had been settled when a relative had come to move the crippled man and his family to happier surroundings. She had been sorry to see them go; she had made money on their keep and she missed the red-haired woman's help. But a greater loss was ahead of her, one to which she would never quite reconcile herself.

Chapter 22

Throughout her years on the farm Mary had gone to school as much as Annie would let her. After the day the Gypsy fortune teller had told her she would some day leave this place and have a nice life, an easy life, she had been more determined than ever to get an education. She loved to read and, in her little girl years, a nice life meant reading as much as she wanted to.

It had been slow going for, year after year, in spite of director Orson Covell's many visits to remind Annie of the law that required all Nebraska children to be in school until they graduated from the eighth grade or turned sixteen, the woman had kept her out of school more days than she let her go. And there had been some times that Mary had tried to forget.

Like the occasion, back in the sixth grade, when she had won a spelling certificate. Ever since the fourth grade she had been trying to win one of the coveted certificates, and failing each month because she had to stay home and work on the day of the spell-down. Then, on the last Friday in March, she had spelled down her class and won. With the treasured paper clutched tightly in her hand, she had run most of the way home.

Annie and Liz were in the kitchen when she hurried through the door. Holding out the certificate to her mother, she said, "See, I won the spell-down this month." Annie snatched the paper from Liz's reaching hand and scowled at it, her lips moving as she slowly read it. Then, raising her slit gaze to the girl's face, she said, "This damn thing means a lot to you, don't it?"

"Oh, yes," Mary whispered, then gave a pitiful little cry of pain, a sound such as a wounded, helpless rabbit makes, as Annie lifted the stove lid and dropped the handsome, scrolled paper into the flames.

And there had been the spring morning in her fifteenth year when she had hurried through her chores and changed her clothes, making ready for her last minute dash to school. Angry because two days of rain had made field and garden work impossible, Annie watched as the girl hurriedly combed her long, dark hair and began the thick braid she wore down her back. "Mary, you lazy slut," she growled suddenly, "you spend too damn much time crimping in front of that looking glass," and snatching a pair of scissors from the kitchen shelf, she caught the braid in her other hand and sheared it off close to the girl's head.

Mary made no sound, that time. Only her stricken eyes showed her understanding of what had happened. But Liz uttered a strangled wail of protest, and Clara was moved to say, "Oh, Mom, *that's* too much." When Annie reached for her buggy whip Liz shut her mouth and turned back to her dish washing and Mary snatched her coat and ran outside. But she did not go to school that day, nor again until fall, when her hair had grown enough for the beginning of a new braid.

Then, in mid-October of that autumn of 1924, in Mary's twenty-first year, Annie told Clara to buy a length of dress goods and a pair of cheap shoes for the girl, as there was nothing in the donation bin fit for her to wear to church on the few occasions they still attended. Sarah made the dress, fitting it to the skinny girl so that she looked a bit plumper, a little less starved.

The first new dress she had had since she came to the farm, sixteen years earlier, Mary put it on the next Sunday morning and came out of her storeroom bed chamber just as Annie came into the kitchen, dressed for church. To her aunt, Mary had been only a possession, another piece of property. But now, as she looked at the girl, her eyes suddenly narrowed even more. With the bright blue of the pretty dress giving color to her face, the woman saw that she was almost attractive. For the first time since her childhood she saw her as a *person* — a person with a higher dollar value.

Why not? She was sometimes short of girls for her parties at the bungalow; and Mary, always at hand, might be useful there.

That afternoon she called the girl into her room and shut the door. Shivering, Mary waited. She knew that, whatever her aunt had to say, it would not be good. Annie put the proposition to her niece, bluntly and plainly.

The girl's eyes widened in shock and she seemed to shrink even more into herself as she backed away. "No," she gasped. "No, no, no."

"Oh yes you will," Annie rasped. "You'll damn well do as I tell you to. You've no call to act so high and mighty as to think you're too good to sleep with any man I tell you to, you bastard. Now get out. I have to think."

Mary crept about the place the rest of the day, numb with fear and despair. What should she do? Who could she go to? Would Frank be able to help her? He had moved back into the beet shack, where he cooked his own meals, and seldom came to the house any more. All the while Annie seemed to be watching her, her hooded eyes glittering.

The next day the woman came to the girl again, but this time her manner was friendly, her voice soft and coaxing. If Mary would be a good girl and help her out at the party Saturday night, she said, she would pay her for it, and all she'd have to do was wear her new dress and look nice. She could sit at the big table with the rest of the guests and eat all she wanted.

"You'd like that, wouldn't you?" The vanilla voice was soft and wheedling as she went on. "The only other thing you'd have to do is go to bed with the man that partners you at supper."

But Mary still backed away, like a colt from the first feel of the bridle bit against its teeth. "No," she said again. "No, I'll die before I'll do that."

"You'll do it alright," Annie promised her grimly, all softness gone from her voice. "You'll do it, so you'd just as well make up your mind to it."

That night, in their little room, Mary whispered it all to her mother. The only time they ever dared talk to each other was at night, in bed and in whispers, for they knew that Annie often listened at their door. They had learned, long ago, that if she saw them talking together she would demand to know what they had talked about — and whip their legs until they told her.

"I'm going to run away again," Mary told her mother. "There's a different sheriff now, and maybe he'll help me. And when I get a job, and a place to live, I'll come and get you."

"Yes," Liz agreed, "you'll have to go. But don't come back for me. Annie will never let me go."

Mary had already run away twice, once when she was seventeen, and again when she was nearly nineteen. Both times she had reached North Platte, and both times she had been turned over to Sheriff Sayman and taken back to the farm, where Annie had whipped her cruelly and threatened to kill her if she ever tried it again.

The next day began as a sunny October Friday. The orchard and the big cottonwoods in the yard were leafless, but the corn in the big field north of the road stood tall and tawny, almost ready for the pickers. Annie put Mary to picking and dressing chickens and helping get ready for the big party in the bungalow the next evening, and the threatening glances she gave the girl kept her cold with dread.

"I'll have to go tonight," Mary whispered to her mother that afternoon, then turned uneasy as a cloud bank began to gather in the north and a chill crept over the valley. If the night was clear there would be a moon, and the girl could not tell, as yet, if it would be good or bad. If she slipped away after everyone was asleep, the moon would help light her way across the miles to town; if she had to run for it a dark and moonless night would be best.

After supper, with the patients fed and in their rooms, Clara went on an errand to the bungalow while Mary, Liz, and Sarah washed the dishes and cleaned up the kitchen. Annie started for the parlor and her rocking chair, but at the door turned suddenly and came back.

"Mary, you won't have to rub my feet tonight. I know you're tired, so you can go to bed as soon as you're finished here."

Mary's mind raced. Such consideration was wholly unlike her aunt. Did she suspect what she planned to do tonight? Of course she did. No one ever put anything over on Annie, she thought as her heart sank.

"Yes," Annie went on, "you just go on to bed and get a good night's sleep. I want you rested and fresh for the party tomorrow night."

"No," Mary screamed at her over the choking tightness in her throat. "I won't do it."

With a quick step to the corner, Annie caught up her whip. "Oh yes you will, you scar-faced slut."

"I won't. I'll never do it. I'll run away."

"Where would you run to? You've no place to go and nobody would have you. You found that out the other times you tried it. You're just an ugly slut and it's no good you thinking you're anything else." The whip slashed through the air at shoulder level. Mary covered her head with her arms and took the cut on her elbow.

"Say 'yes', you damn bitch," Annie roared, "or I'll beat you to death," and she raised the whip again.

"Never," the girl screamed.

The woman's slit eyes glared back at her cowering victim with an insane fury—and so they stood for a long moment.

Liz stood by the sink, frozen in fright and horror. Sarah, reaching to hang up the dish towel, became suddenly still. The hate, fear and tension, thick as summer fog in the room, had penetrated even her silent world. Little Joe, crouching under the table, watched with wide, frightened black eyes.

Then Annie, all self control gone, flung her whip away and caught up the big butcher knife from the work table beside the sink. The blade gleamed wickedly in the lamplight, for Frank kept all the knives and scissors honed to a razor's edge. Holding the knife like a spear, its point before her, the maddened woman ran at the girl. Mary screamed and jumped aside. The knife point missed her stomach but pierced her side at the tip of her hip. Still screaming, she whirled and ran as Annie drew back her arm, ready to strike again.

Then Liz and Sarah, moving together, jumped at the crazed woman and held her arm. "Run, run," Liz shrieked, and while Mary fled through the door into the early darkness, the two women wrestled the knife from Annie who, yelling and cursing, then caught up her whip and laid into Liz with it. And Liz, covering her head with her arms, stood and took the flogging. Every minute that Annie belabored her with the whip gave Mary time to get farther away.

Sarah pulled her son from under the table and slipped away to her room as Clara came back into the kitchen and demanded to know what was going on. Breathless and panting, Annie glared at her daughter for a moment; then, reason returning, she gasped, "Oh, my g—. *Mary, she's running away.*"

At once she became her usual keen, calculating self, organizing her search party and putting it into action. With a final slash at Liz, she ordered her to run to the beet shack and get Frank to help, then lit some lanterns and called the dogs. As they headed for the road and the cornfield beyond it, Liz came running back. Frank, she said, was not coming to help. Spitting curses, Annie scattered her helpers into the field.

Chapter 23

Mary, leaving the house on the run, fled across the barnyard, down the lane and across the road into the cornfield. There, slowed a little by the tall corn stalks, she jumped the furrows until she was well into the field before she turned east, toward town. Then she ran on, between the rows, until a sharp stitch in her side slowed her to a fast walk. As she hurried along she put her hand to her right side, where she had felt the stab of pain from the butcher knife. Her dress was wet and sticky; she wondered how long the cut was, and if she was still bleeding.

Well, no matter. The wound didn't hurt much, just a little stinging, and she had to keep going. Annie would be looking for her any minute now. The night was black dark and the air felt damp and chilly, as if it might rain soon. She was barefooted and had no coat or jacket, but there was no help for that either. She must keep going.

In the darkness it was difficult to keep running straight down the corn row. She kept bumping into the stalks, first on one side, then on the other — and then she heard the first sounds of pursuit, the dogs barking, and Annie calling her, and then Clara, and finally her mother's thin, anxious voice. She knew Liz called her only because Annie had ordered her to, under threat of the whip.

Then Annie called again, her voice honey sweet and smooth, "Mary, I'm sorry dear, sorry I hurt you. Just come back, Mary, and I'll make it up to you, I promise. You won't have to do anything you don't want to, Mary. Auntie wants you to come back." On and on, the vanilla voice beseeched her.

But the coaxing words, "Mary dear," only brought to the fleeing girl's mind the curling lip and contemptuous voice of her aunt when she had said, long ago, "When I call you 'Mary dear' I am really calling you a slut, you dirty little bastard." The memory only made her run the faster.

The voices sounded well behind her now. If she were to get over on the road she could make better time. She figured she was nearly to the east end of the field, anyway, nearly half a mile from the house, and she was sure that Annie would soon have to give up the pursuit, the way her feet must be hurting her by now.

As quietly and quickly as she could, Mary made her way back through the corn stalks to the road, where she began to run again. She could see nothing, but knew she was on the road as long as she could feel gravel beneath her bare feet. If she trod on grass or weeds it meant that she was in the shallow roadside ditch and she corrected her course accordingly.

Behind her the barking dogs and calling voices grew fainter, and then ceased. Suddenly it began to rain, a sharp, cold shower that soaked her thoroughly, then settled into a chilly drizzle. The girl plodded on.

Back in the field the searchers, too, were soaked by the shower, and Annie's feet were killing her. "Let's go back," she panted, "and get into dry clothes and drive back down the road. Tain't likely we'll find her but we'd better try. It'll be better if we catch the bitch before she gets to town and blabs all she knows. If we don't, we'll give it up for the night. It'll take her most of the night to get to town, and if we go after her again at daylight we can track her down the road, and maybe get her back before she does much damage."

The new sheriff was *not* one of Annie's friends, and if the girl got to him with her story the fat might be in the fire.

Mary, too, had thought of the possibility of her pursuers coming after her in the car, and when she heard the Ford chugging down the road she hid in the tall, dead weeds in the fence row at the far side of the road ditch, and again when the car returned. After that she plodded on, cold and wet, her side throbbing sharply now.

Now and then she stumbled into a chuckhole in the road and fell, the gravel stinging her hands and skinning her knees. Toward morning she was falling from sheer weariness, but each time she got up and plodded on. Dimly, she was remembering that, more than twenty years ago, her mother, too, had run away from Annie to get to town and marry her cowboy. She, too, had been ragged and dirty and scared, but she had made it — and Mary, too, was determined to make it in her turn.

Finally she saw a streak of light ahead of her, and then the looming shadow of the Bostwick bungalow beside the road. She began to sob with relief. She had almost made it. Now if she could just find a house with a light on, where somebody was up, she could go in and ask for help. She passed another house, dark and shadowy in the drizzly gloom, and then, a block or two ahead, a light came on. She tried to run again, but she was too cold and numb. Her leaden feet would move no faster.

As she did every morning, Margaret Johnson turned on her kitchen light at five o'clock and began to prepare breakfast for her father who had to be at the First National Bank at six to begin his janitor's duties.

She was stirring up a bowl of pancake batter when she heard something at the door, a sound like something falling against the door. A scarecrow figure almost fell into her arms when she pulled the door open. Calling to her father to come, quick, she helped the soaked, dirty girl to a chair.

Ben Johnson hurried into the room, pulling his suspenders over his shoulders as he came. By then the strange visitor was crying so hard she couldn't talk, deep, hoarse, hysterical sobs that shook her thin body. When the kindly pair tried to question her she only cried the harder. Finally they gave up and called sheriff Benson.

Roused from a sound sleep, the sheriff said he'd be right over. By the time he arrived Margaret had learned that the girl's name was Mary Knox and that she had run away from the Cook farm. The woman passed her information on to the sheriff, who nodded. "Yeah, I've heard that old woman's a devil," he said, his pitying eyes on the forlorn figure.

The sheriff sat down beside the girl and said gently, "Now, Mary, tell me what's wrong. Why are you here, all wet and muddy? And that looks like blood on the side of your dress. What happened?" But Mary only put her face in her hands and shivered. She seemed to have lost the power to speak.

When the sheriff could learn no more from her, he told the Johnsons he would take the girl on to his apartment behind the jail and get her cleaned up. "Then," he went on, "I guess we'll have to call Mrs. Cook and see what we can find out from her."

"No," Mary screamed. "No, no," and began to cry again.

"Wait a minute," Margaret Johnson broke in. "Maybe my neighbor can help us. I think she knows Mary. Let me give her a call."

The motherly neighbor, Myrtle Anderson, came right over, but Mary, dazed by fear and exhaustion, only stared at her blankly.

"Look, Mary," Mrs. Anderson said, "my sister, Lena Meyers used to go to school with you. You remember Lena? She lived with the Spanglers for several years and went to your school. I'm her sister and I want to help you. But you'll have to tell me what happened."

With an effort the girl pulled herself together and focused her eyes on the kindly face before her. Then, in broken, jerky sentences, she related the events of the past few hours. "But," she whispered at the end of her tale, "I've run away before, and that other sheriff always took me back."

"This sheriff won't take you back," the man's voice was rough with the pity he felt. "You come with me and I'll help you. We'll get you cleaned up and have a doctor look at that cut, and then we'll decide what to do."

The sheriff and Mary left and the neighbor headed down the block to her own home. A few minutes later Annie and Clara halted their car in front of the house and came to the door. They had readily followed Mary's barefoot tracks in the muddy gravel to where they turned off the road in front of the Johnson house.

Margaret stood squarely in the doorway, staring coldly at her visitors. "Is Mary Knox here?" Annie asked in her smooth company voice. But before she could explain that there had been a little trouble and Mary had become frightened and run away, and that they had been looking for her most of the night, Margaret Johnson told them the sheriff had taken Mary to the jail, and shut the door.

"Damn bitch," Annie muttered as they went back to their car.

The sheriff's family living quarters were at the back of the big brick jail, and Annie had been there several times in Sheriff Sayman's time. She went there now, and asked for Mary.

"I'll get her," Benson told her as he showed them to chairs in the parlor, then went to another door and called to his wife to send Mary in.

The girl slipped through the door and stood close to the sheriff. Bathed and wearing a robe much too large for her, she looked exhausted, her dark eyes shadowed and the old scar starkly white in her sun browned face.

Before Annie could speak the sheriff said, "Mary, your aunt has come for you. Do you want to go home with her?"

And in the most courageous act of her life, the girl looked straight into the slitted, glittering eyes of her aunt and said, "I'll die before I'll go home with you."

With a hurt look on her face, Annie said smoothly, "Why Mary, after all I've done for you, after I've given you and your mother a good home all these years, you talk to me like this?" Her pain seemed almost more than she could bear. Turning to her daughter, she said sadly, "Well, Clara, I guess we'd just as well go." Swiveling her little eyes back to Mary, she said sweetly, "But Mary, when you settle down and come to your senses and want to come home, you just let Auntie know and we'll come right in and get you."

As she turned heavily to leave, she shot a last question at the sheriff. "What do you figure on doing with her? She's never been away from home before, you know."

"We'll find something," Benson replied.

"Damn that sheriff," Annie muttered darkly to Clara as they got into their car. "If we still had Sayman he would've brought her back."

Chapter 24

Until Mary was gone from the farm none of her co-laborers had appreciated how much work the skinny, silent girl had turned off. Liz and Sarah realized it more than the others, for her work fell to them to do. Even Clara had to help more to keep things going, but Annie swore that she missed her more than the others—for now she had no one to rub her aching feet while they sat in the parlor of an evening. She had made Sarah try it, but the deaf woman hadn't the knack for it either. So she had Liz put a handful of Epsom salts in a half-bushel pail of warm water, and while her feet soaked she crocheted, squinting her little eyes over her many plans for getting her runaway back.

A few days after Mary left the last of the bedfast old men died. But just before it was time to dress the Thanksgiving poultry the county sent another patient to the Poor Farm, kindly old Johnny Beedle. Grown too frail to work for wages, or even for his room and board, but still able, Annie figured, to help pick scalded chickens and turkeys.

Frank still caught and killed the birds and brought them to the shed where Johnny and Cabe scalded and hung them by the feet from hooks in the rafters and stripped away their feathers. At the other side of the shed Sarah and Liz dressed them and took them, clean and trussed, to the kitchen. There Annie went over each one, cursing if she found so much as a pin feather. Her birds were the best to be had in the whole community, and her trade had grown accordingly.

Throughout the process the stocky, scowling woman frequently used her whip on her unfortunate helpers, and even Sarah felt the sting of it now, whenever Annie thought she was slowing up a little. Through most of that cold week before Thanksgiving they worked in the unheated shed. If Mary had been with them they could have finished much sooner.

On the Sunday following Thanksgiving, Harley Costin, Clara and Annie sat over cake and coffee in the Cook kitchen, talking of the courthouse fire and its aftermath. Of Sellers and Bader, whose cases were still pending appeals, of Arlie Aden, awaiting sentencing for his part in the affair, and of the new courthouse.

Enough rooms had been knocked together on the second floor to house and carry on the county's business, but there was no paint anywhere, and no finished woodwork; only raw surfaces, bare plank doors and rough cement floors, while its lofty arched Grecian Doric windows stared blankly out on Main Street.

"It'll prob'ly stay that way for quite awhile," Costin predicted. "The taxpayers are dead set against voting any more money for the building, not even to buy glass for all those big windows. Last Monday we ordered twelve-foot bridge planks to cover 'em, and tomorrow they'll start boarding 'em up. It'll look like hell, but its all we can do."

Annie nodded. She knew how it was; for she stopped in every now and then to squint over the new tax records and note the most recent forfeitures, the latest victims of the edict that all who could not produce a receipt must pay their 1922 taxes again.

"It's been a hell of a mess," the commissioner went on, gloomily, "and with elections comin' up again next year, the voters are likely to clean house when they go to the polls. Damn few of us are going to be back in office, come January, 1925."

"Then we'd better have another party," Annie decided. "We haven't had one since that damn fire and its time we get organized and moving again."

"But whatever happens," Costin told Clara, "you go ahead and put in your bid for the Poor Farm. I'm pretty sure you'll get it if you still want it."

Several familiar faces were missing from that pre-Christmas party: Sylvester Sellers, Arthur Aden, Allen Bader and Tom Cooper. Neither was Emmet Sodman there. Replaced by Evans at the last election, he was no longer on Annie's guest list. But W. R. Munson was there, and Charlie Sayman, who seldom missed a party, even after his own ouster by Benson, two years back.

Annie let it be known, that night, that she would bring all of her considerable influence to bear, and that she would even put up some money where it would help the most, to keep her friends in office, or to help elect new ones who would see things her way.

.

Chapter 25

Following Costin's advice, Clara put in her bid for the contract to care for the county poor for the year of 1924 and, as usual, the competition had been stiff. A May Brown, of North Platte, wanted the contract, and Bertha Dean of Hershey was still battling her determined neighbor, J. Abbott, for the right to keep the county poor.

In a speech before the county commissioners, Abbott stated that, if the contract was awarded to Mrs. Dean, he would present a petition. They didn't want Negroes, Mexicans and the like, roaming their town, he said, and drinking from the public hydrants used by school children.

Why not, he demanded, leave the poor where they are, at the Cook farm, where they have plenty of good, wholesome food, comfortable quarters, and kind-hearted people to care for them? With the run of the farm, and vegetables and fruit in quantity, it's an ideal place for them. Besides, he concluded, if the Poor House was to be located in Hershey, it would lower property values in the whole town.

There was one more bid, submitted on the last day of the dying year by Alara Costin, Harley Costin's wife of thirty-five years. It was accompanied by a "Letter of Remonstrance" against the letting of the contract for the care of the county paupers to Clara Cook, and read:

"Comes now Alara Costin of Sutherland, Nebraska, and herewith objects to the county letting the contract to Miss Clara Cook for the following reasons, to wit:

"1. That your said objector is a taxpayer of Lincoln County and is vitally interested in the welfare of the people of said county and in having said people cared for in a proper manner, with as little cost as possible, and believes, and can produce, facts to satisfy the board that some of the accounts presented and allowed are improper accounts and should not be charged for the care and keep of the poor.

"2. Your objector further alleges that she has reason to believe, knows the facts to be, and can produce the evidence to show, that Clara Cook has failed and neglected to abide by, and fulfill, her part of the contract, and is confident that a change is necessary for the financial benefit of the county.

"3. Your objector further objects to the moral atmosphere, environment, and conduct at said home, provided by Clara Cook for the poor of the county, and respectfully represents to the board that the conduct is improper, illegal, and does not and should not meet the approval of the board.

"4. Your objector further contends that there are other bids more reasonable for the care provided than the bid of Clara Cook, and as a taxpayer and a resident of the county, and as one interested in the welfare of the poor of Lincoln County, objects to the board considering the bid of Clara Cook for this year.

"Your objector contends that she is able to prove all the allegations herein.

Signed,
Alara Costin."

Annie was furious when the letter was published in the *Telegraph*, along with the other county business for that week. There could be no doubt now that Alara Costin, and probably the rest of the community, knew what was going on at the Poor Farm, both in the treatment of the county poor and the goings on at the bungalow. A number of other "taxpayers" got in line and raised their voices in moral indignation, and Jess Evans hung stubbornly to his vote for a change, but Annie had already enrolled Tom Cooper's replacement, Faye Davis, on her side, and knew she could depend on him.

The contract was awarded to Clara. After awhile the outcry died away and life went on as usual at the Poor Farm.

With the coming of spring the three "walk about" old men came out of their cheerless rooms to seek the sunny sides of the farm buildings, soaking up the warmth their stiff old bones needed and enjoying the fragrance of the flower laden lilac bushes. Little Joe sat with them most of the time, none of them saying much. He would have liked to be with his mother, but when he talked to her with his fingers she dared not answer him. *Her* fingers were busy with her planting and weeding and Annie was watching to see that she kept them so.

Little Joe was five now. He had lost his little-boy roundness and become as skinny as the rest of Annie's underfed family, and the sparkle in his big black eyes had been replaced by fear. He stayed as far from Annie and her whip as he could.

Frank had tried a half-acre of cabbage the previous summer, raising the seedlings in his big hot-bed on the south side of the barn. They had made a good profit on the large, firm heads and could have sold more. So this year Annie said they would put a whole acre to cabbage. Setting out the acre of little plants had taken all hands, even old Mrs.

Baker, who enjoyed garden work, and old Johnny and, of course, Cabe.

Most of the hoeing and weeding of the big patch had fallen to Frank, Liz and Sarah. Annie had tried Mrs. Baker and old Johnny at it, but the old woman fainted under the hot sun one forenoon, and the old man could only crawl along the rows, pulling such weeds as he could see with his dimming eyes. The tireless Cabe could not be used at all as a weeder — he pulled and hoed *everything*, vegetables as well as weeds.

Annie held another of her parties on election night. Quite a number of the county officials were among the guests: Faye Davis, Dr. Duncan and W. R. Munson. Nate Elsen, a middle-aged bachelor attorney, a new friend of Annie's, and Charley Sayman and Harley Costin, were there, as well as her former banker, Riley Landers, and several others.

An unspoken rule prevailed at the Cook parties — none of the men invited ever brought his own wife. Most of the guests had their own lady friends and appreciated the opportunity of entertaining them at the Cook bungalow. It seemed more decorous, or more sophisticated, than slipping out of town to a hotel.

The house was crowded, that cold November evening, the guests determinedly festive, as they filled their plates at the loaded buffet table and their glasses from the pitchers of "juice" lined up on the sideboard.

The polls closed at eight o'clock and Annie had arranged to have the "returns" brought out at ten. By then the figures, though not final, would at least show the "trend" for each office. Another of her new friends, Art Haynes, had offered to wait at the courthouse until ten, then rush the figures out to the farm.

A stocky, broad-shouldered man of thirty-five, Haynes, a dealer in real estate, had bumped into Annie that summer when they both went after the same piece of tax-delinquent property. Strangely enough, they became friends over the deal, and that election night it was Haynes who burned up the road to the farm with the election news.

Harley Costin had lost to Ben Esely of Hershey, Faye Davis, Tom Cooper's temporary replacement, had won by a landslide. Sheriff Benson, in office only a few months when the courthouse burned, was re-elected. W. C. Jones, the fiesty county attorney, had so pleased the voters by his vigorous prosecution of Sellers, Bader and Aden that they voted him in again, but Dr. Duncan, county physician for the past fourteen years, had been replaced by Dr. S. A. Reardon, a younger man.

Thaddeus Long, appointed to replace county clerk Aden immediately after the fire, and Ralph Teeman, treasurer Sellers' replacement, had been elected to fill those offices. There had been others in the running and Annie had decided to wait to see who the victors would be before offering them the hospitality of her bungalow. Neither Long, a strait-laced Presbyterian, nor young Teeman, studious, bespectacled former bank clerk, would be good candidates for her parties—but both might be useful.

Costin's loss threw a decided pall over the party. There was nothing left to do but drown their disappointment in bootleg whiskey.

The next day, over cake and coffee at the Cook kitchen table, Costin advised Clara to go ahead and put in her third bid for the Poor Farm contract. "Davis and Esely are good men. I've talked to both of them and they agree it would be a waste of time and money to move the patients so soon. Jess Evans still don't like you," he grinned at Annie, "but two votes out of three still wins."

Chapter 26

Ada Kelly, wife of A. P., publisher of the *Telegraph*, had long been the beloved Lady Bountiful of her community. With the help of fellow members of the North Platte Woman's Club, the Woman's Christian Temperance Union and like groups, she had sought out the town's poor and discouraged and lent a helping hand. So it was to Ada Kelly that Sheriff Benson turned for help for Mary.

Small, plump and bustling, the good lady took charge. Over the years she had taken in numerous unfortunate girls, befriended and trained them until they married and went into homes of their own. Her present house maid, a needy young woman who had been with her for the past year, would be leaving soon to get married, she told the sheriff, so she could use a new girl.

Benson told her as much of Mary's story as he knew, and the woman shook her head in dismay. "It's hard to believe, but I've been hearing things about that Cook place for quite awhile. Now maybe we can learn enough from the girl that we can do something about it."

Mary had her own room at the big Kelly house on West Fifth Street, and the kitchen, large, well-lighted and cheerful, was furnished with every modern convenience. All the rooms were comfortable and attractive with their pleasant melding of good modern furniture with lovely old antiques. She loved the house and Ada Kelly, but it was months before she stopped flinching whenever her employer entered the room and spoke to her briskly. During most of her life the sudden sound of a voice had been followed by the cutting slash of a whip.

Ada Kelly noticed, and noticed, too, that the girl was very reluctant to go to the store or on an errand by herself. She had thought it only shyness and timidity, and that she would soon get over it, but when she realized that it was *fear* she asked, "Mary, what are you afraid of? It's only four blocks to the store, just a nice little walk." And Mary finally whispered, "What if Annie comes along and gets me back? She'll kill me if she ever does."

"*Mary, Annie Cook is never going to get you back. You are twenty-one now and she can't make you go back. I will see to that, and so will Sheriff Benson and a lot of other people.*"

So Mary began going to the store, but walking fast, almost running, and keeping a sharp lookout for Annie's car. If she should see it, and hear that vanilla voice, "Oh Mary dear ____ ," she meant to run for home as fast as she could. The fear of Annie was something she knew she would never get over.

Ada Kelly's plan for getting the whole story of Annie and the Poor Farm from Mary did not seem to be coming to anything, for Mary kept her silence, answering her employer's questions in monosyllables, volunteering nothing. "Poor little thing, she's scared to death," the older woman thought. "What a hellion that old Annie Cook must be."

So she was kinder than ever to Mary. She had already bought her new clothes and helped her shampoo and brush her long, heavy hair and try becoming ways to "put it up." She gave her a handful of "kid curlers" and showed her how to make a row of little curls across her forehead, and bought her a jar of makeup cream and helped her work it into the puckered scar below her eye until the blemish scarcely showed at all.

Mary was almost tearfully grateful for the makeup cream, but when Ada Kelly asked her how she got the scar she only dropped her head and muttered that it was "just a burn," and would say no more.

At first sight of the girl the good woman had been shocked at her thinness. "She's been starved," she told A. P., and set about fattening her up. Mary was hungry, there was no doubt about that, but she seemed afraid to eat all she wanted and her employer had to urge her to eat more, to "have some more of this, Mary, it's good for you." The girl's humped shoulders bothered her, too, and she said, over and over, "Stand straight and tall, Mary, you've nothing to be ashamed of."

With the passing weeks the girl's thin figure filled out. Her skinny arms and legs rounded, her shoulders began to straighten and her dimples showed again as her cheeks plumped. By spring she looked like the girl she should have been for the past half-dozen years.

Ada Kelly was pleased with Mary. She was a good worker, quick and capable, neat and efficient, and had quickly learned her duties in the Kelly home. It was only her silence that bothered the good woman. Watching the girl, she wondered what dark and terrible thoughts and memories were hidden behind her sad and quiet face.

She often brought her little presents, and one sunny April day she gave her a pair of new slippers. "They were on sale, and you have such slim, pretty feet, Mary, so I thought you should have a pair."

"I didn't think my feet would ever be pretty," the girl said, putting on a slipper and holding out her foot to look at it. "I've gone barefoot most of my life and they always looked so big and awful to me."

It was the most she had said at one time in all the months she had been in the Kelly home and Ada was overjoyed. At last Mary was talking.

Many times, that past winter, Mary had wanted to talk, to tell this kind woman what it had been like, living under Annie's whip and tongue. She had felt it would be a relief to tell it all, but each time she tried the old fear overcame her, welling up in her throat and holding the words back. She knew *she should tell—for the sakes of her mother and poor Sarah and little Joe* and all those other poor souls at Annie's mercy. If she told maybe Mrs. Kelly could find a way to help them.

At first Mary talked mostly of her mother and herself, with now and then some mention of Sarah Martin and her little boy. Ada listened, and asked questions, until she had learned all that Mary knew about the unfortunate mother and son. Then she went to see Emma Pulver, who was still bristling over the high-handed way in which Sarah and little Joe had been taken from her.

Justly angry over the whole situation, Mrs. Kelly demanded of her husband that he publish the story in his newspaper, expose the whole thing and wake the people up to what was going on out at the Poor Farm. But A. P. said he didn't see how it could be done. If he wrote a strong enough story to really help any, he'd be in trouble himself. He dared not implicate W. R. Munson, his biggest advertiser, nor any of the county commissioners or other county officials, since he now got all of the lucrative county printing and reports. If he made any of them mad at him they'd take the business to the *Lincounty County Tribune*, whose editor had long been willing to give his eye teeth to get it.

Ada Kelly did not give up. She talked to many people in the months that followed, and pulled a few strings of her own. By March of 1925 she had found a good home for the deaf woman and her son. A well-to-do elderly farm couple in Phelps County, sixty-five miles to the east, wanted a housekeeper and had no objection to the little boy. With the arrangements made, even to the day on which Sarah Martin and little Joe were to be put on the train in North Platte, Mrs. Kelly and two of her W.C.T.U. friends drove out to the Poor Farm.

It was Ada's first trip to the place she had heard so much about. It was a bleak spring day, with a few high clouds scudding across the sky, and patches of snow from a late February storm still pocking the fields and the graveled highway. Carefully steering her big Buick town car between the winter chuckholes, she drove down the lane into the farmyard, forlorn beneath the leafless cottonwoods.

Annie met the visitors at her kitchen door, silencing the snarling dogs and smiling her loose-lipped smile. The big car denoted callers of importance. Ada Kelly introduced herself and her friends, then asked to see Sarah Martin. Annie was not too surprised. Thad Long had already told her of the move afoot to send Sarah, her best worker, away. "Come in, I'll call her," she said, and moved aside.

Two women, one bent, skinny and barefoot, the other tall and shockingly thin, were working in the kitchen end of the big room. A bent old woman was setting the table for the noon meal. "Liz, tell Sarah to come here," Annie said, as she led her callers into the parlor.

Ada saw the barefooted woman tap the thin one on the shoulder, then point toward Annie and her visitors and give her a little shove in their direction. Annie seated her callers and motioned Sarah to them. When the deaf woman understood that they wanted to talk to her, she presented her pad and pencil.

Ada Kelly took it and wrote busily for a little while, then handed it back. The deaf woman read it through, turned back and read it through again. When she finally looked up there was a tired sparkle in her sad eyes. She nodded vigorously, then wrote a quick line or two on the pad and handed it back. She and her son would be ready, she wrote, when they came for her the next day.

Annie, who had planted her solid bulk by the door to watch, now spoke up. "She's not going anywhere," she stated. "She belongs here and I'll see that she stays."

"But we have the arrangements all made and Sheriff Benson is coming for her tomorrow."

"It won't do him any good. I'll get an injunction. They're going to stay here where they belong."

"We'll see about that," spunky Ada Kelly promised as she and her friends took their leave.

Thoroughly upset, Ada went straight to see the sheriff, who listened to her indignant tale and said, "Well, she's a powerful old woman, but I'll see what I can do. She may hold things up for awhile, but I don't think she can get away with it."

So they telephoned the Phelps County people, told them there would be a delay, and asked them to hold the position open.

The first of September had come before they had the matter settled. Annie had fought stubbornly, with injunctions and every device she and the county judge could bring to bear. To please Annie the new commissioners, Esely and Davis, would have voted to leave the Martins where they were. But Jess Evans put up a determined fight to let them go, and with Benson and Long and other officials aware of the fact that the deaf woman could be self-supporting, it seemed best to let them go.

This time it was sheriff Benson who took the news to the Poor Farm. On Monday, September 7, a warm, hazy day, the sheriff drove past ripening cornfields, well pleased with his errand. It wasn't often that anyone bested Annie Cook.

Annie had her crew in the orchard, picking up windfalls and pressing them into cider. As the sheriff's car turned into the lane, she leaned her buggy whip against the far side of a tree and went to meet him. To his surprise, she took the news calmly. "I'll have her and the boy ready," she said.

The sheriff held a brief pencil-pad conversation with the too-thin woman. Once again the news of her imminent release brought a tired sparkle to her eyes. He would come for her on Wednesday, the sheriff wrote. Sarah replied that little Joe was now in school, but that she would keep him home and they would be ready to go on that day.

Back in town the sheriff stopped to see Ada Kelly. "I sure thought the old lady would blow up, but she didn't. Queer, after the scrap she put up last spring to keep the woman."

"Well, I'm just glad it's nearly over," the good lady said. "But I want you to be sure and stop here on your way to the depot. We've got some decent clothes together for that poor woman and her little boy, and a good suitcase to put them in. We don't want them totally destitute when they get to that fine Larsen farm."

The next afternoon Benson called Ada on the telephone, the shock he had just undergone shaking his voice. Annie, he said, had just called to tell him that Sarah Martin was dead. He then repeated the story the woman had just told him. After the noon meal Mrs. Martin had said she had a bad headache and had gone to her room to lie down. Her room being on the west side of the house, she had pulled the blind before she laid down.

According to Annie, she had these headaches often and kept a bottle of medicine for them on a chair beside her bed. She also kept a bottle of carbolic acid on the chair, using it at night to treat an itch on her hands. The bottles were about the same size, and in the darkened room she must have taken a swallow from the wrong bottle.

"I've already talked to Doc Reardon," the sheriff said. "He says it's a plain case of accidental poisoning, and Munson has already brought the body in. She's to be buried tomorrow."

"But what about that poor little boy?" asked Ada. "What will become of him?"

"I suppose he'll have to stay where he is," Benson said. "I wouldn't know what else."

Chapter 27

Little Joe had gone to school as usual, that Tuesday morning, after his mother had scrubbed his face, neck and ears at the kitchen wash bench and combed his hair. It was seldom that any of the clothing from the donation bin fit the boy, but his mother's skilled needle had taken in too-large garments until they fit him neatly. He looked clean and well cared for as he accepted Sarah's good-bye kiss and trotted off to school with his little lard pail lunch bucket.

He had been going to school for a week and liking it. For the first time in his life he was with other children; the teacher, young and pretty, "liked kids," and, best of all, he was out of reach of Annie's harsh voice and stinging buggy whip.

But that afternoon Clara came to the schoolhouse door and held a brief, low-voiced conversation with the teacher. Then the teacher came to Joe's little desk, with tears in her eyes, and told him he was to go home with Miss Cook. He didn't often get to ride in the car and would have been excited about it, except that Clara hurried him into the Ford and got in herself, all without saying a word. When he asked her what was the matter, she replied, without looking at him, that he would find out when they got home.

Frightened and expecting to be punished for something, the boy went into the kitchen where Annie, doing something at the table, turned to him and said, "Come here," then led the way into the room where he slept with his mother. The blind was down and the room shadowed. Annie went to the bed and turned back the sheet that covered it.

Little Joe looked down on the still white face of his mother. Suddenly he wanted to cry, but was afraid to. Annie used her whip on him when he cried, so now he only asked, his voice quavering, "What's the matter with her?"

"She's dead," the woman answered, and spread the sheet smooth again.

A few minutes later Munson's black hearse drove into the yard. The mortician and Annie held a short, whispered conversation, something about a "death certificate" and an "accident," before he and his helper went into the bedroom with a long wicker basket. When they came out, each carrying an end of the basket, the child knew he would never see his mother again. Too frightened now to cry, he watched the men carry their burden to the hearse and drive away.

Since the day he and his mother had come to the farm his life had been neither pleasant nor easy. Now he knew it was going to be worse. In his mother he had had a friend and sympathizer, someone who cared for him. Now he had no one. He was alone. Five years old and alone.

The *Telegraph* reported briefly that Mrs. Sarah Martin, age 40, had died of accidental poisoning on September 8, 1925, at the county Poor Farm, with burial on September 9 in the North Platte cemetery. Her card at Munson's mortuary listed only her name, her age, the physician's name, date of her death and the cost of her burial, $45.00.

The evening that the undertaker took his mother away, Annie put little Joe into the storeroom with Liz to sleep. Frightened, lonely and hungry, he cried quietly into his blanket. And Liz, exhausted from her day at the cider press and still grieving for her own lost Mary, reached over from her cot to his to give him a comforting pat on the shoulder.

The next morning Annie brought his school clothes from his mother's room and told him that, from now on, he was to change in the entryway, hang his chore clothes on a nail by the door, then change back when he came home from school. And, as it had been with Mary before him, he was to get home as quick as he could after school. There was to be no loitering in the schoolyard after four o'clock, no "wrasseling" with the other boys, no "fooling around" on the way home.

The chore clothes the boy put on that afternoon, scrounged from the donation bin, were much too large. He looked like a little clown in the pants, cinched to his skinny waist with a piece of rope and the legs rolled up; the faded shirt, hanging off his shoulders and the sleeves rolled halfway to the elbows.

Little Joe had a right to wonder, after his mother's death, why he had ever been born; for his space in the world seemed to be only a narrow cot in a dark room—and a nail by the door in the entryway.

Now that Sarah was gone there was plenty for the boy to do, helping Liz with the poultry, bringing in fuel for the stoves, feeding the bucket calves after Frank and Liz finished milking and separating— and all to the stinging swish of Annie's whip. Only Frank was always kind and, sometimes, Clara. But Annie kept him away from Frank as much as she could and Clara seldom had time for him.

As she had done with Mary, Annie soon began keeping Joe out of school whenever she had need of him, and greying Orson Covell began calling on her again to talk about it.

One November evening the woman completely lost her temper with the boy and used a board on him instead of her buggy whip, then sent him to bed without supper.

The next morning when she came into the room to get him and Liz up, she brought the lantern with her, dragged the sleepy boy out of bed and ordered him to drop his oversized, long-legged winter underwear to his ankles. Wincing with pain, Joe obeyed, shivering with cold and fright as Annie inspected the results of her handiwork—the black and blue bruises on his back, buttocks, arms and legs.

Her little eyes narrowed to gleaming slits, as she reflected that she must have hit the brat harder than she meant to, then ordered him to get dressed and get at his chores.

After the boy had gone to school she called Orson Covell and told him that Joe had come home from school the day before all black and blue from a beating the teacher had given him with a yardstick. "He prob'ly needed a whipping," the vanilla voice purred, "but I don't think she needed to beat him that hard."

"I see," Covell said. "Well, Mrs. Cook, there's only one way to settle something like this. You be at the schoolhouse at four o'clock and I'll meet you there and we'll talk to little Joe and the teacher."

Covell's car was already in the schoolyard when Annie and Clara drove in, just as the children came pouring out of the schoolhouse. Joe, his dinner pail in his hand, stopped still and seemed to shrink into his too-large jacket when he saw Annie's car in the yard. In her company voice she called to him to wait a minute, and began to ease her heavy body out of the Ford.

The teacher stood in the doorway, surprised and uneasy as she looked at her visitors. A meeting like this probably portended trouble, and with Mrs. Cook one of her callers, she could be sure of it. A new teacher at the Nichols school, she knew Annie only by reputation—and most of what she had heard had not been good.

The westering winter sun flooded the schoolroom as the teacher seated her visitors, then sat down at her desk, facing them. Little Joe slid, hesitant and scared, into his own small desk in the front row.

When the director explained the reason for the visit, the teacher looked astonished, then distressed. "Why, I haven't even seen any marks on the child," she said, "and I certainly haven't touched him."

Covell then turned to the boy. "Now, Joe," he said in his kindly way, "I want you to roll up your sleeves so we can see if there are any bruises on your arms. Don't be afraid. Nobody's going to hurt you. We just want to see if there are any bruises, that's all." But Joe only cowered lower in his seat, his head down, and began to cry in silent terror, the big tears sliding down his gaunt little face.

The director then went to him, picked up first one scrawny little arm, then the other, and rolled up his shirtsleeves. The angry black and blue marks were very evident for what they were. Someone had brutally beaten the child.

"But I never touched him," the teacher protested, "did I, Joe? I'd never beat a child like that. It's inhuman."

Annie sat solidly in her seat and said nothing at all, a knowing, accusing half-smile on her slack lips, her eyes glinting behind their slit lids. Clara, following her mother's lead, also remained silent. The boy went on crying, pitiful, silent, frightened tears, and Covell, still holding the little arm, could feel his trembling.

Turning to the three women, he said, "Well, I guess that's about all. I just don't want anything like this to happen again." He looked at the teacher as he spoke, but she read only reassurance in his eyes, and in the kindly smile he gave her.

Annie led the way out of the room, a suggestion of a waddle in the swaying of her wide hips, as she rubbed her mole with satisfaction. She knew the director hadn't believed her story, but she also knew he would not do anything more about the incident.

Nichols School. Joe Cook, standing next to little girl in white. The shoes Joe is wearing look almost twice the size of the shoes of the boy beside him.

Chapter 28

By the end of Mary's first six months at the Kelly's, her own mother would scarcely have recognized her as the attractive, neatly dressed young woman she had become. Daily use of the makeup cream almost hid the old burn scar, and she smiled more often as the weeks passed. Except for knowing that her mother was still at Annie's mercy, she was happy and content. Sometimes she wondered if all this was really true, and not a dream from which she'd waken any minute to the reality of Annie's whip and curses.

Was this the nice, easy life the Gypsy had foretold for her? It was not that there wasn't plenty of work to do here. There was, helping Ada Kelly care for the big house and entertain her many clubs and friends. But it was pleasant work, caring for lovely things, handling fine dishes and linens, making dainty sandwiches and salads. A far cry from milking cows, or picking turkeys and gagging at the sickening smell of their hot, wet feathers.

It was at this time that an elderly couple, a Mr. and Mrs. William Dauphin, came to the big house one evening to see the Kellys on business. Mary served refreshments before they left and the Dauphins asked about the girl, and "tsked, tsked" when they learned she was from the Poor Farm, Annie Cook's niece, no less. They had heard tales of the goings on there, they said, and were glad that Mary had gotten away. Like many others, they shook their heads and wondered why "somebody doesn't do something about that place."

The Dauphins took a liking to Mary that evening, and on their way home Mrs. Dauphin said wistfully, "I wish Willie would take a fancy to her. She seems a steady sort of girl, not flighty nor afraid of work."

Willie was their twenty-five-year-old son, a late-born lad and a problem his elderly parents did not know how to handle. Maybe, if he were to meet and marry a good girl like Mary he would settle down and behave himself.

Mrs. Dauphin saw to it that they met, and was pleased that young Will seemed attracted to the girl. The following weeks were happy ones for Mary. Will Dauphin was a handsome young fellow, a snappy dresser and a good spender. His new Whippet was parked often at the Kelly's that summer.

Ada Kelly was pleased, too. "Old William Dauphin is a well-to-do man," she told Mary. "He owns several farms and A. P. says he is the owner, or part owner, of a couple of banks."

Totally innocent in the ways of a man with a maid, Mary had neither the experience nor the will power to resist her suitor when he became too affectionate, too demanding. Over and over, he told her not to worry, if anything happened they would be married. And when, in early November, Mary told him she was pregnant, young Will, surprisingly, agreed to go through with the ceremony anytime she wanted to.

After a tearful parting from the Kelly's, Mary moved into the Dauphin home, where Will's mother, a former dressmaker, made her wedding outfit. As she and her future mother-in-law worked on her clothes, Mary longed for her own mother, wishing that poor skinny Liz could be a part of her happiness. But once she was established in her own home, she planned, she would go and get her mother. She didn't yet know how she would get her away from Annie, but she had friends now, the sheriff and Mrs. Kelly and old Mr. Dauphin, and maybe they could manage it.

Will and Mary left the Dauphin home in the Whippet on the morning of December 19, 1924, a bright, clear day, for Sterling, Colorado, where they were married that afternoon.

The newly-weds spent two days in Colorado, putting up at the best hotels and seeing the sights. Before starting home Mary's husband borrowed the rest of her savings, explaining that he had miscalculated on the cost of their wedding trip. And by that time she had learned that the Whippet was his mother's and the money he had spent all summer was his father's.

On their return home Will's father told him he and Mary could have one of his farms in Sherman County, a hundred miles to the east. His renter was moving and he would set them up on the vacant place with everything they'd need to farm, and a second-hand Ford to boot, as Mrs. Dauphin wanted to keep her car at home.

The parents hoped that getting Will away from his old friends, a "fast" crowd at best, would give him a better chance to settle down and become a steady family man. Mary was pleased. She knew all about farm life, and working for Will and herself, on a farm of their own, suited her fine. Only Will was unhappy. He had planned on his father setting him up in a filling station, or a garage, in town.

From the first Mary worked hard on the Sherman County farm, doing all the familiar chores she had done at Annie's: milking cows, tending poultry, sows and little pigs, churning, marketing eggs and butter, putting in a big garden. Will was not much help. Too often he did not come home from town until long after the evening chores were done. Mornings he hated to get up and Mary did the milking alone. She bore it patiently, however, telling herself how lucky she was to be doing the work of her own free will, rather than under the threat of Annie's whip.

When it came time to put in the corn life became more difficult. Mary, nearing the end of her pregnancy, could not handle that, too. Harnessing the team and riding all day on the disc and corn planter was more than she dared attempt. Will got up, grumbling, dragged off to the field late in the mornings and came in again early in the evenings so he could drive into town. He was still planting corn days after all his neighbors were done.

In the end it didn't matter much, for that was a dry summer for unirrigated farms and the harvest was a scanty one. About all they made, that first year, was the money Mary took in for her butter and eggs.

Their son, another William Dauphin, was born in June and the older Will proudly paraded his fatherhood, and for a few days did the chores and treated his wife with consideration. Then went back to his evenings in town while Mary did the chores.

The second year on the farm was even harder for Mary. Now she not only had most of the work to do but a growing baby to care for. There was adequate rain, that summer, but Will's fields were late planted and weedy, the yield poor. That fall he told his father he was through with farming, as it didn't pay, and he intended to come home and find a business more in keeping with his style and abilities.

They did fairly well on the sale of the livestock and machinery and Will used the money to buy a new car and move his family back to Lincoln County. Will Dauphin, Sr., had moved to another of his farms the previous year, out on Bignell Flat, fifteen miles southeast of North Platte. Mrs. Dauphin, in failing health, had stayed on in their town home. So now Will took Mary and the baby to the little house on the Bignell farm and left her there to help his father.

Swallowing her disappointment over the failure of their own farming venture, Mary buckled down to helping her father-in-law make a success of his. She helped with the milking and separating and began making butter again, knowing she could sell all she could make to Ada Kelly and her friends at premium prices.

Under Mary's expert management (learned under the stinging lash of Annie's whip) the Dauphin hens laid longer and more liberally than any of the neighbor's flocks, and their egg cases were always full for the weekly trips to town. Throughout the winter months her father-in-law took her to town in his old Buick to make her deliveries. But Mary, knowing the old man would have to be in his fields, come spring, learned to drive the car herself. Then, with little Bill on the seat beside her, she made her delivery trips; and the best part of each day was the little while she spent over a cup of tea with Ada Kelly in the cheerful kitchen where, for the first time since she was a little girl, she had known freedom from want and fear.

Will came home now and then to stay over night, but as the weeks passed he came less and less often and Mary had to admit to herself that she was glad of it, for each time he came he was more quarrelsome and abusive. Usually he wanted money, and if Mary didn't have it, or as much as he wanted, he swore at her and sometimes slapped her—but never when his father was around.

With her husband away most of the time affairs went well for Mary and she began to sing at her work, her strong, sweet voice drifting out across the Flat. Her father-in-law, unfailingly kind, often complimented her on the beauty of her voice, the quality of her work and on her appearance. When she put on a fresh, starched gingham dress, and put little Bill into clean rompers, ready for a delivery trip to town, he told them they "looked like a million dollars."

The summer rains were timely, that year, and Dauphin, a good farmer, raised a bumper corn crop. By October the laden stalks stood tall and white in the field and, at supper one evening, the farmer told Mary the corn was dry enough to shuck and it was "time for McCassy to show up." McCassy, he explained, was a drifting farm hand who shucked corn on Bignell Flat year after year.

McCassy came a few days later, his old canvas knapsack slung over his shoulder. Dauphin welcomed him back, told him to put the sack in the haymow, and helped him catch up his team. Mary had somewhat dreaded his coming. Remembering some of the old men they had had at the Poor Farm, she distrusted "drifters."

But McCassy was different. A cleanly, middle-aged man of good manners, he was respectful to her and kind to little Bill. Listening to his talk at the table, his descriptions of the places he had been and the things he had seen since he left the Flat the year before, she decided he was only a man with itching feet and a desire to see as much of the world as he could in one lifetime. When he was no longer able to work he would probably wind up on a Poor Farm somewhere. She only hoped it would not be one like Annie's.

One evening soon after he came, the man got up from his chair after supper, took the dish towel off it's hook by the work table and began to dry the dishes for Mary. Tired from her long day's work, and now in the fourth month of her second pregnancy, the young woman was grateful. Every evening after that the hired hand dried the dishes before he went off to his hayloft sleeping quarters.

On a cold November evening that marked the final day of corn-picking, Will came home, walking into the kitchen unannounced as usual. Supper was over, Mary and McCassy were finishing the dishes and Dauphin had gone to make his final round of the barnyard. Will's face darkened when he saw Mary at the dishpan and the hired hand with the dish towel, but he remained civil while his wife cut a piece of pie and set it before him. He ignored his two-year-old son, timidly watching him from his highchair.

McCassy hung up the dish towel, said good night and left for the haymow. Will gave him time to get out of earshot, then jumped to his feet and demanded of Mary how long this had been going on. Before the livid anger in his face, she stepped back, supporting her thickening body against the table.

"It's just like you," Will shouted, "to go getting a crush on a hired man and start carrying on like a common whore."

Mary had seen her husband angry many times, but never like this. Before she could answer him he slapped her, then went on yelling and slapping. As his rage grew he balled his fists and struck her repeatedly, cursing and spitting out vile accusations.

Then the door flew open and his father burst into the room. At a glance he took in the scene, the woman holding onto the table to keep from falling, his son striking brutal blows to her face and body, the terrorized baby screaming in his chair.

"Stop it. Stop it, you bully," the older man commanded, his voice deadly calm as he reached for his shotgun on its supports above the door.

Will halted, his fist drawn back for another blow. Before he could deliver it the double barrels of the old shotgun were leveled at his face and his father was ordering him to get out, fast, and never come back. Dropping his fist, Will scuttled for the door like a scalded cat.

The father waited, the gun in his hands, until they heard the car engine start and its gears clashing in hurried flight. Then, shaken and pale, the old man put the gun down and helped the badly injured young woman to her bed. For the next hour he was busy, cleaning up the blood from Mary's split lips and lacerations and quieting his frightened little grandson.

Will Dauphin cared for little Bill and Mary with the skill and tenderness of a woman, and telephoned her customers to tell them she was ill and would not be able to make her rounds that week. And while she lay abed because of her laming injuries word came that Mrs. Dauphin had died of a stroke at her home.

The old woman had been good to her and Mary was grieved at her death, and doubly so that she was not able to go to her funeral. As soon as she was up and about again she moulded the butter her father-in-law had churned while she was laid up, and drove her regular route the following week.

In Ada Kelly's bright kitchen, she told her friend all that had happened. "To think" she sobbed, "that after all those awful years with Annie, I had to marry a man like Will and have it almost as bad again."

The older woman comforted her as best she could. "At least you don't have to go on living with him. He is out of your life now, and Mary, you are a good looking young woman. You will find a good man yet, and a happy home."

Chapter 29

Clara, kindly and easygoing by nature, under other circumstances would have been the contented wife of a valley farmer and the plump mother of a brood of round-faced happy children. But Annie, with the help of Dr. Myra, had seen to it that she was denied motherhood, and that her best qualities and attributes were twisted into strange and unnatural channels.

During her childhood years, when she had spent most of her time with her father, she had been a happy little girl. Then, as Annie took over and purposely kept her away from the best influence she would ever know, she began, perforce, to change. Her mother instilled in her a desire for money and tried to pass on to her her own driving need for power. That Clara had no feeling for the latter angered and frustrated the mother.

"Just the no-good Cook worthlessness," she raged. "Just like your father. All he wants is enough to eat, a roof over his worthless head and a few rags to cover his nakedness. If it wasn't for me he'd still be sitting here on one of the best farms in the valley and barely making enough to pay the taxes."

And Clara, who had once adored her father, listened and gradually came to feel a kind of contempt for him, but never dislike, such as her mother felt. Instead she pitied him and, as often as she could, brought him presents, small things to make his barren existence a little easier: warm new socks, mittens, especially the soft, double-thumbed husking mittens he preferred, or a Scotch cap with a fur-lined inner band to turn down to keep his neck and ears warm against the bitter north winds of winter. A time or two, noting the frayed collar on his best shirt, the one he wore to church, she bought him a good new one.

But buying presents for her father, or for Mary, Liz or little Joe, was difficult. Annie had to know what was in every sack or package in the car and it was not easy to conceal anything from her. If there chanced to be something she had not authorized for one of the family she flew into a rage and, if she could, destroyed the gift—such as the time Clara bought two pairs of new bib overalls for eight-year-old Joe.

Clara put the car away, then came into the kitchen with her sacks and packages. Annie had already gone to her room to change into her everyday clothes and Joe was coming through the entryway with a basket of cobs for the stove. "Here, Joe, I brought you something," Clara said, and slid a brown paper package across the table to him.

Joe's dark, serious little face lit up in pleased surprise. Gifts or pleasant surprises had been few and far between in his life. Ripping the string from the package and folding back the paper, he let out a little yelp of astonishment. "New overalls. Oh, Clara, new overalls." He held up the top pair, letting the legs unfold, and stared at them in wonder. "Oh, Clara, the first new ones I ever had in my whole life."

"Try them on. See if I got the right size."

In a trice the excited boy peeled off his filthy chore pants and pulled the new garment on over his baggy long underwear. Already he could see himself going to school on Monday, wearing the new overalls. In pure joy he went dancing, jumping and jigging around the old kitchen—and then Annie came in. "What's going on here?" she demanded, and the boy froze in mid-jump.

"Where'd you get those?"

"Clara gave 'em to me," Joe whispered, his face white before the glare in the woman's eyes.

"Get 'em off," she ordered—and waited like a hawk poised to swoop while the trembling boy fumbled the overalls off. Then, swift as her own swinging whip lash, she caught up the two pairs of overalls in one hand, lifted the front lid off the kitchen range with the other and stuffed them both into the flames.

"Ma, what are you doing?" Clara shouted, and the two women were at it again, quarreling and yelling at each other while the brokenhearted boy pulled on his old pants and slipped out of the kitchen to go on about his chores.

Long ago, in her mid-teens, Clara had been interested in boys. Even the trips to Omaha and the interlude with the polite Mr. Watanabe (she had put the business with the section hands firmly out of her mind) had not changed that. She had been quite in love with young Van Lue when she married him, but her divorce, remarriage, and watching Joe Possa walk out the courthouse door, had changed all that and decided her against any further romance.

Now, as she approached her thirty-third birthday, she was satisfied with Harley Costin and his weekly visits. Even though he was twice her age and married, she liked the man. He met some need within her, the need for a friend, perhaps, and she began to toy with the thought of being married to him. It would be pleasant, she decided, for it seemed that the only times she ever laughed, any more, were when she was with him.

He had never mentioned divorcing his wife—but divorce was a two-way street—a man's wife might *divorce* him. That Costin's wife knew about her, and resented her, had been made plain in her bid for the care of the county poor and in the "Letter of Remonstrance" she had sent the commissioners.

In any case, should the future bring about a Costin divorce, Clara meant to be prepared. So, fifteen years after her second marriage, she obtained a divorce from Joe Possa, granted on the grounds of desertion and non-support.

In addition to Costin's visits she had her love for her music and her fondness for driving, but in these, too, there was frustration. Under her mother's iron-bound work schedule there was never time enough to spend at her piano, and neither would Annie agree to buying the new car Clara so badly wanted.

They had bought the first car in 1920 and it was showing its age. Clara studied the advertisements of the latest models as they came out each year, admiring the new body styles and improved driving features. But with Frank to keep the old car repaired and running, Annie could see no sense in putting out the money for a new one. They quarreled about it often.

After his defeat in the 1924 election Costin opened a service station in Sutherland and invited Clara to drive up any time for free refills of her gas tank. Sometimes she asked Joe to ride along when she visited the Costin station. Those times were high spots in the boy's barren life for he had few opportunities to ride in the car, or get away from his long hours in the garden or the poultry houses. As they drove away after one fill-up, Joe asked Clara why she never paid for the gas.

"Oh, I pay for it, all right," she told him cheerfully. "You just don't see me doing it."

The first of each December Clara submitted her bid for the care of the county poor, put together with the help of Costin who still had good contacts at the courthouse. If he advised her to shave her rates a little, as costs declined, or to raise them a bit if he thought the county would stand for it, she did so, always pleased that the contract was in her name and not her mother's. And, year after year, the contract was awarded to her, although her's was not always the lowest bid, for Ben Esely and Faye Davis served three terms on the Board of County Commissioners, and each faithfully did Annie's bidding.

Chapter 30

That fall when Covell made his rounds of the Nichols District, making up his list of pupils for the coming year, Annie told him to enroll the boy as Joseph Cook. Since it was up to her to raise him, she said, he had just as well go by her family name. It would be less confusing, "and anyway," she added, "half the people around here think he's Clara's boy."

Joe heard the conversation and when Covell was gone he asked, with a troubled frown on his face, "But Annie, Sarah was really my mother, wasn't she?"

"No, she wasn't. She was just one of the county poor folks who took care of you when you were little. Clara didn't have time, and looking after you was a good job for that deaf and dumb woman. Anyway, you wouldn't want a deaf and dumb woman for your mother, would you?"

The boy seldom thought about Sarah any more, but now he puzzled the matter over in his mind, trying to remember his reasons for believing she was his mother. He could have been mistaken, he decided. And Annie, smiling and rubbing her mole, was satisfied. The sooner the brat believed he was a Cook, the better. Her control over him would be surer if he thought he was a part of the family.

But when Joe asked Frank about it, the man looked at him for a long while, his sad eyes filled with pain.

"No, Joe, Sarah Martin was your mother," he finally said.

Joe spent every stolen moment he could manage with the tall, quiet man who always spoke kindly to him. But it was hard to get away from Annie for even a little while.

Early that spring she had given him a pair of thin blankets and told him he was to sleep on the kitchen floor by the door of her room. She wanted him there, where she could waken him at night to run out and check on the brooder houses. Liz had done it for years, but she was getting harder to waken and Annie often had to get out of bed and plod to the storeroom to shake her awake. With Joe at her door, she could yell him awake and send him on the errand, and anyway he was getting too big to sleep in Liz's room any longer. So now he could not even slip away evenings to the haymow, or the beet shack, to spend a little while with Frank.

He and Liz could usually visit with the kindly man while they milked the cows, for Annie seldom came to the barn then. But even then they had to be careful, for she had a way of silently slipping up on them in her rubber soled canvas shoes to make sure they weren't wasting any time. Occasionally Joe managed a few minutes with his friend in the beet shack, and those were the best of all; for the man usually had something he could offer the boy to eat, since he cooked most of his own meals there, and they could talk undisturbed about the things that bothered them—until Annie's rough voice called him back to servitude.

On one such visit, Joe, picking at whiplash scabs on his neck and arms, asked, "Why is Annie the way she is, Frank?"

"I don't know," the man said, after a long pause. "When we were first married she was a good wife. She worked hard and was never mean. Then she got sick and went down to Omaha to see a doctor. That was when Clara was a little girl. She was gone quite awhile and when she came back she was—different. She went back to Omaha a few more times when she didn't feel well, and every time she came home more—spiteful, meaner.

"Then she took Clara with her on one of her last trips to the doctor. Clara was a good girl until then, cheerful, happy. But she changed too. Then they bought the big house in town so Clara could go to high school. After that I didn't see too much of her for awhile. Then she wanted to get married. She was only sixteen, but Bill Van Lue was a steady young fellow and when she came to me and asked me to help her, I did. But Annie broke up her marriage and ran Bill off, and after that they began to quarrel, and now they're at it all the time."

The man sat silent for a little while, and Joe had never seen him look quite so sad, so full of pain. And then he went on. "You see," he explained, "Annie isn't happy, hasn't been for a long time, and she doesn't want anybody around her to be happy. All she's thought of, or cared for, for years, Joe, is money. Money and the power over people to make them do what she wants them to. It's a sickness, boy, a sickness of the mind. I guess we should feel sorry for her, Joe. It is a terrible thing to be sick in your mind."

The weary lines in his worn face had seemed to deepen as he talked. Joe, hurting for Frank as well as for himself, reached over to put a hand on his friend's knee and give him a comforting pat or two, but froze as Annie's strident voice reached the beet shack.

"Joe, Joe, where the hell are you? Git here as fast as you can, dammit. Always fooling around when I need ____ ." But the lad's feet were already flying to answer the summons. The man looked sadly after the unfortunate boy. There was so little he could do to help him. As it had been with Mary, any kindness he did for Joe only made Annie mistreat him more.

Joe thought a great deal about all that Frank had told him. The idea that *they* should feel sorry for Annie rather than themselves was a new one. Until now his sympathy had been all for himself and the others who had to live under the woman's abuse. But maybe Frank was right. A sickness of the mind that could make anyone be as mean as Annie was must be a terrible thing.

In the spring of Joe's eleventh year Annie decided that she would have fryers by the first of May, well ahead of any of her neighbors. So she filled one of her brooder houses with rooster chicks in February, while there was still snow on the ground. Each evening at bedtime she checked the brooder house herself, seeing to it that the little roosters were comfortably scattered on the warm, straw-covered floor around the brooder stove.

Toward midnight she roused Joe from his blankets on the floor by her door and sent him out, through the cold and snow, to make sure that all was well in the brooder house, with the heat staying at the proper level. Too much heat could suffocate the little fryers, not enough and they would pile up and smother.

Running through the cold, two or three times a night, Joe peered through the brooder house window, making sure, by the light of a lantern hanging from the ceiling, that the roosters were comfortable. Usually all was well and he could hurry back to his pallet for another nap, until Annie roused him with the rest of the household for pre-dawn chores and breakfast. At school, that spring, Joe went to sleep at his desk more days than not.

Then one night in March, when the young roosters were about half feathered out, there was trouble at the brooder house. The weather had turned unusually cold, almost down to zero, and Joe, peering through the window, saw smoke swirling from under the brooder stove. He ran screaming to the house, and Annie, waddling out of her bedroom in her outing flannel nightgown, ran with him back to the brooder house. The woman and the boy beat out the flames with the empty feed sacks piled in one corner of the small room, but not before quite a number of the little fryers had smothered in the smoke.

Annie and Joe, still coughing and wiping their streaming eyes, looked about them. Most of the roosters, pressed against the walls as far from the still smoking straw as they could get, were all right. But Annie saw only the dead ones. Cursing, she picked up a dead bird and smacked Joe across the face with its smoky body. "One," she said and tossed it aside. "Two," she said as she picked up another, smacked him again and tossed it onto the first. "Three," smack, "four," smack, and on and on until the dead pile numbered twenty-seven.

As bad as his experience with the dead chickens had been, Joe remembered worse; a form of abuse so terrible that he could not bear to speak of it, not even to Frank. It had begun not long after Sarah's death, on an evening when Annie had called him into the room she shared with Clara.

The room held the double bed where the two women slept, a dresser and a rocking chair. Clara was sitting on the bed, a leafless willow switch in her hand, an uncertain, uneasy expression on her round face. Annie, grasping another willow switch, sat down heavily in the rocker and ordered Joe to take off his pants. Trembling with dread, the boy obeyed.

"Now your shirt and undersuit. Strip naked."

The boy froze—until a savage whack from the woman's switch made him do as she said. His face flaming with embarrassment, the child stood naked and shaking before the women. The space between them in the bedroom was small and when Annie suddenly struck the boy across his genitals with her switch he yelled and leaped away, only to be smacked by Clara's switch. And so they went at it, swatting the leaping, crying child across his buttocks and genitals until he was exhausted. The expression of uneasiness never left Clara's face, but the sadistic gleam in Annie's slit eyes showed her enjoyment of the strange rite.

Several times a year Annie repeated the ritual. Clara always helped, unwillingly, Joe was sure, but with the older woman it was pure enjoyment. Her loose lips spread in an ugly, lecherous smirk, she began the play—and with every smack of her switch her lips drew tighter, back and back, until the sobbing child had scarcely strength left to leap away. Each time, as she delivered her last blow, Annie's mouth suddenly relaxed into its normal slackness and, dropping the willow, she dismissed the boy with a curse and a growled, "Git your clothes and git to bed."

His skinny chest heaving with his gasping cries, his buttocks and genitals fiery red, Joe grabbed his garments and ran from the room, to creep into his blankets and cry himself to sleep.

But now, in his eleventh year, there had been no switching for several months and Joe was daring to hope that there would never be another.

Chapter 31

It was the summer after the brooder house fire that Annie held her first prayer meeting in the yard in front of the old house. As with other farm houses in the valley, only the backyard was commonly used. Everyone came to the back door, nearest the road, and few ever came to the front door or set foot in the front yard. So, holding the meetings there was a novel idea.

Joe never knew for sure who suggested the prayer meetings, but suspected it was the Reverend Chauncy Tester, pastor of one of the largest churches in North Platte. A handsome, well-dressed, popular churchman, he had a large following. After meeting him in the spring, the two women began going to his church, not regularly, but often enough to be considered a part of its congregation; and the preacher took to visiting the Cook farm.

The women seemed pleased each time the minister in his low slung, box-like Packard drove into the yard, usually bringing one of his many friends with him. One day the friend was Will Dauphin. Annie was delighted. She had long wanted to meet Mary's husband.

Annie had kept track of Mary's whereabouts since the night she ran away. When she learned of her marriage to Dauphin she had checked up on the young man, learning that he never held a job for long, and that he drove his mother's car and spent his father's money. She had been furious when the couple moved to the Sherman County farm, far out of her reach, and pleased when they came back to Bignell Flat.

When she heard, a little later, that they were no longer living together she had been so gratified that she had made a batch of peach dumplings for supper — and let Joe eat all he wanted of them.

Over cake and coffee in her kitchen, Annie studied Will Dauphin through her slit eyes and, for all his charm and good looks, quickly spotted his faults: sly, mean, lazy and, if need be, dishonest. According to her husband, Mary was mean, bossy, and carried on with other men. Annie and the Reverend sympathized with him, and when they left she tucked a twenty dollar bill into his vest pocket, and another into the preacher's.

They held the first prayer meeting on a pleasant evening in late June. Annie made ready for it by having the grass and weeds in the front yard cut, and provided seats by laying planks across boxes and bales of hay. Frank cleaned and lit the farm lanterns and hung them from the limbs of the tall old cottonwoods. Earl and Lela Comstock, always interested in anything of a religious nature, came early and carried the kitchen work table outside and furnished it with pitchers of lemonade and glasses.

Annie had given a general ring on the party line and invited all the neighbors. Curious about a prayer meeting at profane old Annie's, quite a few of them came. With the exception of one bedfast old man, the seven or eight patients then at the farm, cleaned up and dressed in their rusty best, were seated in a little group up front, where everybody could see that they were well cared for.

For Annie was not unaware of the stories circulating in the neighborhood, stories of abuse and mistreatment of the county poor at the Cook farm. So let the curious come and see for themselves that there was nothing to the tales. She even had Clara cut Joe's hair that afternoon and, after his chores were done, ordered him to get into his school clothes, unworn since the last day of school, and come to the front yard.

The Reverend Tester came with Will Dauphin and two or three carloads of his church people. Altogether it was quite a sizable crowd and Annie was pleased. When most of the people were in their places Frank came to stand at the back of the assembly, and Joe went to stand beside him. From his place he searched the crowd for faces he knew. The Lays from across the road were there, and the Saners from the next farm west, and the Lester McConnell family from a little farther on. Lester McConnell was one of the few people he could really call a friend and he was glad to see him there.

The young farmer, with his wife and several children, had moved onto the old Moore place only that spring. Annie, who sometimes sent him on errands to the neighbors, had two or three times that spring sent him to the McConnells, where Mrs. McConnell, bothered by his skinniness, always gave him something to eat and Lester took time to visit with him for the few minutes he could stay. For he was always under orders to waste no time, to get right home.

The meeting began then, with Clara playing her piano just inside the open parlor door, and the congregation singing several hymns. The preacher then opened the service, welcoming the crowd, reading some scriptures, frequently mentioning Annie and her good works, and then calling for testimonies. There were a few, mostly from Tester's friends who wanted to "help out," and then the meeting was dismissed with prayer.

Annie invited everyone to help themselves to lemonade while she and Clara, with Lela's help, quickly served the patients small glasses of the beverage and hurried them into the house to their rooms. It would be just as well if no one had a chance to visit with them.

When Joe, thirsty for a glass of the lemonade (a rare treat at the farm for any but Annie, Clara and their friends) slipped up to the table Annie made him blink by handing him a big glass of the beverage and putting her heavy arm across his shoulders as she said, "This is our little Joe, and I don't know what we'd do without him."

The boy gulped his drink and slipped away. But when he sought Frank again he could not find him. The hypocrisy of the whole affair, he knew, had sent the honest old man to the quiet of his blankets in the haymow.

Annie and Clara were satisfied with the meeting. On the whole, they believed, it had made a good impression. The Reverend Tester seemed pleased with it, too, and offered to help them hold another soon.

Annie held two more before the summer was over. Their curiosity satisfied, few of the neighbors came back, but their absence was more than made up by the increased attendance from town. Frank still came, to stand in the back and listen for a little while, as if hoping the meetings would get better, hold some real spiritual meaning, and Joe always went to stand beside him, and to watch wistfully when he walked away, wishing he could go with him.

At the second meeting Conley Boyd, a bearded, stocky, elderly man, stood up and gave his "testimony." One of the Reverend Chauncey Testor's prize exhibits, Conley told how he had been a drunken sot until the preacher got hold of him, pulled him out of the gutter and told him of a better way of life.

He described, in raw detail, what it was like to be a sodden drunk, wallowing in his own vomit, hopeless, friendless, headed for a drunkard's grave in the potter's field. Joe's stomach knotted in sympathy with the man, many of the women were wiping their eyes.

But now that he had gotten religion, Boyd said, his mellow voice ringing across the quiet yard, he despised his old ways. Now he not only wanted to live a new life but he wanted to help others live it, too. Neat, clean and well-groomed, the man's testimony was forceful and impressive. Young Joe, as well as most of those on the plank benches, was happy for old Mr. Boyd.

His disillusionment began a week or so later when the man came out to the farm with another of Annie's friends. Dirty and rumpled, he reeked of alcohol. Joe, shocked and sorry, feared that whiskey had gotten the better of the man again and that he'd soon be back in the gutter. He saw the man drunk at Annie's another time before she held her third prayer meeting. But on that night he was cold sober, and as neat and clean as he had been on one night he gave his testimony. Joe was happy to see that he was once again on the right road.

He listened carefully when Boyd got to his feet and gave his testimony all over again, with embellishments, and was bewildered when he said nothing about any backsliding, letting his listeners believe that he had been on the wagon ever since the Reverend Tester had first rescued him from the gutter. When he finished the preacher got up and put his arm across the man's shoulders and made a little speech about the power of God in men's lives.

At the end Joe, watching and listening back in the shadows, said to himself, "Why you old two-faced liar," and wasn't sure he didn't mean the preacher, too. Still, he decided, old Boyd *could* be fooling the preacher, just making sure the Reverend never caught him at his drinking. Then he compared the goings on at Annie's prayer meetings with Frank Cook's quiet pursuit of the teachings of the Man of Nazareth. He knew that his good friend read his Bible daily, then lived what it taught, never taking the Lord's name in vain, and being honest, and kind to every living creature, especially the ones Annie abused.

Chapter 32

Annie liked mean dogs. The first dog, Brute, had had the desired effect, instilling fear and respect in all who came to the farm. When Brute grew old she acquired two more, a mastiff and a German shepherd, huge, powerful animals. Munson brought her the mastiff, Charlie Sayman the police dog.

Old Brute still ran free on the place but the new dogs were chained in the day time, one on either side of the old board walk that led to the kitchen door; the mastiff, larger and more savage than the other, with a heavy log chain. The chains were just long enough to allow the dogs to reach almost to the edge of the walk. As long as callers stayed in the middle of the walk they were safe from the snarling dogs' bared fangs.

The approach of a stranger brought the animals to the ends of their chains, and only those who lived on the farm, or those who came often to it, were spared their threatening display. For Harley Costin they lay quiet, and for W. R. Munson, Dr. Duncan, Faye Davis, Ben Esely, and a few others. But, while they tolerated the family, any of the three animals would attack on Annie's command. All too often the angry woman had set the dogs on Mary, Liz and Joe, and all would carry the animals' fang marks to their graves.

All the dogs ran loose at night and, after the summer when the extra gang had filtered through the darkness to the kitchen door, few people had legitimate business at the farm in the night time. For those who did, Annie issued the terse advice, "Honk your horn if you drive in after we've turned the dogs loose." On party nights, or during prayer meetings, the brutes were kept chained until the last cars had driven away.

Joe hated the dogs, and with reason. Not long after the coming of the last two Annie went out one evening, turned them loose and went back into the house. Joe, coming from the barn a little later, saw the pair, hackles raised, circling each other and growling deep in their throats. When they closed, rolling and tumbling in a vicious fight, it looked to the boy as if they meant to kill each other.

Catching up a heavy stick, he waded into the fray and tried to club the dogs apart. Annie, hearing the racket, came waddling out. "Stop that damned fighting," she yelled. At the voice of authority the dogs immediately gave up their battling and slunk away, as Joe turned, the stick still in his hand, to see the woman bearing down upon him, her face twisted with anger.

Snatching the stick, she began beating him with it, blow after blow, while he crouched, arms over his head, smothering his cries of pain. On his blanket that night, trying to find the position that hurt his bruised body the least, he wondered why she had beaten him. Did she think he had started the dog fight, or that he was hurting her precious dogs with the stick, or what? He finally went to sleep, promising himself that, as soon as he was a little older and a little bigger, he would run away, far away.

Later that summer Clara and Annie, always looking for bargains, found that they could buy "day-old" bakery goods from a local baker's shop for a fraction of the fresh-baked prices. Thereafter Clara brought sackfuls of the stale rolls and cookies home each Saturday and dealt them out to Liz, Joe and the county wards. The hungry folks at Annie's table ate them greedily—until their empty sweetness palled, after which they ate them only because their hunger forced them to.

When school started Joe found his lunch pail filled with the stale, tough rolls and cookies. His lunches had never been anything to brag about, but even plain bread and butter would have been better than the bakery stuff. While he nibbled at his dry pineapple or jelly "Bismarcks" he hungrily watched his classmates eating fried chicken and beef or peanut butter sandwiches.

But the others saw Joe eating the big sugared rolls and cookies— and hungered in turn. Bakery products were a treat in those thrifty farm homes where the mothers did all the baking. Soon the youngsters were trading—Joe's sweets for half a sandwich or a chicken leg.

One warm noon time in late September Joe and his friend, Clarence Berg, squatted by the school yard fence, no more than thirty feet from the road, to open their lunch pails and dicker over a good trade. As Joe handed over a big "bear claw" in exchange for a fried pork sandwich, a car chugged by. He looked up—to see Clara and Annie passing in the old Ford. Annie was looking straight at him through her slit eyelids and Joe cowered. He knew he was in big trouble.

The furious old woman was waiting for him when he reached home that afternoon. While he changed his clothes in the entryway she slashed at his bare legs and shoulders with her whip, shouting "Why was that damned Berg brat eating one of your rolls?"

"I only traded it to him for a sandwich," Joe gasped.

"I'll teach you to trade off your good grub, dammit. You tell those kids about that good bakery stuff and their folks will be wanting in on the cut prices, too, and then there won't be enough to go around."

All through supper Annie raged and swore at the boy. Liz and the half dozen patients cowered at the table; old man Day's hands shaking so much that he was spilling his spoonfuls of soup back into his bowl. Grandma Payne was crying, big tears sliding down her wrinkled cheeks. Only old Jake Potter, deaf as a post, went ahead with his supper, unconcerned.

But even he looked uneasy when Annie got up from her place and lumbered to the back side of the table. Grabbing Joe by the ears, she slammed his head against the wall behind his chair. Again, and yet again, and when she released him and turned away, panting gustily, a bright splotch of blood glistened and widened on the old plastered wall behind him.

Hurt and humiliated as he so often was, Joe still found it in himself to feel sorry for the other discards of humanity who were so unfortunate as to fall into Annie's hands. From those still able to work she exacted the last ounce of their strength and endurance. For the others, the feeblest and most helpless, she had more subtle and even crueler ways to humiliate and degrade them.

There was old man Pitts, a strange, totally bald man who would not eat meat nor use leather. Neither would he take life, not even that of a fly. He wore foul, ragged canvas moccasins on his feet and used a frayed old rope to hold up his pants. His vow to abstain from meat, however, was easy to keep at the Poor Farm, where the patients seldom saw or tasted that article at Annie's table.

For some reason, perhaps only because he was "different," Annie seemed to hate the old man even more than she hated the rest of them, or so it seemed to Joe. At any rate she made him the constant butt of her spite. Often she waited until they were all seated at the table, with their food on their plates, to begin on the bald-headed man.

Ridiculing the careful way "old Baldy" separated the bits of potatoes, carrots and cabbage in his watery soup into neat little piles on his plate before taking a bite, she'd keep on until old Pitts, looking all around the circle, the hurt building in his faded eyes, laid down his spoon and stumbled away from the table.

"Now, with old Twitterpate out of the way, maybe the rest of us can enjoy our meal," Annie would smile as the old man shuffled outside.

After three months or so at the farm, old Pitts was missing one morning. "Son of a bitch," Annie swore. "The old fool's prob'ly run away. Get out and look for him, all of you. We'll have to find the old bastard." With all the household, except two patients too old and infirm to make it out of the yard, out searching, she went to the phone and called the sheriff. "We're all out looking for him," she reported, "but you oughta be here, too."

Frank found the old man before the sheriff arrived, floating face down in the irrigation ditch. At his shout the others came and stood on the bank. Joe would never forget the way the old man looked, his stiffened arms and legs extended, like a frog's as it leaps into the water, the back of his bald head glistening in the slanting rays of the early morning sun, the thin old body rocking gently in the running water of the ditch.

Sheriff Benson and his deputy pulled the body from the water, and Annie plodded off to the house to call W. R. Munson.

Runaways at the Poor Farm were almost routine. They happened every summer and nearly every neighboring farmer had played unwitting host to some frightened, desperate old man. The Bergs had had one come up their lane one morning as they got up, soon after daybreak. A big, raw-boned old man with a very lame leg, he was wet and muddy, barely able to drag himself along. He had slipped away from Cook's about midnight, he said, and had crawled through several cornfields to reach the Berg lane.

Mrs. Berg scrounged up some dry clothes for him and he sat down to breakfast with the family, who had never seen a man put away so many pancakes and eggs at one meal. "That old woman starves us," he told them, "and works the pants off us with a whip."

Not knowing what else to do, Al Berg called the sheriff, who drove out and got the old man. Later that week the old fellow was back at Annie's, by order of the county commissioners, so the Bergs were told.

Another neighbor, Jim Halsey, found an old man hiding in his haymow, one morning, when he went up to put down hay for his work team. This runaway, too, had been most of the night getting to the Halsey haymow. While the scared old fellow wolfed his breakfast, Mrs. Halsey, a meticulous housekeeper, looked him over. She told her neighbors later that she had never seen such a dirty old man. It wasn't just the dirt picked up during his night's crawl through the fields, it was the accumulated filth of months on end, his scabby head, his filthy neck, his encrusted hands.

"Doesn't Mrs.Cook ever make you take a bath?" she asked.

"All the washin' we git is in the horse tank, and then we have to hurry, no more'n a splash or two," he told her.

When he finally finished his breakfast the old man asked Halsey to take him to town, when he had the time, and let him out. He had relatives there, he said, and he knew they would take him in, even though they didn't have much themselves. "They just don't know the way I've been treated at that place. Just don't take me back there. It's a hell-hole to live in." The Halsey's took him to town and let him out.

Annie called the sheriff and reported the man missing. When she was told, a couple of days later, that the runaway had been located and relatives were caring for him, she raised quite a row. But this time the law was against her. The man had "other means" of support and the county could not gainsay that, not with so much criticism of the Poor

Farm beginning to surface and another election coming up.

Old "Crip" Jensen had not been so fortunate, so far as anyone knew. Annie had reported him missing, too, "prob'ly just wandered away," she said. The Poor Farm crew and the sheriff searched for him the first day. The rest of the community joined in the hunt the second day, but no sign of the crippled old man was ever found. "Better look some more, right there on the farm," some of the neighbors said, "maybe do a little digging in the orchard."

Chapter 33

One of Mary's butter, cream and eggs customers was Alma Ritner, owner of the once elegant Ritner Hotel. A friend of Ada Kelly's, she, too, was fond of Mary and often asked her to come in and have a cup of tea with her. One summer day a few weeks after the birth of Mary's little girl, Mrs. Ritner told her they had recently turned the hotel into a boarding home for single men, mostly Union Pacific workmen. The place was full she said, but she was having trouble getting the laundry done.

"Would you know of anyone I could get to do it, Mary?" she asked.

A week later Mary was in the laundry business. Until then she had washed for herself and her family on a washboard at the Dauphin farm. Now she bought a gasoline engine powered Maytag and did the hotel laundry as well as her own, paying for the machine with the extra money. On her Saturday delivery trips to town she left the clean linens at the hotel and picked up the soiled.

For Mary, life on the farm that summer was busy but serene. Will, mindful of his father's ultimatum, delivered over the sights of a shotgun, did not come to the farm anymore. Little Bill tagged at his mother's heels but the baby spent most of her time with her grandfather. From the first the older Dauphin had been devoted to little Irene, even carrying her with him in a basket as he did his chores—bringing her to her mother only when she was hungry.

By the time the little girl was six months old he had rigged a carrying sack for her from an old blanket that he slung to his back. The baby seemed happy there and the pair content. By winter, when she had been weaned, the grandfather could look after her at home while her mother made her day-long delivery trips to town.

At the hotel, one winter afternoon, Mary came down the stairs with a big basket piled high with soiled sheets. As she reached the bottom step a man came through the door in front of her. "Hey," he said, "that basket's bigger than you are. Here, let me give you a hand."

He took the basket from her and the two looked at each other over it's top. Mary saw a man of medium height and build, about forty and darkly handsome. His teeth were white and even as he smiled at her he looked kind, with laugh lines radiating from his eyes. Mary had lived too long with grim hate not to be attracted by kindness when she saw it.

He saw a slender young woman, probably twenty-five years old, with pretty brown hair and eyes. He liked her looks and didn't even notice the scar on her cheek. In the twenty years since that Sunday afternoon in Annie's kitchen, it had faded to a faint puckering that was easily covered with the makeup cream.

The man spoke first. "I seem to have your basket. What am I supposed to do with it?"

"I was taking it out to my car. I do the hotel laundry," Mary explained.

Before long Lewis Cauffman was driving out to the farm on Bignell Flat to bring the soiled hotel linens and pick up the clean, and to sit awhile in the kitchen over a cup of coffee and a piece of Mary's pie. The two laughed often, even though there was much that was not amusing in both their pasts.

Cauffman had heard rumors about Annie and her poor farm, and about her deals with both the old and the new "courthouse rings." Who hadn't? But he swore softly under his breath as Mary told him of her years under Annie's whip. "And it's still going on," she said, "for my mother is still out there. It has been five years now, since I got away, but I think about her every day, and wonder how she is. I haven't heard a thing from her, or about her, and don't expect to unless I happen to run into Uncle Frank in town. But someday, if I ever have a big enough house, I am going to get my mother away from Annie and take care of her."

Cauffman's life, too, had not been without its difficulties. He was part Indian, he said, and his darkness had caused him problems in his boyhood, "back east" where he came from. Soon after arriving in North Platte, five or six years back, he had gone to work for the Union Pacific, and had met a slim, good looking girl at one of the "hotels" on Front Street. She was about his own age, Cauffman told Mary, and probably past her prime for her profession. But she was jolly, easygoing and very pretty—and quite willing to marry him when he asked her.

"She probably knew she'd be out of a job in a few years," he explained to Mary. "I suppose she was looking for a home and security, and I thought she felt about me the way I did about her. But I guess I was just an insurance policy to her." For awhile it had been a good life, he went on. Hazel had put on fifty pounds, and then she had found herself "a lover on the side."

"I didn't mind her extra weight," Cauffman said, "for she was still pretty. But I did mind the other, I guess because the fellow was such a slob and I didn't see how she could stand him." So they had separated and he had moved into the Ritner. They'd be getting a divorce one of these days, he supposed.

Chapter 34

The nefarious course of the county's affairs worked to Annie's advantage as the decade of the Twenties ran out. Most of the new county and city officials, elected after the burning of the courthouse, had proven no more honest than those they replaced. Strongly entrenched by 1927, they managed the return of Charlie Sayman to the sheriff's office in that year's election.

Annie celebrated with a big party at the bungalow. Most of her old friends were there, Landers, the banker, commissioners Esely and Davis, Dr. Duncan, Munson and a fairly new one, Mayor Chester Tetley, and Harley Costin. Among the regulars of the past two years was one of her favorites, Arthur Haynes, a close friend of Sheriff Sayman's.

Only that evening the sheriff, with his arm across Haynes' stocky shoulders, had said to her, "Be good to this fella, Annie. He's a good Democrat but he sure helped me get my old job back." Privately, he had told her that Haynes had friends in high places, friends such as a recent governor of the state, and other prominent people.

She saw a good deal of the man that winter, and came to depend on him more and more. Since buying her first house in town, more than twenty years ago, she had learned a great deal about the darker side of the little western city's social life: its bordellos, saloons and gambling joints, and the people who frequented them, but not until Art Haynes became her friend had she learned the whole of it. Bootlegging, it seemed, was the hub around which it all revolved.

An inveterate gambler, Haynes seemed to have a hand in every illegal business going on in the area, the hidden whiskey stills operating all over the territory, the speakeasies and houses of prostitution, back room gambling parlors and slot machines. Though the profits were huge, Annie learned, his expenses were heavy—protection alone exacted a heavy toll—and he was often broke and in need of a banker who could supply cash in a hurry.

Annie filled that office well, but drove a hard bargain in return, a hefty share of the gambler's profits for herself. And even while she smiled approval on him, the baleful glare from her slit eyes warned him that he'd better be prompt with her cut.

Haynes' Dodge coupe was parked often in the Cook yard while he and Annie went over their accounts and figured out new deals. A gaggle of new resorts had fastened upon the town following the institution of prohibition, establishments known as "chicken huts." Located on the north side of the railroad tracks, most of them were owned, or managed, by Negroes. Fronts for illegal liquor, gambling and prostitution, they were popular and well patronized by whites.

Haynes, laying it all out for Annie on her kitchen table, represented himself as the head of the chicken hut business and "sold her a block of shares." It was an up and coming money maker and it was going to get better, he boasted. Already North Platte was known as "Little Chicago," and its underworld trade was growing fast.

And if North Platte had become the Little Chicago of the West, then Art Haynes considered himself its Al Capone. As a power in the Democratic party and overlord of the town's gangster faction, he was, or so he believed, a potent force in the community. He ran the whole business by "strong arm" methods, he confided to Annie. "As soon as the bastards find out they'd better fork over on time, or get beat up and run out of town, they shape up pretty fast." Annie nodded her approval.

Early in 1929 Haynes, Sayman and Annie began to consider the upcoming city elections, with their possibility of some very close races. Because of the wide open practice of some of its illegal activities, especially bootlegging, gambling and prostitution, Little Chicago was getting some extra attention from the state officials and Attorney General C. A. Sorensen had sent an undercover agent out from Omaha to look into such affairs. When he learned that nine houses of prostitution, twenty-five bootlegging joints and one big gambling house were "all running wide open," he had ordered Mayor Chester Tetley to clean things up—or resign.

Then the town's other mortician, M. J. Filly, had jumped into the mayoral race. Filly had long been irked over the fact that he was unable to get any of the county's dead business. He had several times submitted his bid for the pauper burials, he stated, but even though he regularly underbid his rival, Munson always got the contract. It was time, he declared, for the "town's better element to assert themselves" and elect honest officials who would run things according to law.

It was going to be a rough fight, Haynes and the sheriff told Annie, and it would cost plenty. The woman narrowed her eyes and rubbed her mole, considering, then told them to go ahead, she'd put up the money.

More than anything else Annie still wanted that north Eighty. All other forms of material wealth might be lost, or fail, but good land stayed where it was and rewarded its owner. What with all her expenses, it was taking much longer than she had figured to accumulate the buying price. So, now that she had managed an association with the man who could make it possible for her to acquire the money she needed, she did not intend to let anything stand in her way. With the right officials in office and the right people running things, business could flourish as usual and even the state couldn't do much about it.

Haynes and his Democrats worked hard and, though Tetley made no move to clean up his town, victory seemed assured—until the Saturday evening before election day, when a determined squad of state officers descended on the city. Their swift wholesale raids netted thirteen arrests in the "dive" section of town, and the newspapers made the most of it during the next two days.

North Platte's "better element" hoped the resulting bad publicity for Tetley would defeat him. But the mayor's strong backing by Haynes and his people, coupled with the unpopularity of the prohibition law, defeated the "dry" Filly instead. The ultimatum seemed to be "business as usual."

Annie and Clara celebrated with another big party in the bungalow.

Following the election relative quiet took over until a hot morning in July, when two police officers were sent to the Humming Bird Inn, a chicken hut, to arrest a black man for beating up on the black woman who lived with him and helped him operate the business. Such arrests were routine in that section of town, but this one did not follow the usual pattern.

Seeman, the black, hid in the Inn's attic and when one of the officers, Edward Greene, went up the stairs after him he shot away half the side of his head. The other officer ran outside to summon help. A small crowd had already gathered and the policeman, noting Haynes among them, asked him to keep order and guard the Inn until he could get back.

He returned shortly with more police officers, several firemen and a few members of the North Platte National Guard. By then several armed citizens had arrived to lend a hand, and the whole force entered the building to arrest Seeman. It was never determined whether someone in the arresting party shot the black man, or whether he died by his own hand, but when it was over there were two bodies in the yard, Seeman and Officer Greene, awaiting Munson's dead wagon.

After the bodies were removed and the crowd drifting away, Haynes, acting the part of Al Capone, turned to the young fellows lingering at the scene of the excitement. Officer Greene had been a mighty good friend of his, he told them, and if the North Platte officials weren't going to do anything about his murder, then it was time the rest of them did. To begin with, he declared, all the niggers should be run out of town and the place cleaned up. They'd be doing the town a favor if they went ahead, right now, and took care of it.

It was a ridiculous speech. The murderer was already dead and the town, as yet, had not had time to make a statement of any kind about the affair. But Haynes had accomplished his purpose. He had incited the excitable young people to action and, since there were only twenty or so black households in the town, running them out would not take long.

With some of his young helpers riding on the running boards of his car and the rest following along behind, he drove slowly from house to house in the black section. He did not get out of the car himself, but to each little group of his amateur vigilantes he gave the same instructions, "Don't threaten anybody. Just tell them to be out of town by three o'clock this afternoon if they know what's good for them," and sent them to the door. By three o'clock that afternoon the city was emptied of blacks.

In the Cook kitchen that evening, Haynes boasted that running the niggers out of town had been easy, and that a chicken hut or two could likely be picked up "pretty cheap" because of it.

Due to the fact that Edward Greene, a former professional baseball player, had been a very popular police officer, his shooting made headlines in papers across the state. That he had been killed by a black man, and that the murder had happened in North Platte, "the Little Chicago of the West," added to the sensationalism of the affair.

Outstate interest in the matter would have died quickly, however, except for the fact that the black citizens had been run out of town. It was the Negro exodus that led to what quickly became known as "The North Platte Race Riot," rating headlines across the nation, from the *New York Times* to the *Los Angeles Evening Express.*

Turning the attention of the city and state officials away from himself and his business and onto the town's niggers would help, Haynes told Annie. With Greene's killing taking place in a chicken hut, even one he did not own, any investigation could have been awkward. But now it would center on the "mob" running the blacks out of town and let up on the bootlegging and the rest of it.

"Getting the people stirred up against the niggers will take the heat off the chicken huts for awhile and make it safe to go on running them here. We have a damned good thing going, Annie, and we want to keep it that way."

The pair gloated over the Lincoln and Omaha reports that "Negroes Leave North Platte—Feeling Runs High Following Killing Of Policeman—Thousands Witness Battle During Which Two Die," and "Negroes Flee Mob Wrath, having gathered what belongings they could carry and hit the road while the townspeople looked on, watchful lest some go only a short distance and turn back."

The lurid reports brought Governor Arthur Weaver, State Sheriff W. C. Condit and Attorney General Sorensen (still smarting over his failure either to oust Mayor Tetley from office or make him clean up his town) into the affair, "Calling upon the officers of North Platte and Lincoln County to arrest and cause to be prosecuted all those who have been responsible for the outrage of driving innocent and law abiding citizens from their homes." Sorensen added, "The Negroes weren't to blame. Responsibility rests with those local officials who permitted dives to operate. If there had been no dives there would have been no shooting."

While the town's "better element" indignantly bewailed the unflattering publicity concerning "the disgraceful affair at North Platte," Art and Annie and their cohorts gloated. It was money in the bank for them.

After a busy week in the town, the states' investigators concluded there was no evidence of physical violence toward the Negroes, but plenty pointing to a group of young men and boys who had gone from house to house telling blacks, "Nigger, be gone by three o'clock, and we don't mean maybe."

Following the questioning of nearly one hundred citizens, both black and white, and putting together five hundred pages of testimony, most of it having to do with violation of prohibition laws, the state brought forth its statement that "certain as yet unnamed persons had taken part in the issuance of the eviction demand, but that the state had not yet determined which criminal statute would apply."

By early August the Attorney General's office had made the determination that a "charge of unlawful assembly and disturbing the peace be brought against Arthur Haynes." North Platte's Al Capone was elated. There was to be no investigation of chicken huts and their businesses. As for this picayune charge, no jury in his own community would convict him, he bragged. Not as long as he had personal friends reaching all the way up to a former state governor who would swear to his good citizenship.

A week later, before a packed courtroom, fifteen white witnesses testified that they had been asked to go along with a small crowd of young fellows, all headed for the black section of town, but had declined. Several blacks stated that some white men had ordered them out of town by three o'clock, and that they had fled in terror.

Haynes then took the stand to explain how he had aided the police, that hot July morning, and that he had been the first member of the citizen "posse" to look through the trap door of the attic where the wanted man was believed to be hiding. "No one wanted to stick his head up there while Seeman was hiding there," he stated modestly.

Annie watched closely as the new county attorney, Collis Bell, a beak-nosed, tight-lipped young man took the floor. He hadn't been in office long enough yet for her to make up her mind about him. As the prosecuting attorney, he explained the law as it applied to an instance of unlawful assembly. Further than that he made no comment on the case.

George Gibbs, Haynes' attorney, then charged that the only reason the state had for prosecuting his client was Attorney General Sorensen's *personal dislike of North Platte*, and that the charges against Arthur Haynes were quite as unfounded as the wild newspaper stories that a "mob of armed citizens had run the blacks, including five mothers of newborn babies, out of town in the rain."

After ten minutes of deliberation, the five-man jury found Haynes not guilty of unlawful assembly and disturbing the peace. And by then most of the blacks had returned to town and business was flourishing as never before.

Chapter 35

As he had for years, the Reverend Tester made almost weekly visits to the farm, all that summer of 1930, often bringing Will Dauphin with him. Annie welcomed them both, tucked ten or twenty dollar bills into their vest pockets and filled the minister's car with fruit and vegetables and a dressed chicken or duck when they left.

The front yard meetings in the summer and the bungalow parties in the winter had become something of a tradition. The parties, however had changed since that first winter. Annie no longer furnished the girls, or only rarely, as the men preferred to bring their own "ladies." The "regulars" liked it better that way, and frequently brought her the names of friends who wanted to be added to the guest list.

It gave her a great deal of satisfaction to have a waiting list for her parties. She doubted that that old busybody, Ada Kelly, could say the same for hers — and Annie's guests paid, and paid plenty, for the privilege of partying at her bungalow.

A few months after the chicken hut killings, Haynes told Annie of a new man he wanted her to meet, John Hunter, from up in the Sandhills north of Tryon. John, he said, had two or three years ago finished serving a sentence for stealing cattle in the hills. Prohibition had come in while he was in the pen, and when he got out he had gone into bootlegging in a big way. By taking the heat off some important people involved in the cattle stealing case, John had earned a bundle, Haynes explained, enough to buy himself a big new truck, and he was now running good Canadian whiskey from Canada to Texas.

He was doing well at it, too, Haynes said. "I see that he gets through Lincoln County OK and he's plenty grateful to me. He's on the road most of the time, but he's around once in awhile and I'll see that he gets to one of your parties this fall."

"Do that," Annie said, "and see that he brings some of the Canadian stuff along. It's time we had something better than the rot gut poison Charlie Sayman brings out of those pig pen stills he raids." Later in the winter she asked Haynes when he was going to bring John Hunter to see her. "I've been waiting a long time to meet that fella."

"I know, but he's pretty busy. He's not in town much anymore. Mostly he just stops long enough to gas up his truck, and maybe see that good looking new wife of his. He's making a pile of money though, and sometimes I wonder if he's playing fair with me. Seems to me the damn good protection I give him ought to be worth more than I'm getting."

When, a few weeks later, Annie inquired again as to when she was to meet John Hunter, Haynes shrugged his wide shoulders. "Maybe never." His tone was surly. "I'm about fed up with that bastard. He's getting too big for his britches and thinking he won't have to play along with me anymore. But I'm onto him now, and when I get through with him...." He scowled as his words trailed away.

Then there came a week in the fore part of August when Haynes neither came to the farm nor called. Neither could Annie find out anything about him when she asked around. The week ended with a prayer meeting in the Cook yard, and the gangster was there. When she asked him where he'd been he only grinned and replied, "Busy. I had some important business to take care of, but everything's fine now."

The old woman narrowed her eyes to slits and looked at him for a long moment. "When am I going to see John Hunter?" she asked then.

"Not for awhile, I'm afraid. Old John decided this damn territory wasn't big enough for both of us, so he took off. Last I heard he was going to Philadelphia. Said his wife was visiting there and he was going to see her. I doubt if he'll be back."

"I see," Annie growled. "Well, I wish you had brought him around while he was here, dammit." She had heard that Hunter was a good looking young buck and it bothered her that she had not met the man.

By the end of the month a good many people were asking about John Hunter. His family, from up in the Sandhills, had enquired of the police, who were making enquiries of their own. At the service station where he regularly serviced his cars—the truck in which he made his "runs," and his Chrysler coupe, a custom-made vehicle with two gas tanks—they learned that he had last been there on the evening of August 5.

He had told the station attendant, that evening, that it was the last time he'd be servicing "this wreck," that he was leaving for Omaha the next day to buy a fancy new car, a red Reo Flying Cloud, and from there he was driving on to Philadelphia to see his wife. Others who knew him said that he had been talking pretty big lately, talking of buying a big, expensive car with a lot of speed, and of buying a ranch in South America.

Then his wife came home from Philadelphia and said that she had not seen him. His elderly parents were concerned; John had never before let this much time go by without communicating with them, they said, and they were afraid he'd met with foul play. "Could be," the police agreed. A man in his line of business ran that risk.

The whiskey truck was found, empty, on Hunter's farm, 17 miles southeast of North Platte. The renter, Harold Lozier, reported that John had stopped there on his way to Omaha. After that the double-tanked Chrysler and its owner seemed to have vanished.

At the request of the old parents, John's attorney, Nate Elsen, was appointed conservator of his estate until he showed up again. According to the *Telegraph Bulletin* his estate consisted of livestock on the farm, three "rooming houses" on Front Street in North Platte, 1,600 acres of land in McPherson County, $19,000 in cash in a lock box at the First National Bank, and a small checking account, for a total of $24,000.

No one believed that Hunter had gone to South America without his money. Many believed that he was dead, "done away with," and some said they were sure they knew who had killed him. But there was no proof, and no body, dead or alive. Nate Elsen sold the cattle and horses off the farm, claimed Hunter owed him money for past services, and kept the proceeds. Months later John's Chrysler coupe showed up on an Omaha garage parking lot, but no one seemed to know who had left it there. That fall the renter, Lozier, and his wife moved to California and "the Hunter case" became another unsolved mystery, which Annie sometimes mentioned to Art Haynes, who only shrugged.

Chapter 36

In Joe's twelfth summer Annie decided he was big enough to work a team and cultivator and help Frank in the cornfield. Many farm boys of twelve, and even younger, handled teams and machinery on the valley farms. But Joe was skinny and undersized for his age, hardly larger than a ten-year-old, too slight to lift the heavy harness to the backs of the big work mares.

The lad was willing, even eager, to work in the field, and with Frank to harness his team for him each morning, he could manage. The long hours in the field were hard, even for a man, but the boy was grateful to be away from the sound of Annie's harsh voice and the weight of her ever ready whip hand.

Old Bess and Betty, the team Joe drove to his cultivator, were gentle and dependable and there would have been no problem, except that Betty had one bad habit. When Joe, with her bridle in his hand, went into her stall to put it on her she managed with unerring certainty to lean against him as he passed and pin him to the side of her stall. She never tried her trick on Frank, only on the boy, so Frank not only harnessed the mares but bridled them as well.

But after the noon meal one day, Annie put Joe to another task, one that kept him busy until well after Frank had gone to the field. The mares were left unbridled to eat the hay in their manger until Joe was ready for them. He bridled old Bess and gave her a friendly pat on the rump as he left her side of the stall, took Betty's bridle from its hook and tried to dash past her before she could lean against him. As usual, she was too quick for him and her heavy body caught and squeezed him against the plank wall of her stall. Scarcely able to breathe, he squirmed and wriggled to free himself, then swung the bridle hard against the mare's legs and panted, "Get over, you big lummox. Let me outta here," and swung the bridle again.

"Beat one of my horses, will you? You dirty bastard, I'll show you what it feels like," came Annie's angry shout as she snatched the bridle from him and swung it down hard, bit first, on the boy's head. At the same time the mare stepped over, releasing him. Dazed by the blow, he almost fell in the stall as the woman tossed him the bridle and snarled, "Now git on out to the field, you runty maggot, and don't ever let me catch you beating that mare again."

With his sleeve Joe wiped away the blood running into his eyes from the cut on his head, pulled the mare's head down and tugged the bridle on over her ears. The cut stung and his head throbbed and ached, all that long, hot afternoon as he guided the team down the corn rows.

Annie held another of her prayer meetings that evening. Joe, at the horse tank, tenderly soaking away the dried blood from the gash on the top of his head, saw the first cars arriving and the visitors making their way to the front yard. As he went on cleaning his aching wound, he thought of some of the other times Annie had lashed out at him with whatever object she happened to have in her hand.

There had been the evening her temper had boiled over while she was busy at the kitchen range and she had snatched the long stove poker from the woodbox. Swinging around, she had struck him across the mouth with the steel rod, cracking his four front teeth and splitting his lower lip.

Or the time, early that spring, when he had tried hiding from her wrath in the hay loft, crawling far back in the pile of hay and hoping she would not find him. But Annie never gave up. When he did not answer her angry calls and she could not find him elsewhere, she had come puffing up the steep stairway to the loft. Catching up the nearest pitch fork, she had plowed heavy-footed across the floor and stabbed the sharp tines viciously into the hay. Joe held his breath and made himself as small as he could, but when the fork came dangerously close, he crawled out of the hay and took his punishment — always worse if it was delayed — and especially harsh this time because she had had to haul her bulk up the hay loft stairs.

As he dribbled water from his fingers over his gashed head, he recalled another evening when he had tried outrunning the woman, hoping to find a hiding place where he could hole up until she cooled off. Scuttling across the yard and dodging behind the big chicken house, he scrambled onto a barrel at the corner and clawed his way up onto the roof of the building. As Annie panted by below, he slid up to the peak of the roof and peeked over the ridgepole to watch her.

Cursing fiercely, she peered about her in the dusk. A few yards away Frank and Liz had lately built a haystack. A pitch fork still leaned against the stack and she grabbed it up in her stubby, powerful hands. Then, screeching threats and curses, she began stabbing the long, shining tines deep into the hay. From his perch on the roof, Joe watched, his stomach scrunching every time she slammed the sharp tines into the stack. If he had been hidden there she would have impaled him like a chicken leg stabbed with a fork.

"She could've killed me," the boy thought hopelessly, "and she probably will, someday."

As he finished washing the dried blood out of his hair and straightened up, the words of the first hymn of the evening came to him from the front yard. Frank no longer came to the meetings and Annie explained to those who asked for him that he was not feeling very well, that summer.

Old Boyd, he knew, would be at the meeting, still giving his testimony and offering long prayers for all other "wrongdoers." He had seen the man half-drunk at Annie's again that spring and knew he was "pulling their legs," as Annie called it, and getting away with it.

After each meeting it gave Joe a sick feeling in the pit of his stomach to watch the visitors shaking the man's hand and purring over him the way they did. So, this evening, he took off his shirt and patted the water out of his hair, then slipped away to his blanket on the old kitchen floor. He was in no mood to listen to the preaching, or to old Boyd proclaiming the joys of his new life.

Chapter 37

By 1932 drouth and depression had fastened a grim hold on the Great Plains. The prices of grain and cattle had plummeted, banks were failing, thousands were out of work and people everywhere were tightening their belts. But Annie, with a finger in so many pies, was one of the few who continued to make money.

Year after year Clara had submitted her bid for the care of the county poor. Although other bids, some at lower rates, were annually turned in, the contract was regularly awarded to her. And, with the increasing hard times, more people were being forced onto the pauper rolls.

So, when even Annie could crowd no more bodies into the available bedrooms in the old house, she and Clara decided to move into the kitchen bedroom in the bungalow and turn their old room over to the incoming patients. By taking Liz with them they freed the storeroom for patient use, too. For Joe the move was simple, he had only to carry his blankets to the new location on the dining room floor outside Annie's door. On party nights she sent him back to the kitchen in the old house to sleep. For Liz there was a folding cot in the bungalow kitchen, after the dinner dishes were done.

By then, in spite of Annie's attempts at camouflage, the Cook Poor Farm had become notorious across the county, and beyond. At every community gathering, whether of club, church group or lodge, Annie and her place were as much a part of the conversation as the dry weather, dust storms and hard times. Every visitor to the farm seemed to come away with a new story, some strange thing seen or suspicioned.

The three old men who, at one time or another, had been found floating in the Cook irrigation ditch, were facts; but whether or not they had wandered away from the house and fallen into the ditch, as Annie claimed, was a question. It *was* possible, of course, and there seemed no way to disprove her story, but there were suspicious folks who said the woman could just as well have pushed the old fellows in, now that they were no longer able to work.

Another fact was Orson Covell's account of his visit to the farm, one winter's day, to see why Joe hadn't been to school for nearly two weeks. While he talked to Annie in the warm kitchen an old man had come out of one of the bedrooms and asked if he could, please, leave the door open so it could warm up in his room. "We're all cold in there," he pleaded. But Annie had clumped across the floor and ordered him to get back in his room and stay there, then pulled the door shut and locked it with a key she took from her apron pocket.

Even stranger was what happened to Steve Kash's nephew, Allen Porter, a teen-age town boy who spent his summers on the farm. Directed by his uncle to drive over to the Cook place and bring home a potato digger Annie had borrowed, Allen had hooked up his big team, Bill and Charlie, and driven the half mile to the Cook farm.

The lad had worked old Bill and Charlie, a gentle, well-broken pair, for the past two summers and had no trouble with them, but that day, when he reached the Cook lane, the team had balked at turning in. Never before had the big horses hesitated to do his bidding. Now, with a loud "giddap" and a hard slap of the lines, he pulled them around and urged them into the lane. Halfway to the house the team shied away from a wagon box on the ground beside the road. The horses' legs, he noted, were trembling.

From his seat on the wagon Allen could see down into the box, and was startled at sight of the skinny old man lying there, his eyes wide open, his face covered with flies. He could tell that he was alive, for his chest moved gently up and down with his shallow breathing.

Urging his team on to the end of the board walk, where the two big dogs raged at him, pulling on their chains, he pulled them to a stop. Before he could decide what he should do, Annie opened the door and came out. Silencing the dogs with a harsh command, she turned her slit eyes on her visitor and asked what he wanted.

Young Porter explained and she pointed toward the barn, then led the way to the potato digger and helped him tie it to the back of his wagon. Climbing quickly back to his seat he headed for the lane, where the uneasy team again shied away from the wagon box and the old man with the flies swarming over his face.

How can he lay there like that, looking at the sun? The lad wondered—and then had his hands full with his team as the pair broke into a run, whirled the wagon and the trailing machine out of the lane, around the corner and into the road that led home. Out of control and running away, the big team, lathered and dripping sweat, clattered into the home barnyard a few minutes later.

At the questioning look on his uncle's face, Allen explained the unseemly speed on a hot afternoon. The older man did not seem surprised. Nodding, he told the boy to be sure and let the horses cool down before he watered them, and turned away.

Then another neighbor, Minnie Bales, bought a setting of goose eggs from Annie and put them under a chicken hen to hatch. When, at the end of the required brooding period, not a single egg hatched, she took a close look at the clutch—and found a pinhole in every egg. "Nothing is too low for that mean old witch to do," she told her husband.

"Witch" was a term more and more often applied to the old woman. Children at play in their home yards panicked and ran into the house when they saw her car coming down the road. If they were playing in the school yard at noon or recess and her car came by they ran to the schoolhouse to cluster on the steps by the door until she was out of sight. Those who had to walk past her place on their way to and from school left off their "fooling around" to hurry, with averted eyes, until they were well past the lane.

When they talked of the "old witch" it was in hushed voices. Ila Albers said she had once been right up to the house. Since she lived a mile and a half from the schoolhouse, a long walk for a ten-year-old, if anyone going her way came along and offered her a ride she was glad to accept it. On the fall day that a neighbor stopped for her, just after she left the school yard, she had climbed gratefully into his car. When they came to the Cook farm he told her he had to see Mrs. Cook for a minute and turned into the lane.

"I was scared to death," Ila told her eager listeners. "All those big dogs, barking and tearing around. I knew I oughten to be there, right in the old witch's yard, but I didn't dare get out and walk on home. Then Mr. Doyle came out and we left, but I was still shaking when I got home."

The Johnson girls, Doris and Arlene, could do better—they had been right *in* the old witch's kitchen. Their mother, who befriended the whole community, included Annie and Clara in her neighborly circle; and one afternoon took her little daughters with her to call at the Cook farm.

Annie had been friendly and seemed glad to see them, they said, and after seating them she had cut a big slice of chocolate layer cake for each of them. "It looked good, but we were afraid to touch it," the girls said. "Mama ate hers, but she knew how we felt, so she told the old witch it was too near supper time and would spoil our appetites. So she wrapped it up for us to take home, and when Mama told her we'd have to be going because it was Brother's birthday and she was making him a special supper, she wrapped up another big piece for him. But when we got home, he wouldn't eat his either, so we gave it all to the dogs."

Chapter 38

Joe liked most of the patients who lived at the Poor Farm. Kind, lonely old men and women who could no longer care for themselves, most of them had no families. A few, however, were like the old widow, Mrs. Fees, who, with tears in her faded eyes, told him how her son had persuaded her to deed her farm to him. In return he was to give her a home and care for her as long as she lived.

In time the son had needed her room in the house for his growing family. He had then promised that, if she would move to the Poor Farm he would pay her board and room there so she wouldn't have to work. He had paid the first year's allotment, she said, and then the hard times came on and he had failed to come up with the second payment.

"The first year he used to come to see me and make sure Annie wasn't working me, but now that he doesn't pay he doesn't come any more—and Annie's mad and takes it out on me."

Even as a boy Joe knew that he would never understand how Annie, and sometimes Clara, could *enjoy*, as they seemed to, the cruelties they put upon the helpless old people. He would never forget the grief of the sweet old lady who had once known far better times. On the day she arrived Annie took her into the small room she was to share with another old woman, pointed out her bed, and the dresser drawer where she was to put her possessions; then watched, sharp-eyed, as the grey-haired woman unpacked her old valise.

Lifting out a garment, the woman held it up for Annie to see, fondly eyeing its shimmering brown and gold colors as she said, "Mrs. Cook, this is my paisley satin waist. I've had it for years but it still looks like new."

Annie's lids drooped lower over her glinting eyes. "Humpf," she sniffed, "it looks like a batch of crook-necked squashes to me." The light faded from the old lady's eyes as she started to refold the waist and put it in the drawer. "Wait a minute," Annie growled suddenly, "let me see it again," and she snatched at the garment. Involuntarily, the old woman's fingers tightened on her treasured bit of splendor from the past. There was a ripping sound as the frail old satin gave way, and a sharp cry of protest from its owner. Without a word Annie flung the ruined blouse on the bed and plodded out of the room.

Another old woman, fitted with a new set of false teeth shortly before she came to the Poor Farm, had been extremely proud of her new dentures—until the spring day that Annie took them away from her and threw them over the backyard fence into the Halstead cornfield, where Annie had Liz and Joe throw the hens that occasionally died in her henhouses. When he found the hens, Floyd Halstead, one of the few neighbors who was unafraid of Annie Cook, picked them up and threw them back onto her side of the fence.

But this time the farmer, approaching on his four-horse disc and unaware of the little byplay in the Cook yard, disced the teeth under the rich black soil as he passed, while the old woman, her hand covering her toothless mouth, wept bitterly.

Nor would he forget the old man, bedridden for a week or more, who one evening begged Clara for a cookie while she was feeding him his watery oatmeal gruel. "Oh, I guess you can have a cookie," she told him, and went to the kitchen to get it.

"Here, Joe, take this cookie to old Hutch," she told the boy. Joe gave it to the old man, who took it in his claw-like hand, looked at it wistfully—then died without taking a bite of it.

Nor old Jasper Ormsby, a Civil War veteran. Old Jasper was one of Joe's special friends, and when the old man, after nearly a year at the farm, could no longer get out of his bed he looked in on him as often as he could, bringing him a drink of water, straightening his dirty, rumpled blankets, or just sitting beside his bed when he had a few minutes to spare.

One winter's day Joe saw Dr. Duncan's car in the yard when he came home from school. Hurrying into the entryway, he changed his clothes in the freezing cold and went into the kitchen. The doctor sat at the table with Annie and Clara, drinking coffee and eating apple pie. Joe's mouth watered hungrily, but none of them paid him any attention as he slipped past them into Mr. Ormsby's room.

The old man's eyes were shut and his face the grey color of the wood ashes Joe carried out in the ash pans every day. The boy started for the bed, then stopped. The old body on the bed was shaking, a hard, rapid shuddering that shook the iron bedstead. After one second look Joe ran back into the kitchen.

"What's the matter with Mr. Ormsby? He's about to shake his bed to pieces."

The three at the table looked at him, then the doctor said, "What! Isn't that old fellow dead yet?" He got up slowly and went into the room, shutting the door behind him. When he came out a few minutes later he said, matter of factly, "He's dead now."

As Annie plodded to the wall phone to call Munson, she curtly ordered Joe to get at his chores and be quick about it. He felt more lonely than ever as he hurried through his work in the cold winter dusk. He would miss the old man—and he would not soon forget the way it had been at the last—the queer, ashy color of Mr. Ormsby's face and the awful shaking of the thin old body. What, he wondered, had Dr. Duncan done to him in that closed room? He recalled a few other times when the doctor had been called to the farm. They had lost a patient each of those times, too—sick old men no longer able to work.

"Seems like we lose a patient every time old Doc Duncan comes out here," Joe said to Frank and Liz over the swishing of milk into their pails in the frigid cow barn that evening.

But he said nothing of any of this to anyone else. To the community he was only the silent, shabby, undersized lad with the big, scared eyes who lived at the Cook place. When anyone tried to talk to him, even when Annie and/or Clara were not present, he only nodded or shook his head and shied away. Many dubbed him "that bashful boy from the Poor Farm," a few others figured he was scared, scared almost to death.

But in later years, when it was all over and the Cook Poor Farm was a part of the past, Joe would remember, better than anything else, the fighting that constantly went on between Annie and her daughter. A never ending battle, or so it seemed to the boy on his blanket by their bedroom door. Their arguing, screaming and cursing went on for hours, night after night, and few of their quarrels ever seemed to be settled.

It seemed to Joe that they fought about everything: whether or not to buy a new car; the treatment, or mistreatment of the patients, including himself; the plans for the day and money, *especially money.* But not about Liz, Liz was Annie's property and she would brook no interference there.

Clara, as the bookkeeper, knew most of the details of her mother's business and enjoyed "faulting" her whenever she could. Annie could not stand criticism and the two often came to actual blows and hair-pulling bouts. When the combat became physical Joe pulled his blanket over his head and shivered, hoping they were not going to kill each other.

Annie's treatment of the patients was, on a daily basis, far more severe than Clara's, but he knew that the daughter, too, could get furiously angry. As on the day that old Lars Petersen turned up missing from his job of cleaning the cow barn. Clara, in the old Ford, found him near the west boundary of the Cook farm, plodding along the road toward Hershey. Ordering him into the turnrow space at the edge of the newly planted cornfield, she followed him in the car, screaming at him to go faster.

In a shambling run, the frightened old man was doing his best to keep ahead of the car, but the farther they went the angrier Clara became. Halfway down the turnrow, Frank and Joe, taking the slack out of the fence between their field and the neighbor's cow pasture, saw it all. As the old man and Clara passed them, Joe saw that she was actually foaming at the mouth, an ugly yellow phlegm spewing from her lips as she yelled curses and bumped the stumbling old man fleeing before her.

Joe would never forget the look he saw on Frank Cook's face as the pair went by—a sadness beyond description. "Poor girl," the father whispered, then turned away.

That night Annie tore into Clara for chasing old Lars with the car. Clara defended herself by reminding her mother of some of her own brutalities toward her patients—and they were at it again. More than anything else, however, it seemed to Joe that the two women quarreled over their money. There was often a great deal of cash on the farm, mostly in bills that they kept in the paper sacks and counted often, making sure the total balanced with the figures in Clara's books.

Many a night he watched them bring out the money sack from its hiding place, pour the money out on the dining room table and count it. The scene was always the same, both of them counting bills into piles of one hundred dollars each and lining the piles up in rows that covered the table. Thousands of dollars, all to be finally stuffed back into the sacks, fitted one inside the other until the money bag was six or seven sacks thick.

Then one night, in the midst of a violent quarrel, Annie struck a match and held it to the money bag as she snarled, "All right, we'll see what becomes of your damned money." Clara's jaw dropped and she stood frozen as the paper began to burn. Then she lunged at her mother, snatched the bag away and rubbed out the fire.

After that one or the other of them so frequently set the money sack afire that it began to seem like a silly game to the boy; for one of them always put the fire out before it reached the money. Why did they do it, he wondered. Neither of them intended to let the money burn.

Chapter 39

By 1933 Lewis Cauffman was tired of hotel living and restaurant food. "I'm buying another house," he told Mary on one of his visits to the farm on Bignell Flat, "and I'd like to have you come to town and be my housekeeper."

Times were getting harder. The stock market crash of 1929 had left its mark on even the heartland communities such as central and western Nebraska. Both the banks in which Dauphin had an interest had closed their doors and he had lost some of his farms. The new house he had planned to build for Mary and her children had been given up until things got better.

Times were leaner in North Platte, too, and Mary had lost some of her produce customers. Due to lay-offs on the railroad, fewer men stayed at the Ritner and there was less laundry. Paid by the piece, Mary's checks were smaller now.

Her father-in-law urged her to make the move if she wanted to. He and Irene would get along fine, he said. From the first there had been no thought in the mind of either that the little girl would leave her grandfather. Since babyhood she had spent all her waking hours with him, tagging after him around the farm all day, riding back and forth across the fields with him in the stout wooden boxes he bolted to the frames of the machines he used, even taking her naps in the boxes. When they came in at the end of the day, Mary bathed and shampooed the dusty child and put her into clean clothes for supper. Now, the old man said, he would do the same and they'd be fine, if she wanted to move to town.

So Mary and young Bill made the move, but one day each week she drove Cauffman's Chevy out to the farm to take groceries, do the laundry in her Maytag, and do the baking for the pair for another week.

It was Mary's move to town that gave Annie the excuse she had long been looking for. For sixteen years Mary had been her "property" and she had in no way forgiven her for running away. But with Ada Kelly, and then old man Dauphin, looking after her she had not dared move against her until now.

It was a good thing, she told herself, that she had held onto Will Dauphin, making him one of the "regulars" at her parties and giving him spending money now and then. Smacking her loose lips over the news that Mary had left her little daughter with old man Dauphin and moved in with Lewis Cauffman, would finally turn affairs her way, she felt certain.

She sent at once for Will and told him it was time he sued Mary for divorce and demanded custody of his children. He had the best of grounds, she said, what with Mary deserting her little girl and "shacking up with Cauffman like a common whore." She was willing to pay all the expenses of the action, she assured him, and would be glad to give his children a good home until they were grown.

On the first day of September Will filed his divorce petition and asked custody of the children. Sheriff Sayman served the court summons on Mary two days later.

Although pleased that Will was instituting the action that would free her from him, Mary was stunned by his declaration that he had "always conducted himself towards his wife as a faithful, chaste and dutiful husband," while she had "treated him with extreme cruelty, calling him vile, indecent and vulgar names and cursing and swearing at him." He had gone on to claim that she hated him and would never live with him again as his wife, and that she had committed adultery and was even then living in a state of adultry and was morally unfit to have custody of their two children. He wanted custody, he stated, "to care for, control and educate" them himself.

Sitting in her kitchen in Cauffman's house, Mary held the paper in her hands, remembering the slapping and cursing she had taken from her husband, his drinking and womanizing, the awful last beating that had put her to bed for nearly two weeks. Will had things turned around, laying all his own actions at her door. Will's father agreed with her, when she drove out to the farm to show him the summons.

"But don't you worry," he told her. "I'll never let him get these children."

The Dauphin divorce and custody case came on for trial the following February. Appearing for Mary were her father-in-law, several neighbors from Bignell Flat and her good friends Ada Kelly and Alma Ritner. From her seat beside her attorney, Mary stole a quick glance across the room at Annie and Will, and then did not look their way again.

Annie, in her shapeless old wool coat and crocheted cap, looked confident and sure of herself. Beside her Will, well-dressed and dapper as always, wore a self-satisfied, triumphant smirk. Mary did not miss the fact that the Reverend Tester flanked Annie on her other side.

With the preacher's help, the woman was certain that Will would be able to prove adultry against his wife and win custody of the children. No judge in his right mind could rule otherwise. The boy was nine now, the girl six, old enough to earn their way on the farm; but it was the hurt she could do Mary, thankless brat that she had turned out to be, that filled Annie with satisfaction. By the time she was done with her she would be mighty sorry that she had been so ungrateful to her good old aunt—running away, and then telling tales about the way she treated her patients. Yes, with the preacher on their side, Will couldn't lose their custody case.

Young Dauphin testified to Mary's cruelty to him and her unfitness as a mother. The preacher earnestly gave his reasons for believing her to be an unsuitable mother. County Attorney Collis Bell's cross-questioning, however, showed their testimony to be questionable.

Then Mary's supporters were called. Their vigorous defense of the young woman was impressive, but it was old William Dauphin's testimony that clenched the case.

In his rusty blue suit he sat in the witness box, leaning forward in his earnestness, his blue eyes dark with wrath. Mary, he stated, had endured much abuse from his son, who had not supported her or the children; and in the end he had been forced to order him out of the house to protect her from physical abuse. She had been a good mother, he went on, one of the finest, and had taken employment in the Cauffman home only to support her children. He concluded his testimony by declaring that the children would go to their father only over his dead body.

The court awarded young Dauphin his divorce, then found him "able-bodied and capable of working to support his family." Accordingly, it awarded custody of the children to their mother, ordered their father to pay Mary $10 per month in child support, and assessed all costs of the action to him.

Annie could not believe it. She should have worked on that judge, a new man, elected at the last election, but she had been so sure of the verdict, so sure that Will would win. Well, she would take care of the judge at the next election, and she would have plenty to say to that beak-nosed Collis Bell, too. As for Will Dauphin, he had been but a weak stick at best and she would be better off without him. And Mary—the final glare she turned on her was one of pure hatred.

Mary did not see it, for she did not look her aunt's way again until after the woman had turned to leave the courtroom. She had not had a good look at her in the ten years since she ran away; now she saw that she had gained a good deal of weight and walked like an old woman, plodding flat-footed and heavy toward the door.

For days Annie vented her fury on Joe and Liz and the patients, then set herself to planning what she could do to Mary to make up for the courtroom defeat. When the preacher and Will next came to the farm she had her plan ready. Not much of a plan, but it would do for starters. Will was to go to his father's farm and get Mary's washing machine.

"My old machine is playing out," she told him, "and I have all this washing to do for the patients. Mary still owes money on that Maytag, so I'll pay it off, take the machine and call it square."

It was a weak plan and she knew it; and Will knew that she lied, that Mary had paid for her washing machine long ago, but the minister beamed on her and praised her generosity.

The mild, dry winter of '33-'34 had merged into a rainless spring and the long, steep road up Bignell Hill was deep in dust when Will, with the preacher beside him, plowed his way to its top in a borrowed Ford truck. He was of two minds about his errand, wanting to please Annie and hurt Mary, but at the same time fearful of his reception at his father's house. Having the minister with him would, he hoped, keep his father from shooting first and asking questions later.

To his great relief there seemed to be no one home when he drove into the yard, then he saw the old man, with a team and corn planter on the far side of his cornfield. "We'd just as well go ahead and load the machine, and if Dad and Mary don't like it they can complain to Annie," he told the preacher.

From his field Dauphin saw the truck drive into his yard. At the end of the corn row he turned out of the field and headed his team to the house to see what was wanted. By the time he reached the yard the two men had the Maytag loaded and were tying it down.

"What's going on here?" the older man demanded.

Blustering, red-faced and scared, the son delivered his message. Without a word the father stepped inside the kitchen door, took down his old shotgun and told the pair to "Git, and be quick about it." The little truck sputtered to life and sped away, swirling clouds of dust into the air behind it.

"I should've made the rascals unload that machine," the farmer said aloud to the thinning dust cloud. "Your mama isn't going to like me letting it go," he told little Irene as he put the gun away and they got back onto the planter.

Mary was furious—but helpless; for she knew that with Annie behind the abduction of her machine no one at the courthouse would do anything about it. "Never mind," Lewis Cauffman told her. "I'll get you a new electric washer and you can do the washing here in town and take the clean clothes out to the farm. That old washer will give out one of these days anyway. Let it break down on Annie's hands."

Chapter 40

Times were desperately hard, all across the land, that winter of '33 and '34. As far back as 1932, 11,000 jobless World War veterans had begun their bonus march on Washington, and fifty-six of them, riding an old bus from California, had camped one night in North Platte's small city park. By winter the local Salvation Army was feeding up to forty men a day at its bread and soup table.

When, that summer, an empty building and the necessary equipment had been offered for a public canning kitchen, local citizens had promptly formed a "Relief Committee" to do the work. The *Telegraph* had notified its readers and asked for donations of fruit and vegetables, to be canned and stored for the benefit of the jobless during the coming winter.

Annie had wasted no time in letting the committee know that she would be happy to donate to the cause; and had willingly posed for her picture beside the truck load of summer apples, cabbages and tomatoes, picked and loaded by Liz, Joe, and the able-bodied poor, then waved it on its way to the canning kitchen.

Through the years Joe had noted that whenever Annie was especially generous in any way, she usually found some other way to save something in return. That fall it was Floyd Holbrook, her neighbor on the east, (owner of the field where Liz and Joe were ordered to throw the hens that died, or drowned in the stock tank) who made up the difference.

On a mild September evening Annie ordered Joe to fish a drowned hen out of the tank and throw it over the fence, then stood eying the tall corn stalks, each with its heavy down-turned ear of corn. "Joe," she said suddenly, "that corn is about ripe. Get a sack and climb over the fence and fill it."

"Won't that be stealing?" the boy asked.

"What if it is? I've given a hell of a lot of stuff to that canning kitchen this summer and that Holbrook hasn't given a damned thing. Let him help a little, too."

Joe climbed the fence and filled the sack, and the next morning Annie fed the corn to her chickens. From then on, until Holbrook picked the field, Annie sent the lad over the fence in the dusk of evening to fill his sack with free corn for her poultry.

The parties Annie and Clara held that winter were bigger and gayer and more frequent than ever before, and there were no signs of hard times there. Lela Comstock labored long and hard to load the big table in the dining room with choice foods for the guests. And Sheriff Sayman, who had periodically raided the county stills, kept the gatherings well supplied with the liquid evidence he confiscated. Then when the 14-years-long experiment with prohibition came to an end in December, 1933, the sheriff had on hand enough evidence to keep Annie's parties well oiled for some time to come.

With most of the sumptuous fare raised on the farm by free labor and prepared and served by a woman who received no cash, the elaborate meals cost Annie very little. At the same time the rates she charged for the parties, including the use of the three guest rooms, were so high that each one netted her a satisfying roll of bills for the money sack.

The "regulars" at the parties now included many of the most influential and respected men in North Platte. A new guest, that winter, was Anton Black, owner of the town's most exclusive women's wear shop. In exchange for the favor of entertaining his current lady love at the bungalow, he filled Clara's closet with stylish and expensive dresses.

Another was Mike McCarl. A friend and gambling partner of Art Haynes, he had recently built North Platte's first night club on the outskirts of the town. Mike had been to a few parties the winter before, but this season he brought with him a new lady friend, Violet Hornby, the town's leading madame, and a strikingly beautiful woman. Tall and slender, with sloe-black eyes and raven's wing hair, she moved with a slow, willowy grace and wore wide-brimmed picture hats.

Her first appearance at the bungalow set off a landslide of pleas for invitations to the next party. Violet came one more time and Annie was elated. She found it most gratifying to be able to pick and choose from among the city's most prominent men, including a former United States senator.

On the Sunday before the next party, Mike and Violet went pheasant hunting in the Sandhills north of town and Mike accidentally shot the lady in the leg, shattering the bones between the ankle and the knee. By evening he had her in a private room in the small city hospital, with special nurses on duty around the clock. In spite of the closed door and the rigid secrecy, the rest of the hospital staff soon knew the identity of the patient in the private room, and that the town's finest surgeon had amputated the shattered limb.

That night a young nurse, on duty alone except for the special nurse in the closed room, had her chores finished and her patients settled by midnight. Then, feeling the need of a snack, she decided to go to the basement to get an orange from the crate kept there. Switching on the light at the foot of the stairs, she was startled at sight of the madame's leg, black, swollen and bloody, in the coal bucket before the furnace, awaiting burning with the trash next morning.

That dawn the nurse told her relief, "If I hadn't known that was a *whore's* leg in the bucket I could have gone on by it to get my orange. So I had to go without the orange."

Violet came to no more of Annie's parties that winter, and by the next winter there were no more parties.

Chapter 41

The North Platte Irrigation Company, owner of the second oldest water right in the state, was especially hard hit by the hard times. Controlling most of the county ditches, including those that ran through the Cook farm, it was managed by a board of three directors, elected from among farmers who owned water rights in the company. All water users paid for their water when they paid their taxes, and any user two years in arrears had his irrigation water cut off—a sure inducement for "paying up" if it could possibly be done.

Each spring the company had to borrow money to cover the expense of opening, cleaning and repairing the ditches and their headgates. By the end of the year, with all taxes and irrigation fees paid, the board could expect to "break even." In former years the company had borrowed its operating funds from one or the other of the city banks, but by 1934 one of the banks had closed its doors and the other two had little money to lend, leading to a situation made to order for Anna Cook, whose money sack was bulging.

As more and more farms and other businesses failed and no longer paid taxes, school and irrigation districts, formerly on a cash basis, were forced to pay their teachers and other workers and suppliers with county warrants or I.O.U.s, to be made good when enough taxes came in.

Both Art Haynes and the banker, Riley Landers, had suggested to Annie that she get into the irrigation warrant business. The warrants were gilt-edged, one hundred per cent sure, they said—unless the whole county went broke. Their only drawback was that purchasers had to wait up to three years to cash the county's promises to pay. Haynes, always short of cash, could not afford to wait; neither could the two remaining banks, dangerously close to bankruptcy while they waited for the rains that would bring prosperity to the valley again.

To Annie it looked very good. Not only could she gather in the ten per cent discount on the warrants, but the additional seven per cent interest on the early spring loan to the irrigation company for its operating expenses. She and Clara lost no time in visiting the three directors, all valley neighbors. Annie's terms were the same as the bank's had been—with one exception. She would lend them the $14,000 they needed at the usual 7% interest, *provided they agreed that she, and only she, cash the warrants issued by the North Platte Irrigation Company.*

One of the directors, a well-to-do farmer, had formerly cashed a good many of the warrants himself, usually at full face value for the ditch riders and other hard-pressed ditch laborers. He knew that the Cook women would grant no such favors but would demand every ounce of their pound of flesh; and all three officials knew that the deal stank, but there was no other way to go. They had never needed water more desperately than in that dry winter and spring of '34 and this slit-eyed old woman seemed to be the only one who could meet their need. So they signed Annie's contract, hired a crew of ragged, hungry men and put them to work opening up the ditches.

Since the county warrants had come into use people who had a little money to save or invest had bought them because of the high interest they paid, more than double that paid by banks and many other investments. One such couple had been Harley Hood and his wife. He worked for the Union Pacific, she clerked at the J. C. Penney store. Between them, even in 1934, they could save enough in a few months to buy a ditch warrant. But when Mrs. Hood presented her money that spring for another warrant she was told that "Mrs. Cook buys them all now." Complaints were numerous, angry—and useless. Annie Cook controlled the ditch business.

But all was not well on the Cook horizon that spring. In fact Annie could see several clouds there. At the last election she had lost another of her commissioner friends, Faye Davis. And the man who replaced him, John Snyder, was definitely not a supporter. Now there was only Al Dancer whose backing she could be sure of.

After eleven years of housing the county poor the old house at the Cook farm was in bad shape, the floors and beds encrusted in vomit and urine; and the current patients, unwashed for months, in even worse condition. Word was getting back to her that more and more people were complaining to the commissioners and other officials about the state of affairs at the Poor Farm.

Over the years they had been "inspected" annually, but someone at the courthouse had always warned them in time to have the place and the patients cleaned up a bit, and a "gift" ready for the inspector. But now, with all the parties going on at the bungalow, it was plain that Liz and the one able-bodied old woman at the farm could not keep up with the work there, and still care for the old house and its inmates. Clara and Annie were agreed on that, but bitterly at odds on what to do about it.

Clara said she had all she could do, cooking for them all, and that they should hire some help. With times so hard and so many out of work, extra help wouldn't cost much. But Annie wouldn't hear to such notions and the noisy quarrels went on.

By February one of the patients had become a problem. A man not yet fifty, he was so crippled by rheumatoid arthritis that scarce a joint in his body would bend and he suffered constant pain. The two women argued endlessly over what to do with him. Clara, abetted by Dr. Reardon, held out for hospitalization, but Annie was determined to keep him where he was. Perhaps she hoped that, like old "Crip" Jensen, he would just disappear. In the end Clara won the argument.

The staff at the little city hospital was horrified at the man's condition, his entire body crusted with dirt and every rib protruding. Although he was Dr. Reardon's patient, the outraged head nurse called the hospital doctor, Glenn Waltemath, in to have a look at him. To the doctor, and everyone else who came into his room, the poor man made his plea to be sent to the home of his cousin in "Shanty Town," North Platte's poorest section. "Pat don't have much," he said, "but it's a lot better'n Annie's, and *I'll kill myself before I'll go back there.*"

Her own "Irish" aroused by the plight of her patient, Head Nurse McCullough saw to it that he went to the cousin's shack, and that they had "beef bones and brisket" for their soup pot the rest of the winter.

Soon after the man from the Poor Farm was dismissed from the hospital, Dr. Waltemath invited Miss McCullough to go with him "to have a look around at that Poor Farm."

A raw March wind blustered across the dry fields, rolling tumble weeds ahead of it and raising clouds of dust as the doctor put his car over the bumpy roads. Braking to a stop at the end of the old board walk, the doctor and the nurse sat in the car until Annie came to the door to silence the savage barking of the chained dogs.

Single file, and careful to stay in the middle of the walk, they passed between the snarling dogs and faced the slit-eyed, grim-faced woman, who asked them what they wanted. The doctor replied that they only wanted to look around, and she moved grudgingly aside to let them in.

Blandishments and gifts would do no good today, she knew. She thought of asking them if they had a search warrant but decided against it. Better just to let them look around a little, then get rid of them. Things were very bad, for there had been no warning this time — but she still had her supporters at the courthouse: the one commissioner, the county judge, Morgan Shay, Collis Bell, Sheriff Sayman, and old Dr. Duncan's replacement, S. A. Reardon — enough, she hoped, to insure that Clara could hold her contract. After all, it would be the word of a nosey doctor and nurse against hers and her friends at the courthouse.

The visitors were shocked at what they saw that day. Five old men crowded into the bedroom that had once been Annie's, two of them bedfast. The other three, though able to get about, were sitting on their cots, kept indoors that day by the chilly weather.

"Why are you sitting here?" the doctor asked.

"Annie won't let us sit no wheres else," one of the men answered dully. "We can be outdoors or in here, one or the other."

"Then why don't you open a window? The stench in here is terrible." The doctor edged his way to the smeary window and shoved on the sash. When it didn't move he took a closer look. The window was nailed shut.

The two old women in another room were somewhat cleaner and more tidy, but no less thin and hopeless than the old men. A very pregnant girl was helping Clara in the kitchen, a youngish man, able-bodied but dim-witted was busy at outside farm chores.

The doctor went to the commissioners meeting the following Monday to report on his visit to the Poor Farm. The three men listened attentively and Al Dancer, the chairman, thanked him and assured him they would consider his information. "We sure will," Snyder, the newly elected commissioner from the east end of the county, put in. "I'm planning a visit out there myself, soon."

That evening Dancer drove out to the farm to tell Annie and Clara about the doctor's report and to advise them to try to spruce the place up a little, and maybe feed the patients a little better. The new commissioner was suspicious, he said, and with the doc stirring things up there might be some investigating soon.

Annie had been worried about that new commissioner ever since his election the previous November. A retired farmer, he had been hostile and suspicious at their first meeting. So the Cook women looked at their problem from all sides—and argued violently as to how much improving they could afford to do.

Commissioner Snyder's interest in the Poor Farm related especially to one of the patients, old Steve Carter, Annie learned when, accompanied by the third commissioner, Raymond Hunter, he came to the farm a few days later. Hunter was a fence straddler, as she knew from past dealings with him, but the new man was plainly unfriendly and, in spite of her watchfulness, managed to talk to old Steve alone for a little while. The old man, another homeless bachelor, had worked for Snyder and his neighbors, off and on, for years, and the commissioner did not mean to let him be mistreated now.

On the way back to town he said, "Ray, something has to be done for those old folks out there. They are starving to death. Even my dogs live a lot better than they do."

"I suppose so," Hunter replied cautiously, "But what can you do?"

"We can get them away from that old woman and that dirty hole they live in. Send them somewhere else."

"But how are you going to do it? It'll cost the county more and the taxpayers will raise a howl, hard as times are now."

"We'll find a way. I'm not going to stand for what's going on out there. It ain't human, making folks live like that."

But the commissioner was a little late—the matter would soon be taken out of his hands.

Chapter 42

All that dry and dusty spring, Frank and Joe, with the help of the big, slow-witted patient, worked in the dry fields. By mid-May they had the beets, corn and gardens in and the orchard sprayed. Annie had filled her brooder houses as usual, and one bedfast old man had died. Art Haynes and the Reverend Tester came frequently to the farm and Annie planned to start her prayer meetings again in June.

On a hot evening late in May, Joe, now fifteen, finished his chores, washed for supper and slid wearily onto his chair at the table, facing the west kitchen window. Clara, at the stove getting supper, paid no attention to him. The patients, awaiting Annie's coming and her call to the table, had not yet come in from the yard.

Joe, staring dully at the dark window, was suddenly startled to see an open white hand, palm facing inward, moving slowly across the window. With a chill running up his spine, he sat up straight, his eyes wide, as the hand again moved across the window. At the third passage of the ghostly white hand, he jumped to his feet, sending his chair skidding behind him, ran outside and around to the west side of the house. There was no one there, and no one to be seen within the circle of light cast by the kitchen lamp.

Joe ran on to the poultry houses where Annie and Liz were making their last rounds and shutting the doors. "Annie," he croaked in a shaking voice, "I just saw a white hand wave three times at the big window."

"You saw no such thing," the woman snapped back. "Where the hell do you get such crazy notions?"

The lad ran to the barn then, where Frank was forking straw bedding under his horses. Breathlessly, he blurted out his vision of the white hand. The old man leaned on his fork, studying Joe's terror-stricken face by the light of his lantern. Then he spoke slowly and carefully. "Boy, that was a death call. In three days somebody here will be dead."

"But Frank, a lot of people have died here and I never saw that white hand before."

"That's because, this time, it will be somebody besides one of the poor folks. But if I was you, I wouldn't say anything about this to anyone else. Nobody would believe you anyway. So let's just wait and see what happens. And now why don't you go on in to supper?"

But the memory of the white hand, sliding across the wide window, filled the boy with a nameless terror, numbing his body and turning him so awkward at the table that he let the butter dish slip from his trembling hand. The dish went up-side-down on the table and Annie exploded, ordering him to leave the table and give his supper to the dogs.

Hungry and scared, he hunkered on his blanket that night while the women yelled and cursed in the bedroom. *Who was to die in three days?* This was Saturday night. Sunday, Monday, Tuesday. Someone would die on Tuesday. Would it be Frank? He thought the old man would be glad if he *was* the one. He had been so quiet, so discouraged, all this spring, what with the long dry spell and the women quarreling all the time. He no longer hummed under his breath, the old hymn tunes he loved so much, nor sang little snatches of "Jesus, Lover Of My Soul," or "When The Roll Is Called Up Yonder."

Or maybe he, Joe, would be the one. After all, *he* was the one who saw the hand. It could have been a warning for him, all right. Well, he guessed he wouldn't mind so very much either. Just to be done with Annie and her abuse, with being hungry all the time, and tired and scared. A good, long, quiet rest would be pretty nice.

Then, again, maybe it would be Annie. There was a lot of comfort in that thought and he hung onto it, trying to imagine what life without Annie would be like. Finally he fell into a troubled sleep, disturbed now and again by a shouted string of curses from one or the other of the fighting women.

Sunday passed, and Monday, and Joe thought of little else than the white hand at the window. All Tuesday morning he and Frank worked in the potato field. There had been barely moisture enough in the soil to bring the little plants up; and now, to keep them alive and growing, they were ditching and irrigating between the rows.

"First time I've ever had to start irrigating in May. First time in 43 years," Frank said, scanning the cloudless sky where the sun, hot enough for July, blazed down on the dusty valley.

Under the breathless heat, Joe shed his shirt. His dark skin didn't burn and the air against his sweaty hide felt good, but he would have to remember to put the shirt on again before he went in to dinner. Annie wouldn't stand for his coming shirtless to the table. He had tried it once—and had to feed his dinner to the dogs because of it.

All morning his mind had been heavy with dread. *Today was the third day.* Near mid-forenoon he straightened his aching back and looked toward the house. "Look, Frank," he exclaimed, "there's Doc Reardon's car, turning in to our place. "

"So it is." Frank shaded his eyes with his hand and watched the doctor getting out of his car. Then, a strange urgency in his voice, he said, "Joe, go shut off the water. I'm going in to see what's the matter."

Joe ran to the big ditch to shut the water gate, then hurried across the field to the house. Liz stood under the big tree nearest the kitchen door, a dazed look on her face. "What's the matter? What's happened?" he panted.

With an effort Liz focused her staring eyes on Joe's face. "You won't believe this," she said slowly, "but Annie just killed Clara."

"How?"

"Well, they'd been fighting all morning," Liz replied, picking her words carefully. "Finally, Clara yelled to Annie, 'I don't give a damn what you do,' and she run outta the kitchen to the yard, here. Then Annie grabbed the lid lifter off the stove and run after her. I come out, too, and I saw Annie throw the lifter at Clara. It hit her right here," Liz put her hand to the right side of her head, a little toward the back, then paused again, as if it were hard for her to find the right words to go on.

"Well, then Clara begins to run around this tree, around and around, two or three times, like a chicken with it's head cut off, and then she just fell down dead." Liz's voice trailed away and she shook her head a little, as if still not believing what she had just described.

So the hand had been for Clara. He had not once thought that it might be Clara.

Then Liz roused herself and pointed to a spot near the base of the tree. "See," she whispered, "see the blood on the ground. That's where her head was when they picked her up."

Joe saw the stain, dark and wet looking on the bare ground. Then Liz began to whisper again, "After Clara fell down Annie put her hand over her mouth and just looked at her for a minute, and then she run into the house and came back with a bottle of Lysol. Then she sent me in to get a towel to wrap around Clara's head. What do you suppose she wanted with the Lysol?"

The kitchen door opened and Dolly Saner and Mrs. Lay seemed about to come out, then changed their minds and went back inside and shut the door.

"How'd they get here so quick?" Joe asked.

"Well, after Annie wrapped the towel around Clara's head, she went in and called the doctor and Munson. They listened in when they heard the phone ring, and then they come over as fast as they could. They're helping take care of Annie. She's carrying on something awful," Liz finished drearily.

Joe walked around to the other side of the tree and leaned against the friendly old trunk for a little while. His insides were shaking and all he could think about was the HAND. All the time it had been meant for Clara. Why couldn't it have been for Annie? When he felt a little quieter he went into the house.

Clara was on the old kitchen couch, a clean sheet spread over her. Annie sat on a chair by the table, with Dolly and Mrs. Lay working over her, one of them wiping her face with a wet cloth, the other rubbing her wrists. The doctor was at the sink, mixing something in a glass. Frank was not in the room.

Annie did look awful, her sagging jowls a pasty white, her little eyes closed, her loose lips twitching. He turned and walked slowly to the cot. As he put out his hand to lift the sheet from Clara's face, Annie's whisper came, low and menacing, "Don't touch that sheet," and then a despairing.wail, "Oh, my poor Clara, my poor baby."

Joe dropped his hand and turned back. The doctor was at the table with the glass. "Here, Mrs. Cook, drink this. It will help a little." He put the glass to Annie's lips and she took a sip, then pushed it away and lumbered to her feet. "Joe, I want to see you a minute," she said and plodded toward the storeroom. Joe followed her inside and she shut the door.

"Listen now, and listen good," her voice was low and urgent. "I want you to go get the money sack and hide it in the fruit cellar. That's where we'll keep it 'til this is over." She told him where she and Clara had hidden the sack that morning. "Now git, and don't let anyone see you."

They went back into the kitchen as Munson and his helper came through the door with the dead basket. Annie screamed and the mortician stopped to pat her shoulder and speak a few soothing words.

"Please," she choked, "please don't take her away. Can't you do whatever you have to right here?"

"I'm sorry, but hot as it is today, I'll have to embalm her right away, and I can do that best at my place in town."

"Oh, no, no, not to my poor Clara," Annie wailed. Then, opening her eyes to their usual slits, she said, "Well, all right, but I want you to bring her home before night. I want her right here tonight, where I can look after her myself."

"Yes, I can do that," Munson promised. But as they turned to the couch to put Clara in the basket, Annie went into another outburst of sobbing and moaning, with the doctor and the neighbor women working over her. At the same time she managed to dart a quick, sharp glance at Joe, who still lingered in the kitchen. From long experience, he interpreted the command in the woman's slit eyes and scuttled away to find and hide the money sack.

Annie was still sitting at the table when he came back. She was quieter now and the medicine glass was empty. She shot another sharp, questioning glance at Joe. He nodded and she seemed to relax, then roused to ask the doctor to call Munson and tell him to be sure to bring her poor Clara to the bungalow. "I want her right there in the parlor where I can take care of her."

Next, she asked Dolly to call Mable Johnson and have her come over. "I want her to sit up with me tonight in the parlor with Clara."

Chapter 43

Mrs. Lay and Dolly Saner started cooking dinner for the patients, and then Lela Comstock came, told Annie not to worry about a thing, and took over in the kitchen. Annie said she didn't want anything to eat and that she'd like to go to the bungalow and lie down. Before she left the kitchen she told Liz and Joe to get back to work, to hoe the garden or clean the big chicken house, or something.

All afternoon cars came to the yard and people, many of them carrying plates and pans of food, protected by dish towels with their four corners knotted on top, came and went from the bungalow.

Liz and Joe did the chores alone that evening. Frank did not come to help and they had not seen him. He had only stayed in the kitchen a minute, Liz said, just long enough to look at Clara on the couch, then spread the sheet back over her head and leave.

He was probably out walking somewhere, Joe figured, maybe down by the river where no one would see him, and where he wouldn't have to talk to anybody. He could imagine something of what the man must be feeling. He had to know how his daughter had died—and be driven nearly crazy by his helplessness to do anything about it. It had been that way with Frank for a long while, the lad knew. From halting words dropped now and then by the father he understood that he dared not report on his wife's cruelty to the patients (even if he could get anyone to listen to him) because it would also reflect on Clara, and he could not bring himself to do anything to hurt her. But maybe now, with Clara out of it, he would stand up to Annie and do something about it, maybe he would even go to the authorities with the true story of her death.

Munson brought Clara back while Liz and Joe were milking, and when they finished the chores and went to the bungalow they found her coffin set up in the parlor between the big windows. Although Joe had seen many dead people, including his own mother, at the Poor Farm, this was the first time he had seen a body made ready for burial. Clara's casket was beautiful, all shining silver-grey, and lined with softly pleated white satin. Her shroud was a lacy pink cloud, like the sunsets he and Frank sometimes took a few minutes to watch from under the big cottonwoods by the barn. Her hair had been nicely combed and she lay a little on her side, her head turned just a little toward the viewers. "That's so the place where Annie hit her won't show," Liz whispered to Joe.

She looked nice, the boy thought, much younger and very peaceful, even pretty. She didn't look at all like the angry woman who, only last night, had been yelling cuss words at her mother. He stood a long time beside the expensive coffin, remembering many things: He thought of the dead woman as she had looked, frothing at the mouth while she chased old Lars with her car, bumping him along the turnrow, or, not very long ago, chasing another old man with a pitchfork.

Then he remembered the times, not a lot of them, when she had looked at her father, or at him, with a kindly, even affectionate expression on her face, and the time she had brought him the new overalls. Then he thought of the hand again, and how it had been meant for Clara all the time, and he shivered a little.

He turned away from the coffin and saw that Mrs. Johnson was there with Annie, and that there was a great deal of food on the table. After the custom of the valley at such times, the neighbors had brought in cakes and pies, sandwiches and salads. For the first time in weeks Liz and Joe and the patients would go to bed with full stomachs.

There was another woman there, too, a nurse in a starched white uniform. The doctor had sent her out to look after the bereaved mother and keep her sedated so she wouldn't feel her awful grief so much. While Liz and Joe were eating, the nurse went to the kitchen to fix her patient another glass of medicine. Motioning Joe to her, Annie whispered to him to get the lantern from the entryway and go check on the money sack. She was still awake when Joe came back, her slit eyes seeking his nod of assurance.

The nurse coaxed her to the davenport and made her comfortable there with several pillows under her head. With quivering lips she declared that she would not sleep a wink that night, not with her poor Clara dead in her coffin, but she admitted that she did feel a little better. The medicine had helped. The nurse brought coffee for herself and Mrs. Johnson, then settled herself in an overstuffed chair. Mrs. Johnson sat near the casket.

Joe got his blanket and rolled up in it in a corner of the dining room. From where he lay he could see Clara's gleaming coffin — and he wondered what Annie was *really* feeling. He was sure she hadn't meant to kill Clara. Her daughter was too important to her and to the operation of the Poor Farm. He knew the contract was in Clara's name and he wondered what would happen now. Who would cook for them? Who would keep the books? Where was Frank? What would he do now? Then, too worn out with all the happenings of that long, hot day to wonder any more, he dropped off to sleep, the first sound, quiet sleep he had had in a long, long while.

When he wakened at dawn, the usual time for getting up in summer on the farm, Annie was sound asleep on the davenport and the nurse was dozing in her chair. Only kindly Mrs. Johnson was awake, keeping the vigil beside the casket.

On his way to the barn Joe ducked into the cellar to check on the money sack. He knew that would be the first thing Annie would want to know. Frank was putting the cows in the stanchions when Joe came in. His face looked old and gaunt, his cheeks hollow and his eyes sunken. Joe wished there was something he could do, or say, but he could think of nothing.

Lela Comstock was in the kitchen, getting breakfast, when Joe and Liz finished the separating and put the cream in the icebox. Dolly and Mrs. Lay were back at the bungalow when he went in to report to Annie, who was carrying on because she had waked up and remembered that her poor Clara was dead. The nurse was coaxing her to take some more of her medicine.

As soon as he could get Dolly alone for a minute, Joe asked her what had happened to Clara. Liz's story had seemed clear enough, and he well knew that the lid lifter and the stove poker were two of Annie's favorite weapons. Since she and Mrs. Lay had helped carry the dead woman in the house they must know how she had died—and he wondered what they were going to do about it.

At Joe's question the woman gave him a startled glance, then looked away while she considered her answer. Finally she asked, "Didn't you see all the blood out there?" Joe nodded. "Well, that's all I know about it," she said and walked away.

When Joe saw Frank heading for the potato field he went along. The young plants needed water, he knew, for this new day promised to be as hot and cloudless as the one before it; but he also sensed that, even more than the potatoes needed water, the tormented father needed to be busy.

The miles he had walked the night before had helped, but, weary though he was, he could not rest. Neither could he talk to the people who came to bring food, to offer sympathy, or to satisfy their curiosity; not with the knowledge he carried in his heart. So he had to work.

Seeing him out in his field while his only child lay in her coffin, some of the visitors wondered at him, wondered why he wasn't at the house with his grieving wife, why he couldn't let the farming go, at least until after the funeral. But there were a few who, like Joe, understood and respected the father's need to grieve alone.

The funeral was held in the old Methodist church in Hershey on Thursday afternoon. Munson came for Clara with the hearse, and two other big black cars, one for the family and the second for the pall bearers, instructed to meet at the farm for the ride to the church.

A few people were already in the church when the little procession arrived and the bearers carried the casket to its place in front of the pulpit. Munson opened the satin-lined lid above the dead woman's face, then went back to the car to bring the family in. With Munson on one side and the nurse, in a fresh uniform, on the other, Annie was helped into the church and seated in the front pew. Liz and Joe took their places beside her, and Frank, too, sitting in the same pew with his wife for the first time since she had burned the mole off Mary's face.

Frank, who had not come to the bungalow while Clara lay in state there, now got up from his seat and went to the coffin to bid his daughter good-bye. Joe ached for the old man as he watched him go, his usually straight shoulders sagging in the rusty old navy blue suit. At the coffin he bent over Clara and caressed her face with his calloused old fingers, then put his hands gently on her shoulders and held her while he kissed her still face again and again.

Joe, peeking from behind his hand at Annie, saw that she was sobbing softly into her handkerchief, and then was chilled by the malicious glint he saw in her little eyes as she watched her husband bidding farewell to their daughter. Frank came back to the pew and sat down, bowed his head and put his hand over his eyes.

The church was filling rapidly as the minister, C. E. Austen, accompanied by the Reverend Tester and a former pastor who had served the church when Clara was a little girl, took their places behind the pulpit.

With her handkerchief still pressed to her quivering lips and the nurse patting her arm, Annie watched her friends come in. Judge Shay came, and Collis Bell, Thaddeaus Long, Sheriff Sayman and Nate Elsen. Several former county commissioners were there, Emmet Sodman, Ben Esely, Faye Davis, and, of course, Harley Costin, all sitting together in the front of the church across from the family. The pall bearers were all prominent men, neighbors, and businessmen she and Clara patronized. The whole turnout was a testimony to her standing in the community.

The flowers were gratifying, too, many wreaths and handsome bouquets from neighbors and townspeople; a fine bouquet from old Dr. Duncan, another from Munson, a large wreath from a group of courthouse employees. She was especially proud of the blanket of roses she had had Munson order for her. It covered the whole lower half of the coffin with its pink loveliness.

The service began with a prayer, and then a hymn, sung by some woman Munson had hired. As the singer sat down and the Reverend Austen came to the pulpit with his Bible, Annie stood up, stumbling a little and swaying on her feet, then plodded up to the coffin and bent over it, weeping bitterly. For a little space everyone sat in stony silence, then Munson, in the back of the church, leaped to his feet and hurried to the woman's side. Gently, he put his hands on her heaving shoulders and began to draw her away. "Now, now, Mrs. Cook, now, now," he soothed as he led her outside.

"The old fraud," Joe said to himself, "she's putting every bit of that on." Frank, his hand over his eyes, did not move.

The flustered minister began again, then paused respectfully while Munson brought Annie back to the pew and seated her. On her way up the aisle she noted that Art Haynes and his wife were in the audience, and the banker, Landers, and several other well-known people.

The funeral procession from the church to the North Platte cemetery was a long one, so long that Annie ordered Joe to count the cars behind them as they turned the corner onto the highway. At the graveyard she was pleased with the four-place lot she had had Munson buy for her, the day after Clara's death, in the best section of the big burial ground.

Standing there at Clara's open grave, Joe looked out across the cemetery at the many handsome monuments and tombstones, most of them decorated with limp and faded bouquets and sprays of flowers. Placed there the day before, Memorial Day, most of them had wilted almost instantly under the blazing sun. He knew his mother had been buried here, but he didn't know where. He had never been to her grave and he wondered if anyone had remembered to put a flower there.

Frank stood beside him, his sunken eyes dry, deep lines of grief and weariness etching his face. The undertaker placed a folding chair for Annie, still sobbing gently into her handkerchief, and then stood on one side of her, the nurse on the other, as the minister said the final prayer.

Back at the farm, when the last sympathizer had finally gone, Annie dismissed the nurse and watched her drive away. Then she sent Joe to the cellar for the money sack. There were enough of the funeral "baked meats" left to feed the family and the patients that evening and the next day, she figured. Friday afternoon she called Lela Comstock and asked her to come over and take charge of the kitchen again for a day or two, until she could decide what to do.

Frank, Joe, Liz and the slow-witted patient did the chores and went ahead with the farm work. Except that Clara was gone, it was as if nothing had ever happened.

Chapter 44

The birth of the Dionne quintuplets on May 28, 1934, preempted the *Telegraph*'s headlines and most of the rest of its space on Wednesday, the 30th, leaving only room for a brief item on the death of Clara Cook. For the next several days the paper was filled with almost hourly reports on the precarious survival of the "quints," and it was not until June 5 that space was allotted for a brief recap of the funeral, followed by the statement, "The immediate cause of death was suffocation, resulting from fluid entering the lungs, physicians said. County attorney Collis Bell said an inquest would not be necessary. The death appeared purely accidental."

However the *Daily Bulletin*, a small rival paper, gave the death considerably more space as soon as it learned of it, and on Wednesday, May 30, published the following:

Clara Cook Dead
Victim Of Poison

"Victim of a tragic error, Clara Cook, 38 years old, died yesterday morning at the county Poor Farm for which she held the contract for its operation, after an inmate of the home allegedly prepared a dose of disinfectant for her, thinking it was the medicine she had requested. County Clerk Thad Long, Commissioner Al Dancer and County Attorney Collis Bell investigated the accident. Bell said later that he did not believe an inquest would be necessary.

"According to witnesses, Miss Cook had been busy working in the kitchen and had just prepared to bake bread. While so occupied she asked one of the aged inmates to prepare a dose of medicine which she was accustomed to taking. The inmate, by mistake, poured poison into the glass. Miss Cook swallowed the poison and immediately began choking and coughing. A physician summoned from North Platte said that the liquid had entered her lungs and had practically suffocated her. The investigators did not learn the name of the inmate said to have administered the fatal dose.

"Miss Cook was the daughter of Mr. and Mrs. Frank Cook who own the farm about eight miles northwest of town. It has been the site of the home for the county poor for several years. No steps will be taken to determine who will take care of the poor until after the funeral. It was explained that Mrs. Cook may continue to operate the farm, or new bids may be advertised. At present there are six aged county charges who are inmates of the farm. The funeral will be held Thursday from the Methodist church at Hershey at 3:30 P.M."

With Clara in her grave due to a "tragic accident," the big question in the community was the disposition of the county poor. Would they stay on at Annie's, or would a new home be found for them? On June 5 the *Telegraph* ran the commissioners notice that bids for the care of the county poor would be taken until June 11.

Annie considered resubmitting Clara's last bid, but changed her mind when Dancer came to the farm to tell her that, although he had held out for keeping the inmates where they were, Commissioner Snyder, still stirred up by his visit to the farm, had threatened to bring some influential citizens such as Ada Kelly and the state senator from their district in to inspect the place.

"So now," he told her, "it looks like your neighbor, Jack Haugland, will get the contract. Anyway, we'll be moving the old folks in a few days."

On June 12, under the headline, Brisk Bidding For The County Poor Farm, the *Telegraph* reported: "Seven bids were opened by the county commissioners yesterday in answer to their advertisement for someone to operate the Lincoln County poor farm. Until recently the poor farm was operated by Clara Cook near Hershey, but her accidental death due to drinking poison necessitated the re-opening of bids.

"Mary L. Brower submitted a bid so high that the commissioners indicated she will have scant chance of receiving the award. She asked $14.50 per week per inmate, or slightly in excess of $2 a day. When it is considered that a man and wife on the relief rolls receive only $2 per week for food, it can easily be seen that the cost she estimated is excessive.

"Other bidders were Emma Sutherland, $7 a week; Jacob Haugland, $6; Laura Foster, $5; Mrs. Ray Humphrey, $6; Mrs. John Brose, $5.50; and Lydia Kantz, $7. All the bidders except two live in North Platte. Haugland has a farm 11 miles southwest of here. Lydia Kantz lives at Sutherland. Commissioner Al Dancer stated that pending acceptance of one of the bids, the commissioners will investigate the homes offered for care of the poor and govern their decision by the desirability of the location as well as the low bid."

The commissioners made their selection, the Haugland farm, and moved the county poor there immediately. Annie was glad to see them go. Liz and the one old lady able to work hadn't had time to do much in the way of cleaning them up and she knew the Hauglands would have plenty to say about the condition of the old folks they inherited.

It no longer mattered to her what they said about her. She was above and beyond mere gossip, and that was all they were, anyway, a bunch of gossips. A new story would soon come along and they would forget all about Annie Cook and her Poor Farm. Besides, she had bigger fish to fry—as soon as she could clear up the present mess and get at it. The north Eighty would soon be hers.

Looking back on it while she studied Clara's books, she could see that she had made good money on keeping the county poor, these past twelve years. In addition, it had kept her in contact with all the important county officials and helped her turn many a neat profit on the side. And quantities of the supplies she had bought and charged to the county, sheets and towels, flour and soap, many things, were still stored away, unused.

She could see now that it would have been a mistake to try to keep the county poor any longer. She had found that out soon after the funeral. Without Clara to run the kitchen there would have been no profit in it. Without Clara many things were going to be different. She was going to miss her daughter much more than she had thought. She (Annie) had done no cooking for twenty years and she would miss the good bread and cakes Clara had so handily turned out.

Also, she soon realized, when she threw that lid-lifter she had set herself afoot—for now she had no driver. Yes, she had plenty to do and she had better be about it.

Chapter 45

With Clara and the patients gone the farm seemed empty and too quiet. Where there had sometimes been as many as fifteen people at the table there were now only three, Annie, Liz and Joe, for Frank never came to the house anymore.

When Annie told Joe, the day after the patients left, that he was to be her driver now, he was overjoyed. At school some of the boys his age, and even younger, bragged that they drove their father's cars, and Joe had longed to get behind a steering wheel, too. The few times Clara had taken him with her in the car without Annie along, he had watched her every move with the clutch and brake and knew that he could handle them if he ever got the chance.

So small for his fifteen years that he could scarcely see over the steering wheel, Joe sat as tall as he could and would have managed well enough if it hadn't been for Annie who, although she had never driven a car in her life, immediately took over the driving of that one.

After his first few trips as Annie's driver, Joe spilled out his frustration and disappointment to Lester McConnel. "She makes me drive the way *she* thinks it oughta be done. Like when we have to slow down and she makes me use the brake until I almost kill the engine. Then, just before it dies, she lets me use the clutch. I keep telling her it's so dumb to do it that way, but it don't matter—it has to be done the way *she* says, and every time she tells me what to do she gives me a whack on the head."

Lester sympathized as he always did, and counseled patience. It would all be better some day, he said. But Lester had problems of his own, that hot, dry summer. His wife was not well and supporting a growing family was becoming daily more difficult.

Joe drove Annie to town the day she went in to pay Clara's funeral bill. She usually made him wait in the car while she took care of her business, but this time she ordered him to come with her to carry in some cream, eggs and the dressed hen she had brought the undertaker.

Munson came out of his office to greet her in the waiting room. His broad Irish face all smiles, he took her into his office and seated her before his big desk, where she took a roll of bills from her handbag and asked how much she owed him.

"Eight hundred dollars," he told her. "Clara's funeral was one of the nicest we've ever had. Everyone thought it was beautiful."

Annie counted out the bills, then asked about the death certificate. "Well," the mortician replied slowly, "you know how she died and I know how she died, but I've signed this the way you asked me to, 'accidental poisoning'," and he took the paper from his desk drawer and handed it to her.

From the mortuary Annie ordered Joe to take her to the monument works, across the road from the cemetery. There she spent quite awhile selecting a proper memorial stone for the Cook plot, and ordering it carved and put up with all possible speed. When told that it was in place, she had Joe drive her in to see it. An impressive granite block, it bore the one word, COOK, in large letters. Beside the big stone was a low granite marker engraved with the words, "Clara, beloved daughter."

Annie was pleased. The Cook stone was larger than any other in that section of the cemetery. "I'll be buried here, too, someday," she told Joe, "and Frank and Liz." Then she stomped away to the car to be about her business.

By then word was getting back to her that the Hauglands had been outraged at the condition of the six old folks so recently consigned to their care. That they were filthy beyond belief and that Jack had had

The Cook tombstone. Clara's headstone at left. Frank and Anna are buried in the center lots. The 4th lot, meant for Lizzie, remains unoccupied. (Courtesy Robert Messersmith.)

to cut their hair off close to their heads, the two old women, too, as it was so matted, dirty and full of lice and dog ticks.

In spite of Annie's determination not to let anything they said bother her, it did and she was in a foul mood on the early June day that a pair of insurance men came to the farm. Joe and Annie were in one of the chicken houses, catching and crating young roosters to sell to a poultry firm in town; for she no longer had enough help to dress out her fryers for her select customers.

The morning was oppressively hot and Annie was cussing as she snared the young roosters' legs with her hooked wire. "Who in hell do they think they are, telling things like that?" she said of the Hauglands, as a man in a business suit came to the chicken house door.

"You'll have to wait," she told her callers. "We've got to finish loading this crate. The truck is on the way and these chickens will die in this heat if they have to be shut up very long."

While the wilting men wiped their perspiring faces and waited, Joe and Annie finished their task and helped load the crates on the truck. Then the old woman led the way to the kitchen and put out a pitcher of lemonade for her visitors. She did not offer Joe a glass, nor did he expect her to. To Annie, as he well knew, he was just another of her possessions, like a piece of furniture maybe. He got himself a drink of water at the pump and sat down on a corner of the woodbox to wait.

Annie brought the policy she carried on Clara to the table and began to argue with the men. The face value of the policy was $10,000 but she was claiming double indemnity because of Clara's accidental death and the men were asking a lot of searching questions. After awhile one of the men said he was going out in the yard to get a breath of air and, as he got up from his chair, motioned Joe to follow him.

Standing under the big cottonwood, almost on the spot where Clara's blood had soaked into the dusty ground, the insurance man asked Joe what he knew about Miss Cook's death, and he told him. The knowledge that Annie had killed her daughter had been a burden since the day it happened. He knew the doctor and the undertaker were going along with Annie's version of the death (each believing that he would one day inherit a fine Eighty if he did).

He knew, too, that Frank had said nothing to anyone, and he suspected he knew the reason. With Clara buried and the broken place in her head forever hidden, few people would believe such an impossible story, and if they did Annie had only to declare he was crazy, insane, his mind gone because of his grief, and that would be that.

But these insurance men were different. They were strangers, they didn't know Annie. Maybe *they* could do something if they knew the truth. So he told them the story as he knew it, and felt relieved at the telling.

Back in the kitchen the man faced Annie with his new information, and then quailed before the blazing wrath in the woman's slit eyes as she told him "that bastard kid is a damned liar. He makes up stories and he wouldn't know the truth if he met it in the road." Anyway, she raged on, she had the death certificate, signed by the acting county coroner and the doctor. The agents could talk to them if they doubted her word, or to anybody at the courthouse, or in the whole community, for that matter. They would all back her up. Or was he going to take the word of a snotty bastard brat in place of hers?

While the agent stammered an apology, Annie turned to Joe and ordered him to tell the gentleman that he had lied. Cowering before the menace in the glinting eyes, the lad obeyed.

The men signed the papers insuring payment of the double indemnity Annie demanded, then bid her "Good day" and scurried away. And when they were gone she gave Joe the worst beating of his life, using the buggy whip, her fists, a stick of stove wood, anything she could get her hands on. He was lame and sore for days afterward.

When the insurance check came Annie bought the north Eighty, along with the privilege of harvesting that summer's crops, including twenty acres of beets. For nearly forty years she had coveted that land, good irrigated corn and sugar beet land. Although Joe never understood Art Haynes' part in the transaction, he knew that he had been of help to her in making what they called a "sharp deal."

The Lays, who owned the land and lived in the tall two-story house across the road and a little way west, left for California as soon as the deal was closed. They had been good neighbors but Annie was glad to see them go. They knew too much about Clara's death and other things she'd just as soon keep under cover. Like the other neighbors, they had been afraid to tell what they knew — not with Annie sitting over there with her high-powered rifle, where she could shoot their bull in his pasture, or burn them out some dark night, and they had known she'd do it if they gave her any reason to.

Ownership of the north Eighty made Annie feel so good that, at Haynes' suggestion, she bought another car. The old Ford had been giving considerable trouble lately, refusing to start at times and breaking down occasionally, and Haynes knew of a "damn good bargain," a repossessed 1931 Dodge. That she was using some of Clara's life insurance money to pay for the car that she had refused to let her buy when living, did not seem to bother her.

By then the Comstock's ancient car had also given out and Earl was walking to his handy-man jobs at Annie's and other places. Shortly after installing the Dodge in her garage, Annie called Earl to ask him to come over to do some work for her. Explaining that he had promised to help a neighbor that day, a paying job, he told her he could come tomorrow. No deal, she told him, he could come today, or not at all, ever again.

He walked the two miles out to the farm and Annie showed him the work she wanted done, nothing that couldn't have waited until tomorrow. But when it was done she told him she had something for him, then took him to the old Ford, parked under a cottonwood beside the barn. "Earl," she said graciously, "I want you to have my old car. I don't need it now and you can get a lot of good out of it, handy as you are at fixing things."

Comstock quickly tinkered the engine to life and drove the car home. A few days later Annie called him back again, and while he worked on another part of the farm, she gave Joe a cup of sugar and told him to pour it into the old Ford's gas tank. "It'll make it run better," she said.

Joe stared at her. "Annie, you know it'll gum up the engine so it won't run at all," he told her.

The woman's eyes began to glitter as she reached for her whip. "You heard me" she gritted. "Now do as I tell you, you damn bastard, and don't give me no more of your damn back-talk." Her lips slackened into a half-smile as she watched the lad pouring the sugar into the gas tank.

Annie, Liz and Joe still slept in the bungalow, where the woman took the money sack to bed with her and kept the rifle beside her pillow. Joe now had a bed of his own, a folding cot in a corner of the dining room. Annie had never gotten around to putting water in the new house, so they ate their meals in the old kitchen as they had always done.

As he had for so long, the Reverend Tester still came to the farm, scattering the hens as he swung the big Packard into the yard, and Annie still tucked $20 bills into his vest pocket and smiled slackly at him. But there were no prayer meetings that summer, and no more parties in the bungalow when the farm work was done that fall—even though Annie made Liz clean the whole house once a week as usual.

And Annie still had her good cakes to share with her friends, Art Haynes and the preacher and any others who might drop in. It was all much as it had been before Clara's death—except that Harley Costin's little roadster seldom stopped in the yard any more.

All she had to do now was call Lela Comstock and ask her to bake a cake although, since she had made Joe sugar the old Ford's gas tank, she usually had to send him to Hershey to bring back the baked goods. Otherwise, until he could get hold of another old car, Earl walked out with the cake. Then Annie would tell him that it would all be worth his time. That all this, with a vague wave of her thick hand, would someday be his. "And it may not be long," she might add. "Since I lost poor Clara I don't feel that I'm much longer for this world."

Before the summer was over she had her good bread, too. When she had mentioned to Thad Long how much she missed the bread Clara used to bake, he had quickly volunteered to keep her supplied. "My wife bakes fine bread and we'll be glad to see that you get a loaf every week," he told her.

Chapter 46

After Clara's death Frank worked harder than ever in his fields and gardens, laboring from dawn to full dark, that hot, rainless summer, ditching the precious irrigating water to every plant he could reach. Joe helped him when he could, when he wasn't driving for Annie. But there was a difference in the old man now. He was as kind and considerate as before but he never sang at his work any more, and seldom spoke. When the lad asked him a question he seemed to have to come back from some far place before he answered.

Liz, too, seemed frail, that summer, although Annie appeared not to notice, except that she no longer made her clean the bungalow— there wasn't time enough for that and her outside work, too. Nearly sixty now, and more bent, she had to pause often as she shoveled manure from the barn or chicken houses, and lean against a stall post or wall for a minute, her hand to her aching back.

That fall Joe helped Frank haul the beets from the north Eighty. Frank didn't ask him to, but neither did Annie say anything to stop him, so he lent the old man a hand until the job was done.

Up at 3:30, those chilly November mornings, Frank fed and harnessed his four horses while Liz and Joe did the milking and separating and Annie got breakfast. Joe helped hitch the double teams to the big beet wagon, loaded the evening before with six tons of the big, sweet vegetables, then climbed to the seat beside Frank for the drive to the Hershey beet dump.

Sometimes they were first at the scales, awaiting the seven o'clock opening, sometimes there were one or two wagons ahead of them. If they were told to "go over the dump" the unloading was quick and easy, but if they had to unload on the huge beet pile Joe worked hard, scooping as fast as he could swing his shovel to save Frank all he could.

Joe's first trip over the dump had been scary, for the long, sloping trestle, thirty-five feet above ground at the top, shook and shivered with every forward step of the four horses. Clutching the side of the seat with a white-knuckled hand, he kept his eyes on Frank. When he saw that neither the man nor the horses seemed alarmed, he relaxed a little and watched with interest as the wagon, halted on the platform at the top, was secured with heavy chains, the platform tilted and the load dumped. A minute, or two later they were going down the other side with the empty wagon.

Loading the big wagon was the hardest part, for Joe was small for such work and swinging his loaded shovel as high as his head was exhausting labor, though he did it willingly, well aware how much it saved the old man. Two loads a day, hauled to the dump; and the third, loaded by lantern light and waiting to be hauled the next morning, was a long days' work.

Even Annie could see that getting the beets out was too much for the failing old man and the undersized boy, so that winter she rented the north Eighty to Les McConnell.

Joe had hoped that after Frank was rested from the grueling work of the beet harvest, he would be more like he had been before Clara died, humming or singing little snatches of hymns, reading his Bible, visiting with him when they had a little time together. But there was no change.

Most evenings that winter, after his chores were done, Joe went to the beet shack for a little while before bedtime. For the most part his old friend sat quiet, saying little and, though he picked up his worn old Bible and held it open on his knees, he didn't read it much. Just sat staring into space; and the boy, hurting for him, did not know what to do to help.

The mild winter of '34 and '35, with little snow to dampen and protect the parched fields and pastures, merged into another dry spring. With the March winds, dust storms raged across the prairies, blacking out the sun and the daylight so that chickens went to roost at mid-day and lamps and lanterns had to be lighted.

In Washington President Roosevelt was asking for millions in drouth and farm relief. Annie rented out the farm ground on the home place and ordered only two hundred pullet chicks for one of her brooder houses. Two hundred hens were about all that Liz could care for, these days, and eggs brought so little, that it hardly paid to keep hens. But she had outdone the neighborhood with her poultry for so many years that she couldn't quite bring herself to give them all up. The noisy guineas hiding out their nests and looking after themselves still had the run of the farm, but the turkeys, ducks and geese were gone.

Frank, Liz and Joe planted the potato patch and the gardens and put out their cabbage plants, but Joe frequently had to leave the others to do the work while he drove the car for Annie, for her business took her often to town, and up and down the valley, that spring.

The new courthouse, finished at last, was a handsome building and Joe liked to drive by it. The men who had burned the old one down had served their sentences, and Lincoln countians, tired of the eyesore in their midst, had finally voted the funds to tear the bridge planks from the tall windows and replace them with glass.

That summer they didn't always have irrigation water when they needed it. With no rain for two summers, and little snow in the mountains the past winter, the river no longer carried enough water to keep all the valley ditches full and the Board was forced to ration the reduced supply. By turns, the farmers on the ditch had their water shut off for a day, and on those days Frank, suffering right along with his wilting potatoes and cabbages, worked his way along the rows, often on hands and knees, savagely yanking out every upstart weed that dared rob his precious plants of a drop of water.

Joe sympathized with the old man, and even more with the ditch riders who, it seemed to him, worked hardest of all for their meager pay, tendered weekly in county warrants.

In spite of their "ditch rider" titles, these men *walked* the ditch banks, tending the water gates and maintaining the even flow of water. Rationing made their work even harder and they were weary, hot and dirty when, at the end of each week, they came to the Cook farm, some on foot, some in beat-up old cars, to trade their warrants for cash, less ten percent.

Their knocks on the back door usually brought Joe or Liz. Asked to tell Mrs. Cook they had come to "sell" their warrants, the boy or the bent old woman, more often than not, brought back the message that she was busy and would be out when she could. And if Art Haynes' natty roadster was parked in the yard they knew why the old woman was too busy to see them, and that their wait would be a long one.

So the tired men waited, sometimes until the sun went down. And sometimes Annie sent word that she couldn't see them at all that day; they'd have to come back tomorrow. Rough treatment, Joe thought, for men whose families lived from warrant to warrant, waiting for them to bring home the very bread they needed for supper that night.

He felt sorry for them as he watched them go, some cursing, some with sagging shoulders and tears in their eyes. "There's no end to the ways that old woman can think up to hurt people," he said to himself. And wondered again why someone didn't kill her, or why God didn't strike her dead. Why couldn't the Hand have been for her?

By the summer's end Annie could see that she would have to hire a man to help get the potatoes, cabbages and apples in; for under Frank's loving care his few acres had yielded abundantly. But he no longer had the strength to dig and chop, or lift and carry, the produce to the cellars and granaries.

When Annie mentioned her need of a hired man to Sheriff Sayman he told her of a man who had been in to see him that day. A farmer who had lost his farm to the bank that summer, and his wife to childbirth and overwork a little later. With several dependent children to support, "the poor cuss needs a job bad and would work for small wages," he said. Annie told him to bring the man out.

He came the next day. A gaunt farmer by the name of Henry Moore, he was, like scores of other men in the county, dispossessed and hopeless, barely hanging on. At the Cook farm there was plenty to do. Carloads of people still came out from town to accept the Cook largesse, or to buy what they needed. The stores took the rest, but it all had to be dug, cut, or picked, cleaned and sacked.

Prices had never been lower. With many people working for rock bottom wages, and the rest on bare-bones "relief," the merchants had to sell at prices their customers could afford to pay—and Annie sneered at the scanty sums Frank's produce brought in for the money sack that fall. Actually no more than it cost her to hire the extra help, she complained.

Frank seemed not to notice. He had grown the fruit and vegetables for the pleasure their growing gave him, and had welcomed the weariness he felt at the end of each day, as if he had labored only to make himself too tired to think, or feel, by night.

Chapter 47

With the spring of 1936 the rains came again. With the help of Henry Moore, and with less irrigating to do, the garden work was easier, but even so Frank barely made it through the summer, puttering doggedly at his hoeing and weeding, keeping his vegetables healthy and growing. By September he seldom went to the gardens any more but sat instead, of an afternoon, in the west-facing doorway of the beet shack, the legs of his old overalls pulled up to his knees.

The hot sun felt good on his legs, he told Joe, and the boy nodded, concerned over the appearance of the old man's swollen limbs, the skin stretched tight and shiny from ankle to knee. When he urged him to see a doctor he only shook his head and said there was no need.

Annie paid her husband no attention whatever. When Joe ventured to ask her if she shouldn't have the doctor out to see him she only snorted and told him to mind his own business.

All fall Joe saw to it that the sick man had wood and water in the shack, and something to cook in the old black kettle on the back of the little stove. When, in mid-September, he saw that more was needed he took it upon himself to move him, with his Bible and his few other possessions, to the old house, where he cleaned out a bedroom for him.

Frank made no protest when Joe told him he was ready to take him to the house. It was a slow trip, with several rest stops between the beet shack and the back door. At one stop the old man sat for a little while on a stump facing the bungalow, empty now, and silent all year long except at night when Annie, Liz and Joe went there to sleep.

Joe had heard the tale, making the rounds of the neighborhood these days, that Annie kept the bungalow spic and span and the big dining room table always set with the fine china and glassware, as she had done when Clara was alive. But, as Joe could have told them, there was only dust on the table now, and a few odds and ends Annie left there.

While he waited for Frank to gather his strength for the rest of their journey, Joe wondered again why the woman insisted on sleeping in the bungalow. It would have been much easier to clean out the other bedrooms in the old house and sleep there, especially in winter when snow covered the ground and they had to leave the warm kitchen and tramp across the yard to the bone-chilling cold of the unheated house.

He wondered, too, what Frank was thinking, or if he even saw the big house whose door he had never entered. But he said nothing and they presently moved on toward the old house. Annie set another place at the table that night; otherwise she ignored her husband's presence. Joe helped him to the table, where he ate only a few bites, then helped him back to bed.

By October first the old man's strength was almost gone and Joe could see that the end was near. He was thankful that Annie didn't require his services that day and that he could spend most of it at the bedside of his old friend, watching for the change that he knew was coming soon. He lay unmoving, his eyes closed, his grey beard spread neatly over the blanket Joe smoothed across his chest. His breathing was even and shallow and he could not tell if he slept or not.

Late in the afternoon Liz went to tend the chickens and Henry to milk the cows. Annie plodded about the kitchen, getting supper. Suddenly the old man opened his eyes and whispered to Joe that he needed to get up. The lad helped him to the old chamber pail, then back to bed. Exhausted, the sick man lay quiet for a little while; then, clutching Joe's hand, he spoke again.

"Joe, I have something to say to you. I want you to be a good boy, Joe, because I am leaving you now. They are waiting for me and I am going home, so I have to tell you good-bye." His weak voice faded away, the light went out of his eyes and an expression of utter peace settled over his worn face, wiping out the lines of care.

Joe held the bony old hand for a little while, silently saying his own good-bye, then went to the kitchen where Annie stirred something at the stove. "Frank just died," he told her. She said nothing as she turned and stumped to the old wall phone to call Munson.

Annie did not bring Frank's body home. There was no place for it on the farm he had bought with such high hopes nearly half a century earlier—neither in the old house that he had left years ago for the haymow and the beet shack, nor in the new house that he had never entered.

While his body lay in state in a plain wooden casket at the mortuary, Mary called to pay her last respects. She went late in the evening, when she was sure there would be no other visitors, for she did not want to meet Annie there, then or ever.

For a long time she looked at the gentle old face, remembering her Uncle Frank's unfailing kindness to her and how deeply he had sorrowed for her on the many occasions of Annie's cruelty. The time she burned the mole off her face, all the times when her legs bled from her cutting whip lash, the time she cut off her hair, and burned her spelling certificate, the list could go on and on.

She did not know what she would have done if Uncle Frank had not been there to help, to heal her cuts with a soothing salve he kept behind a feed box in the barn, and her other hurts with quiet words of sympathy.

She remembered the times he had read to her from his Bible, and then explained the passages so that she understood them; and the times they had sung together. She could still hear his deep, clear baritone rolling out the stirring words for "When the Roll is Called Up Yonder." He was there now, she thought, answering to the roll call of his own name in Heaven. And she was glad, for she knew that the old man, like herself, had had plenty of Hell on earth. Except for her mother, he had been her only real friend for fifteen long, hard years. With a gentle pat on his cold forehead, she bid him farewell.

The funeral was held in the Hershey church where he had attended services for so many years, and where he had sung in the choir in happier times. The Reverend Chauncey Tester was in charge, assisted by the church's pastor, C. L. Carpenter. When Munson had asked Annie what hymns she wanted him to select, she had told him to use whatever he liked. Joe had then asked if he could name the songs, and had chosen Frank's favorites: "Face to Face," "A Perfect Day" and "Jesus, Lover of My Soul."

The church was filled with the friends and neighbors who had liked and respected Frank Cook throughout the years. Many of Annie's friends were there, too, and the usual crowd of curiosity seekers, attracted by anything that had to do with Annie Cook.

Annie didn't bother to "dress up" for Frank's funeral. Since Clara's death she hadn't paid much attention to her appearance, nor had she worn her corset since her daughter's funeral, and she wore only loose carpet slippers now because her feet hurt so much.

Joe and Liz were the only relatives sitting with Annie in the front pew, reserved for mourners. Liz, the neighbors noted, seemed to be shrinking with the years, getting smaller and more bent; while Joe, with his downcast, frightened dark eyes and ragged thatch of black hair, didn't seem to be getting any bigger. A strange trio, the beetle-browed, scowling old woman; bent, skinny old Liz and the thin, timid boy.

The sun was low in the west by the time the funeral procession reached the cemetery, where Frank was laid to rest beside his daughter, in the shadow of the big granite stone that bore the single name, COOK, in large letters.

Chapter 48

After her husband's death Annie sold his big teams. They didn't bring much—they were old, and tractors were replacing horses in the valley. But she kept old Henry on to help Liz with the milking and care of the cows and other chores.

Her off-farm business, the houses in town, her real estate deals and the warrants took most of her time. Few people had the ready cash on hand during the hard times of the '30s to buy the school district and irrigation warrants with which the county paid its bills. But Annie always did and more and more people sought her out, warrants in hand.

But it was her business with Art Haynes that interested her most; it not only made easy money for her, but there was an element of risk about it that she relished. Outwitting the law—and making money at it—appealed to her, like thumbing her nose at the law and its officials.

Haynes hurried up the conclusion of many of his real estate deals by arranging to have Annie in his office when a potential buyer came in. Explaining smoothly that, though Mrs. Cook had come in to purchase the same piece of property, he would still honor his agreement with the first buyer, provided he could conclude the sale immediately. It usually worked.

Most of her dealings with the gang lord were conducted over her kitchen table or, occasionally, in his office on Main Street, upstairs over the Duling Optical company. But climbing the stairs to Haynes' office was hard on Annie's feet, and slow because of her bulk, so more and more often they worked the scheme with Annie at home in her kitchen.

Art had two phones on his desk and a signal button on the floor beneath it. With a slow or hesitant client in his office or on the phone, he had only to press the button with his foot to let his girl in the outer office know that she was to call Annie and tell her to make a call on the other phone. When her call came in a moment later, telling him she was ready to close the deal on the same piece of property, it often resulted in a sale.

On a grey afternoon in late November, some six weeks after Frank's funeral, Liz and Joe were sorting apples in the kitchen. With Frank unable to give the orchard his usual care, that summer, the crop had been scanty and poor.

When Haynes' car came suddenly into view and turned into the lane, Annie, at her desk where she could bring her books up to date and, at the same time, see that Liz and Joe didn't dawdle at their work, sniffed in surprise, (usually he called before he came out) then waddled to the cupboard to take out half a layer cake and two cups. When Art came in she was cutting two generous wedges.

"Have a chair, Art," she said, reaching for the coffee pot, and to Liz and Joe, "you two git on out and help Henry."

With a wistful look at the cake, the ragged pair went out. Through the window the two in the kitchen watched them crossing the yard toward the barn.

"That kid's been here a long time," Haynes said. "I'd think he's about old enough to go it on his own."

"Yeh," Annie growled, "but he's got nowhere else to go, and anyway, he thinks this place'll be his when I'm gone. He'll stay around."

"I wouldn't be too sure," the man said.

"You look upset," Annie said abruptly, peering at him through her slit eyelids. "Anything wrong?"

"Well, yes, there is. It's that damn Greek, Sam Pappas. He runs that Oasis restaurant on Main Street, but it's only a front for his gambling tables in the back room. The thing is, he's raking in too much of the business. I'm the one that pays for protection in this burg, one way or another, and he's cutting in on it by too damn much. But if I have him closed down it will probably stir up the bluenoses in town and they'll wind up closing me down, too."

"I see," Annie muttered, rubbing her mole. Art had opened his Vet's Club within the past year, a first class establishment on Main Street, with drinks and entertainment under dimmed lights in the front room and gambling in the back room. The Club had been doing very well and she could understand Haynes' anger at the competition. Furthermore, anything that hurt her friend's business hurt her, too, making her cut smaller — and that she could not have.

After awhile she looked up, her eyes glittering between their folds of puffy flesh. "There's two Sam Pappases in town, ain't there?" she asked.

"Yeh. The other one runs that little Coney Island eating place, or works there anyway. They call him 'Coney Island Sam.' They're cousins."

"Ain't this Coney Island Sam the one that's mixed up in a sodomy case? With a boy they're sending to the reform school?"

"That's right. They're holding the kid in jail now, 'till Sayman gets time to take him to Kearney."

"Do you suppose you could scare this gambling Sam Pappas out of town by accusing *him* of sodomy and threatening to have the kid testify against him before Sayman takes him to Kearney?"

Haynes' gloomy face brightened. "It might work," he agreed. "I got Carl McKenzie appointed to the police force last summer. He'll do anything I tell him to, and Dave Baxter will help. We got him elected to the city council a year ago and had him appointed Police Commissioner. Pappas is afraid of me anyway, and if Carl and Dave and I lay it all out for him, plain, he'll probably agree to get out of town rather than face a court case. In Nebraska the penalty is about twenty years in the pen for sodomy. Yeh, it's pretty sure to work. I'll get right on to it."

They finished their cake and coffee and talked awhile, smoothing their plan. The sky had darkened even more and it was starting to rain — cold, wind-driven bullets of rain that made the gang lord hang on to his hat as he ran for his car.

Haynes called the councilman and the police officer into his office the next day. Both agreed that his plan should work. Baxter and McKenzie were to pick Pappas up at his rooming house, one of the seedy old hotels on Front Street, and take him to McKenzie's third floor room at the old Ritner hotel on the coming Sunday night.

Pappas was a small man, past middle age and frail. Faced by the councilman, a prominent, well-to-do businessman, and by the police officer, a big man with powerful arms and shoulders; and by Haynes, the most feared man in the county, the Greek was sure to see things their way and agree to save his hide by leaving town at their invitation.

The following Wednesday afternoon Haynes was back in Annie's kitchen. The plan hadn't worked, he told her.

In uniform and driving a police cruiser, McKenzie, working his regular four to midnight shift, had picked Pappas up a little after eleven o'clock, Haynes related. "He had Baxter with him, and when they told the Greek they had 'something in his interest' to tell him, he came along without any trouble. At the hotel Bax called me, and by the time I got there they were waiting for me in Mac's room.

"Mac bolted the door and then said, 'All right, Pappas, lets have it. Tell us what you've been doing to the boys in this town.' The Greek looked scared, all right, but he said he hadn't been doing anything to the boys. So Mac laid it all out for him, the sodomy charge, the twenty years in the pen and the kid over in the jail, ready to testify against him, and told him that if he'd get out of town, and stay out, we'd drop the charges and keep still about the whole thing.

"But that damn Greek wouldn't scare. He just claimed he hadn't done anything like that. So Mac got a little rough. He started hitting Pappas and the blood began to squirt. When he tried to fight back Bax grabbed one of his arms and asked me to hold the other one. But that cock-eyed little Greek was slippery as an eel, all bloody like he was. He got away from both of us and slid the bolt on the door and got out in the hall. And there was a fella out there, one of the roomers, I guess, and he looked scared to hell when he saw the Greek.

"Mac and Bax drug him back into the room, and then he began to beg, but he still wouldn't admit to anything, so Mac hit him again, a time or two. Then I said this wasn't the way to do it, that we'd better go to the police station and get the kid and settle it there.

"So that's what we did. The Greek was still bleeding some and his face was swelled up pretty bad, but I told the night officer that there had been a little disagreement and asked him to bring the Harden kid in so he could identify Pappas. A man went after him, but that damn Greek still stood there and wouldn't admit to a thing.

"They came right back with the kid, and what does the damn kid do but stand there and tell us we have the wrong Greek.

"Well, I did what I could to patch things up then. I got Pappas and Mac to shake hands and we left. It was after midnight by then, and Mac's shift was done, so we all went home and I thought that would be the end of it." North Platte's Al Capone shrugged his shoulders, then spread his hands helplessly before Annie.

The woman waited, rubbing her mole, her narrowed eyes calculating.

"I guess Pappas was in worse shape than we thought," Haynes finally went on. "Somebody from the police station took him home — and we made a mistake there. We should've looked after him ourselves, for the old woman that runs his hotel thought he looked pretty bad and took him to the hospital — and now that damned new county attorney is onto it and snooping like hell. It don't look good," he ended flatly, his angry, worried eyes seeking assurance from the squat old woman across the table.

Annie rubbed her thumb back and forth across the blue mole as she considered the matter. "Yeah," she said finally, "it looks like you let it get outa hand all right." But she was worried, too.

The new county attorney, Sam Diedrich, was a different breed of man from Collis Bell. In office more than a year now, he couldn't be bought and he hated gambling in all its forms. He had campaigned on his promise to clean out gambling and prostitution in North Platte and Lincoln County, and had won over Bell in spite of all that Haynes and his political henchmen could do.

"You think Pappas will talk to Diedrich, tell him what happened?"

"I'm afraid he already has. I went up to the hospital yesterday to see him and he told me Diedrich had been in, asking a lot of questions, and he said he was telling him the truth. I told him McKenzie wasn't going to like that, but the damn fool said he couldn't help that, he was going to tell what happened to any son-of-a-bitch that asked him."

"Hmm," Annie pulled at her mole and Haynes looked away. "Well," she said finally, "it looks like you better get yourself a lawyer."

Haynes nodded. "I know, but he's going to want some money and I'm pretty short right now."

Annie's eyes narrowed again, but she knew she'd have to help him—the money for his defense was her insurance that he would not bring her name into anything he might have to reveal.

Chapter 49

The story broke the next morning, November 25, under the front page headline "Diedrich Says He Will File Charges In Mystery Beating." According to the story the county attorney had spent all day Wednesday investigating the circumstances surrounding the case and taking statements from the persons involved. As a result he intended to file criminal charges in the beating suffered Sunday night by Sam I. Pappas, who had been in St. Mary's hospital since early Monday morning.

One event followed fast on the heels of another for the next few days. On Friday the mayor, Dale Duncan, Jr., son of Annie's old friend, Dr. Dale Duncan, Sr., ordered Carl McKenzie relieved of his badge and suspended indefinitely from the police force.

A picture of the beaten man appeared in Saturday's paper, with the names of his assailants. The portions of his face not covered by bandages showed swollen and dark. At a hearing the following Monday morning the three men were charged, made their indignant pleas of "not guilty" and were dismissed on bond of $5,000 each. They were ordered to be in county court on December 6, with Judge Morgan Shay in charge.

Haynes and his colleagues had a week in which to make such "arrangements" as they could. The gang lord spent a portion of it in Annie's kitchen and, by the time they were due in court, was his old arrogant self, boasting confidently that he would never be convicted of any crime, nor spend a day in jail.

The hearing opened before a crowded courtroom on Tuesday, December 7, with an overflow crowd in the wide hallway outside. Annie was there, with Joe beside her, sitting well to the back, attracting as little attention as possible.

Haynes was represented by his friend, Collis Bell. Havland, Call and Havland, an old successful law firm, represented McKenzie. Baxter employed his cousin, Charles Baxter, partner in another of the city's prestigious law firms. County Attorney Samuel Diedrich, assisted by his long-time friend, Attorney Milton Murphy, was pitted against North Platte's best.

That evening the city council met in regular session and two councilmen, stirred anew to righteous wrath by the recent events, demanded to know why no report had been made to the council in response to a petition presented to that body a month ago. The petition, signed by 168 citizens, demanded that all public gambling in the city be stopped.

Mayor Duncan informed the council that he had already instructed the police to stop all such activity and that he didn't know of any gambling now going on. Police Chief James Bechan backed him with a statement that only card games were now in operation, no slot machines or other table devices.

But the councilmen, remembering too many other so-called "clean-ups" in the past, and not convinced that the present action was any better, proposed that a special investigator be hired to look into local gambling conditions, obtain evidence, if any, and report at the next meeting. The council then went into executive session to name and hire a plain clothes officer to conduct the investigation. It looked as if the "better element" was deadly serious in its intentions to clean up Little Chicago.

The next day Attorney Baxter did his best to convince the court that the matter presently before them was merely "an everyday sort of street fight, with no arms involved" and no real harm intended. The whole thing, he said, was just a case "trumped up by Diedrich to hurt three well-known and prominent men."

Diedrich and Murphy questioned Pappas for only thirty-seven minutes, while the attorneys for the defense tried for nearly two hours to shake his story. Tim Glines, night clerk at the Ritner, testified to the presence of all three defendants in Room 25 on the night of November 21.

The defense attorneys then called the county attorney to the stand and tried to show that the whole affair was an attempt by Diedrich to "get" Haynes. But, in the face of the evidence, and with the frail little Greek, just out of the hospital and still looking "peaked, right there in the courtroom, the judge had no choice but to charge the "well-known and prominent men" with kidnapping and assault and battery, with intent to do great bodily harm.

Judge Shay, plainly worried and unhappy, continued bail for the three at $5,000 each and set the date for the trial on January 6, 1938. Haynes' wife and a friend, Charles Parson, a prosperous cafe owner, raised his bail; Baxter's family put up his; and McKenzie's father mortgaged his house to raise his.

On Friday, December 17, Mayor Duncan announced that the council would get its report on gambling, if any, going on in North Platte at the regular Tuesday evening meeting. The special investigator, "whose identity has been carefully guarded," had been at work since the last meeting, he said.

But the many citizens who searched their newspapers the next Wednesday were disappointed—the report was not there. "Just the same old runaround," they grumbled. A week later a big headline announced that forty witnesses might be put on the stand in the Pappas case.

The usual big crowd turned out for the annual Christmas night ball at Jeffers Pavillion, the huge Union Pacific-owned hall on the north side of the tracks. The ball was in full swing when Sam Diedrich and his wife arrived a little before midnight.

The spacious central dance floor, well filled with waltzing couples, was marked off from the rest of the big hall with a white picket fence, inset with wicket gates where officials stood, dropping the nickel-a-dance fees into the deep pockets of their canvas aprons. The wide area outside the fence was crowded with festive guests, many with flasks in their hip pockets, greeting each other with zest and gusto.

As the county attorney and his wife made their way down the north side of the fence, exchanging salutations, they came face to face with Spark Haynes, husky son of the gang lord and an amateur boxer of local renown. In response to Diedrich's nod of recognition, the young man replied with a string of obscenities.

"Can't a man speak to you civilly without being cursed?" the tall county attorney demanded.

"Not after all the damn lies you've been telling about my dad," the burly young boxer retorted, and swung a balled fist into the face of the older man, knocking him backward onto the picket fence.

His lip cut and bleeding, Diedrich had almost regained his balance when Spark swung again. The surrounding crowd, surprised into immobility by the sudden attack, watched as young Haynes battered the county official against the fence, bending him backward over the pointed pickets.

Diedrich's wife, Lorene, was the first to recover her wits and try to stop the one-sided affray by pounding on the attacker with her handbag. Then a bystander or two took a hand, and by then the police assigned to cover the ball came boiling out of the men's room, where they had been having a little nip, and shoved their way up through the crowd.

Diedrich, bloody and groggy, was taken to the hospital with a concussion; Spark Haynes, defiant and cursing, to the police station where he was booked for assault and battery. Under a picture of the battered Diedrich in his hospital bed, the morning paper carried an account of the unequal fight, and the report that Haynes had been freed on $1,000 bond. The Pappas trial, the report added, would now have to be postponed until the county attorney should be able to attend.

Chapter 50

By mid-January forty-seven witnesses, Mayor Duncan among them, had been lined up for the trial, which began in February, with the recovered county attorney and his assistant in charge of the prosecution. Since the accused men had asked for separate trials, Haynes, still smoothly confident, was the only one at the defendant's table.

On that first day the jury was taken to the old Ritner, where they were shown the bolt on the door and the various stains, said to be blood, splashed about the room, the hall and the stairway. Haynes swore that the whole thing was a frame-up and that someone had put the bolt on the door of Room 25 *after* the so-called beating.

"Coney Island Sam," the other Pappas in the now famous case, then testified that McKenzie had recently stated "We are going to run all the ____ Greeks out of this town and white people are going to run it for a change," bringing the second taint of racism into an affair connected with the gangster.

On the following day the identity of the private investigator was revealed. A man by the name of John Deacon, he was a former state deputy sheriff. On the stand he testified that he had known Art Haynes since 1933 and that, the past summer, he had made plans with Sam I. Pappas to establish a "recreation parlor" or gambling room in Ogallala. While fitting the place up, he said, Haynes called him into his office on August 9 and said, "Don't you know you can't do any business in western Nebraska without consulting us? We are running western Nebraska." "We," Deacon said, meant Art Haynes and Pat McHugh, Haynes partner in the Vet's Club.

He went on to testify that Haynes had said to him "If you'll get rid of that damn Greek for us, we can use you," and that he had boasted of "running all the niggers out of town." Sheriff Sayman and the city police judge were members of the Vet's Club, he said, and Police Officer McKenzie had gambled at Pappas' gambling den in the back of the Oasis. Deacon had, indeed, been at work.

Dr. S. A. Reardon, the county physician, next stated on the stand that he had treated Carl McKenzie for an injured arm on Monday morning, November 22, and again the next day, that his arm was swollen and causing him considerable pain, and that he said he had "hurt his arm while subduing a man he was arresting." McKenzie, the doctor said, had claimed compensation from the county for his visits to his office.

Defense Attorney Baxter declared the altercation had come about because Mr. Haynes was attempting to gain a confession from a "moral degenerate" who was debauching the youth of North Platte, and that gambling, as charged by the prosecution, had nothing to do with the matter.

Mayor Duncan's testimony was brief and inconsequential. He merely told that, as soon as he had learned of the trouble at the Ritner, he had suspended officer McKenzie from the force until he could learn more about the matter.

It then came out that Tim Glines, night clerk at the Ritner, who had testified at the November hearing, had since disappeared and could not be found.

Milton Murphy, in his summation for the jury, stated that the whole affair was staged to force the defendant, Sam I. Pappas, to admit to sodomy, have him identified by the Hardin boy and sentenced to the penitentiary for twenty years, and so get him out of the way. "The real reason behind all this was gambling," he concluded. "Sam Pappas was running a place in competition to Haynes' Vet's Club and he had to be eliminated."

In a masterly speech to the jury, County Attorney Samuel Diedrich told the twelve good men and true that Art Haynes had, for many years, been running the crime syndicate in Western Nebraska and that, when he set out to "get" Sam Pappas, his competitor, Officer McKenzie had been his tool for the job, "the same as a loaded gun trained on his enemy."

After keeping its followers on the edges of their chairs for eleven days, the trial ended at 9:22 on Saturday evening and the jurors retired to their locked room. Nearly two days (forty-three hours) later the jury announced it had reached a verdict.

The verdict, read at 4:38 on Sunday afternoon, caught the people unprepared and only twenty-three spectators were on hand to hear it. Haynes, "though tense and somewhat pale," said nothing during the fifteen minute proceeding which ended with the verdict, "guilty of assault with intent to do great bodily harm." He immediately filed an appeal for a new trial.

Carl McKenzie was the next member of the trio to be tried. Sixty-five citizens were examined before twelve could be found to serve as a jury. Before another packed courtroom, Sam I. Pappas testified that he and Art Haynes had not liked each other since "bootlegging times," when Haynes had tried to make him pay "one dollar a gallon for protection."

Then a Woodford Oliver, who had occupied a room across the hall from McKenzie's room at the Ritner, testified that on the night of November 21 he had heard a racket in Room 25, "like someone putting a drunk to bed, or throwing a drunk out, like a scuffle going on in the room, and then out in the hall." Then he heard somebody say, "Set down, you ___ Greek. I'm running this, not you. I'm boss around here."

"And then I heard somebody say, 'Don't Curly, don't hit me again.'" McKenzie's friends called him "Curly."

George Razes, a friend of Haynes, next testified that Haynes had sent him to Pappas' room at the hospital, the day after the fight, to tell the Greek to "forget all about the affair in Room 25."

When the next two witnesses were called the court reported that they had left town and their whereabouts were unknown. One was Tim Glines the night clerk, the other was the maid who, on Gline's order, had washed up the blood stained walls, floors, bedspread and curtains before dawn, that November morning.

Annie, sitting in the back of the courtroom, already knew about that — she had given Haynes the money that paid their way out of town.

Most of the five days of the trial were highlighted by the "feuding" of Baxter, council for the defense, and Murphy, the state's council, with the former repeatedly provoking the latter into "unbecoming retorts and breeches of etiquette." Both were frequently admonished by the court for their "intemperate language and misconduct." The audience loved it, often breaking into laughter and delighted catcalls.

McKenzie's story was that Pappas had caused all the trouble by striking him, an officer of the law trying to do his duty, and that he had struck back only in self-defense. As to anything that happened *after* that night in Room 25, or anything he had said or done, such as visits to the doctor and remarks made there, he simply did not remember.

"You see," the burly ex-officer explained, "after the Mayor kicked me off the force I got drunk and stayed drunk for several days."

The case went to the jury at 4:44 on Saturday afternoon. Twelve hours later, at four o'clock on Sunday morning, the weary dozen reached its decision. As soon as the officiating attorneys were located and present in the courtroom, the bailiff read the verdict "guilty of kidnapping and assault, with intent to do great bodily harm."

This time, too, there were few people in the courtroom and the town had to wait until Monday to read the account in the newspapers. The impact was stunning. While guilt on the assault charge carried a sentence of only "one to five," guilt on the kidnapping charge, in the wake of the Lindberg baby kidnapping, now carried a *mandatory sentence of life imprisonment*. Poor old Mac, he'd really done himself in, this time.

His attorney quickly filed a motion for a new trial—on the grounds of misconduct on the part of the county attorney, the special prosecutor, the jury, and the courtroom audience. The purpose of the deliberate baiting of Murphy by Baxter, McKinzie's attorney, now became clear. Because of it the audience had laughed and become "boisterous," preventing a fair trial.

In the face of the first two guilty verdicts, Councilman David Baxter in March filed for a change of venue for his trial and was advised that it would be held on April 5 in Tryon, county seat of neighboring McPherson County.

Lincoln County officials, the defendant, his attorney, witnesses and interested spectators, then prepared to make the thirty-five mile drive north to Tryon; but the morning of April 5 dawned with a heavy snow storm in progress. By noon, after hours of shoveling through drifts and plowing through snow, the cavalcade made it to the McPherson County courtroom, which turned out to be so small that only the judge, the jury and the attorneys managed to crowd into it. The few family members and sensation seekers who had braved the storm to attend the trial had to cool their heels in the hall, or in other offices.

There being no hotel or public hostelry of any kind in the little ranch-country town, the Judge called a recess early in the afternoon, after which the entire court and the visitors plowed their way back to North Platte.

Back in the little courtroom the next day, the charge of kidnapping was dropped and Baxter was tried only for assault and battery. The jury received the case on Saturday afternoon and, after everyone else had gone home, convened in the little courtroom. At one a.m. on Sunday morning the twelve announced their verdict, "Guilty." Baxter's attorney at once filed a motion for a new trial, alleging many errors. His motion was granted and a new date of April 27 set.

In the meantime the case of Jeffrey (Spark) Haynes vs. Samuel Diedrich came to trial. The young man's father and his friends had had time to do their homework well. Of the scores of witnesses whose names had been taken at the Christmas ball after the "fight," some could not now be found; the rest, taking the stand one by one, declared they had seen nothing out of the way that night.

"Yes," a few said, "there had been a commotion of some kind but it hadn't amounted to anything." Only one couple, a young farmer and his wife, had the courage and the honesty to describe the beating administered to the county attorney by the husky young pugilist.

With so little evidence that there had actually been a fight, Judge Shay said, a light fine against young Haynes for disturbing the peace was all that could be assessed.

Chapter 51

Baxter's second trial was only a week away when, at dawn on the morning of April 21, Annie, Liz and Joe hurried across the yard from the bungalow to the old house. Over at the barn Henry was turning the milk cows into their stalls.

The old box telephone on the wall was ringing impatiently when they came into the kitchen. Annie stomped across the floor to answer it as Joe picked up the milk pails and started for the door. "Wait, Joe," her sharp command stopped him. She listened a minute longer, then hung up the receiver. "Liz and Henry can do the milking, Joe. I need you to drive for me. Get the car."

As Joe headed the car into the lane to the road, Annie spoke again. "We're going to the Sirek place. They're digging up John Hunter's bones out there this morning." She said nothing more, dropping into a deep reverie of her own and paying no attention to Joe or his driving.

Joe knew the Sirek place by sight. He had driven past it on some of his trips with Annie. A large white house, a huge red barn and other good outbuildings, it dominated the valley from its location at the foot of a high, rugged hill some seventeen miles southeast of North Platte.

The road followed the section lines, south, then east, south again and east again, past towering old Sioux Lookout, the highest hill of them all, then east and south again. A few farmers were already in their fields, listing corn in long, straight rows, their teams leaning into their collars. Meadow larks called their cheery greetings from fence posts and Joe enjoyed himself while he could, free of Annie's bossing for once; driving the Dodge as it should be driven, and darting a quick glance at Annie now and then.

The old woman sat with her eyes nearly closed, going over all she knew of this whole affair. Remembering the winter, six or seven years ago when Clara was still alive, when she had urged Art to bring the bootlegger king to her parties, and how he had kept putting her off. There had finally seemed to be bad blood between the two, and then Hunter had disappeared, just dropped suddenly out of sight. She recalled that his truck had been abandoned on the Sirek farm, and his car found, months later, in an Omaha parking lot, but no one had seen the king of Nebraska bootleggers again. And then Art had phoned this morning to tell her Sheriff Sayman and a crew were digging Hunter's bones up from a grave in the Sirek barn. Art had sounded excited, but not surprised.

Annie rubbed her mole vigorously. She had always suspected that Art Haynes knew more about John Hunter's disappearance than he had let on.

At the farm the yard was full of cars, and of people milling about, in and out of the big barn. Haynes, waiting just outside the wide barn door, came to meet them. He seemed pleased over the discovery of the remains of the dead man and the big stir it was causing.

"How did Sayman know where to look for Hunter?" Annie asked him.

"A woman told him. Pearl Whittaker. She used to be John's girl friend, and last night she went to Nate Elsen — he's John's lawyer — and told him he'd find John's bones under the cement floor in Sirek's barn, the third stall from the front door. In August, she said, it would be seven years since John disappeared and she was turning in her information now, before the statute of limitations runs out. With his skeleton as proof that he's dead, she hopes his estate can be settled. She says she's going to put in a claim in the name of her crippled daughter. She says the girl is John's.

"Elsen told Sayman what she said and he got a crew of farmers together and they broke up the cement in the third stall and went to digging. And sure enough, they found old John right where Pearl said he'd be." Haynes finished.

"Humph," Annie sniffed, then gave him a sharp glance. "Maybe this will help you, take the heat off you and Mac and Baxter for awhile."

"Could be," Haynes agreed cheerfully. "Let's go on in the barn and you can see where they dug old John up." He pushed his way through the crowd and stopped at the edge of a gaping hole. Beside it was a box containing a skull and a heap of bones. Annie noted the large, jagged hole over the right temple, then turned her attention to three men sifting earth through a square of window screen.

"What are they doing?" she wanted to know.

"John used to wear a big solitaire diamond ring all the time, but it wasn't on any of the finger bones they've found so far. They're still trying to find it, but if it's not here I guess it means that someone took it off him before they buried him," Haynes told her, then hurried off to fetch a folding wooden chair for her to sit on while she watched.

Now and then the men with the screen winnowed a slender finger bone from the powdery earth and tossed it into the box, but that was all. There was no ring of any kind.

Several of Annie's friends came up to speak to her and talk briefly, the banker and Collis Bell, Thad Long and Judge Shay. The Mayor waved a well manicured hand as he walked by, then Sam Diedrich and Milton Murphy came in and nodded to her from the other side of the grave. A moment later Ferd Sirek bustled into the barn. He'd been over at the house, he said, telling the county attorney all he knew about the affair.

Sirek, a muscular middle-aged man who, twenty years earlier, had enjoyed local prominence as a "prize fighter," was making the most of being the center of attention this morning. Questions came at him from all sides and he claimed to be glad to tell all he knew about this affair.

Yes, he'd owned the farm for about ten years now, ever since he'd bought it from old H. P. Sorensen in 1928. One of the best improved farms in the valley, he'd bought it through Art Haynes, which was how he'd come to know Art. He'd bought the farm for an investment and had rented it out right away. Then his renter moved and Art found another for him, young Harold Lozier, one of John Hunter's right hand men.

He remembered the deal very well because Lozier had paid him $1,000, cash on the barrel head, for a one-year lease on the farm. They had closed the deal in his (Sirek's) car on March 1, 1931, right in front of the First National Bank, and Lozier and his wife had moved into the big house the next day. Yes, he'd figured all along that Hunter had put up the cash to lease the place and stock it, and that it was just a front for operating stills and running bootleg whiskey.

He'd stopped in unexpectedly one day that summer, he explained, and caught Lozier working on a still he'd set up in a cave he'd dug in that third stall. The still wasn't working very well; there didn't seem to be enough oxygen in the cave to make the fire burn the way it should.

Sirek said he'd ordered the hole filled in, and then he'd found that Hunter had a big still in the hog house, out behind the barn, so he'd ordered that one taken down, too. He'd stopped in a few days later to make sure his orders had been carried out.

The cave in the barn had been filled in and leveled off, he said, and the still in the hog house was gone. But it still scared him to think what might have happened if the sheriff, or some of the government revenue men that were always snooping around, had found those stills before he did.

He said he'd asked Lozier that day how John was, and he told him he'd gone to the Sandhill lake country on a fishing trip with two or three friends, some North Platte big shots. Then the next day the story came out in the papers that John had disappeared.

For a little while after that Lozier seemed to have a lot of money. He had lost several hundred gambling in town, and then he and his wife took off for California. "And that's why I don't think they'll ever find that diamond ring in the hole, there. I'll bet John wasn't wearing it when they put him in it."

"Well, that's about it," Ferd concluded his story, "except that, so late in the year, I couldn't rent the farm out again, so I moved here myself. I've been here ever since, running this here dairy," waving his big hand at the rows of stanchions in the barn. "The wife and I decided to go into the dairy business, instead of straight farming and hogs. So we bought a herd of Holsteins and a milking machine, now that we had electricity out here. Then the government said we had to have a cement floor before we could sell the milk, so we put one down, a good thick one, and it's turned out to be a pretty good business."

At noon the earth sifters also concluded the ring was no longer in the grave—if it ever had been—and gave up the search. The crowd broke up quickly then, and Joe was glad to be headed for home. He'd had no breakfast and the forenoon had been a long one.

Chapter 52

The evening *Telegraph* and the local radio station put out the story essentially as Joe and Annie had heard it at the Sirek barn that morning. The paper ran its account under inch-high headlines, "Skeleton Found Under Six Feet Of Earth," with pictures of the grave, and of the skull, showing the large, jagged hole over the right eye and temple where the "death blow" had been dealt. A three-feet long iron bar, found beside the skeleton, was assumed to have been the "instrument of death."

The paper carried the additional information that County Attorney Sam Diedrich and Sheriff Charlie Sayman were already on their way to California to pick up Harold Lozier and his wife and bring them back to North Platte. Hunter's aged parents, it was also noted, were grateful that their son's body had finally been found and that he could now be given a proper burial. That, however, would have to wait until the state was through with his bones, important evidence in the upcoming trial.

The officials had no more than lodged the Loziers in the county jail, charged with the murder and robbery of John Crider Hunter in August, 1931, when the cases of Haynes, McKenzie and Baxter came on for trial in District Court on April 27.

District Judge I. J. Nisley opened the proceedings by denying Baxter's appeal for a new trial and sentencing him to two years at hard labor in the state penitentiary at Lincoln. His attorneys appealed and he was released on bond of $3,000, put up by his family. McKenzie, too, was denied a second trial, with sentence to be passed at a later date. Haynes, however, was granted a second hearing, to take place a week later. With his hat at a cocky angle, he left the courtroom in high spirits, claiming confidently that he would be proved innocent of these ridiculous charges and would never spend a day in jail for the alleged beating of Sam Pappas.

Speculation and rumor ran wild, that spring, concerning both the Pappas case and the murder of John Hunter. Although the state had charged Harold Lozier with the killing, citing robbery as the motive, many believed that a rival liquor gang had done away with the king of bootleggers. Hunter, it was said, had been making $20,000 a month, entirely too much for *one* man, even in those days of wide open traffic in the illegal business, and had to be put away.

But, whoever did it, most people agreed, he had had help. Hunter had been a good-sized man and one man could hardly have managed the murder *and* the burial, "six feet under," even with the grave already dug. Filling a hole the size of the cave in the Sirek barn would have taken one man a long time. So, even if Lozier was guilty, who else had been involved? There was no shortage of names—and that of Art Haynes was often mentioned.

Art and Annie conferred often, that May, over her kitchen table or, once in awhile, in Haynes office while Joe cooled his heels in the car on the street below. (If he was not in his seat behind the wheel when she came out there would be the Devil to pay.) For the most part they were satisfied with the way things were going, even if it didn't look too good for Baxter and Mac. With all the publicity, business at the Vet's Club was better than it had ever been.

On May 3 heavy headlines announced that a lie detector had been brought to North Platte for use in the Hunter case. Such a machine had never before been used in Lincoln County—in fact there were only twenty-eight of the devices in the United States—and to have one in North Platte was big news, attesting to the importance of the case. Rented by the day, the detector was quickly put to use.

Harold Lozier, first to be tested on the machine, was questioned for two and one-half hours by the county attorney and his assistant, and by his own attorneys, George Duncan, brother to the mayor, and Bill Shuman. Mrs. Lozier was next, and then Ferd Sirek and several others were put through the test, "with nothing proved either way."

From the beginning the Loziers had been wholly cooperative, returning willingly to Lincoln County and freely answering all questions. On the detector they stoutly maintained their innocence of the murder, or any knowledge of it—and the machine backed them up.

At this point Art Haynes demanded that he be questioned on the lie detector to prove his veracity in the Pappas case. But by this time the machine was needed elsewhere and, at $100 a day, Lincoln County had already run up a $500 bill, so his request was denied.

In Annie's kitchen that night they congratulated themselves. They had expected the denial, but his willingness to be questioned on the detector should strengthen his defense, they agreed.

On May 6 Haynes' appeal for a new trial in the District Court was also denied by Judge Nisley, who stated bluntly, "In view of the heinousness of your offense I am awarding the maximum sentence allowed by law in an assault and battery case. Do you have anything to say for yourself before I pass sentence?"

The stocky gangster squared his shoulders, looked the judge squarely in the eye and declared, "I am an innocent man. And as to gambling, I've never had anything to do with it." It was a pity so few people had made it to the courtroom, that early morning, to hear him. His attorneys immediately appealed the case to the State Supreme Court and he was released on $4,000 bond, signed by Charles Parson and his wife.

"He owes me," Haynes said of his bondsman, over cake and coffee in Annie's kitchen. "He owns three restaurants, all doing good business, and I've put up plenty of protection for his back-room gambling, more than he's paid me for."

Annie was relieved. She had been worried about having to go Art's bond herself, for she wasn't sure he would stand tied if the going got really rough, the next time around. He was still boasting that he'd never spend a day in jail for the beating of Sam Pappas and she was inclined to believe him—even if it meant jumping bail to prove it.

The following day Judge Nisley denied Carl McKenzie's motion for a new trial and sentenced him to sixty days in the county jail on the assault and battery charge. His friends and family, present in the courtroom that morning, were relieved. But the judge wasn't through.

"Mr. McKenzie, do you have anything to say for yourself before I pass sentence upon you on the charge of kidnapping?" He asked sternly.

"Yes sir. I was only doing my duty as an officer," the heavy-shouldered ex-patrolman declared. There was a brief pause as the judge wrote in his record. Then looking grimly at the defendant, he passed the sentence, "...hard labor in the state penitentiary for the rest of your natural life."

McKenzie wilted and his face turned grey as, involuntarily, he turned to look at Haynes; but that individual was looking at the judge, who was reminding the three defendants that they had until August 6 to appeal their cases to the state supreme court. If the appeals were denied, he said, they were to appear in district court on or after October 3 for final pronouncement of sentence. If new trials were granted they would be held at the same term of court.

If Judge Nisley's sentence should stand, McKenzie was to serve his sixty days in the county jail, then be taken to Lincoln to serve out his life sentence but, pending the appeal, he was released on $5,000 bond, again signed by his father.

Most citizens thought McKenzie's sentence too heavy, but new headlines in the *Telegraph* quickly turned their attention in another direction. "Investigation of the Hunter Case Is Jeopardized as Funds Dwindle, Commissioners and County Attorney Say."

Because of the heavy costs of the Pappas case, the report said, no new roads could be built in the county, that summer, and other services would have to be drastically cut. Even further prosecution of the Pappas case might be impossible, should the supreme court order retrials for the defendants, and the Hunter case might have to be dropped, too.

The news was a let-down. To leave the whole thing hanging and let the defendants in the Pappas case go free was upsetting to those who believed them deserving of punishment for beating the little Greek. And what about the Loziers, now being held in solitary confinement in different jails? Had they killed Hunter, or not? Would anyone ever know? And what about the badly needed roads that would not be built or repaired? The general feeling was one of having been short-changed by somebody, somewhere.

Ten days later, after the refusal of the county officials to make any further comments on the matter, the *Bulletin* complained in inch-high headlines, "Mystery Shrouds Hunter Probe. A silence as deep as that which hung over the mystery of the disappearance of John Hunter for seven years last night veiled the next developments in the investigation of Lincoln County's latest sensational mystery."

That spring of 1938 had been a busy one for Lincoln County officials. Sheriff Charlie Sayman, what with hauling prisoners here and there, serving subpoenas, keeping order, and all his other duties, had been so occupied that he barely had time to file for re-election to another term of office before the five o'clock deadline on the last day of May. County Attorney S. S. Diedrich, even busier, made his filing at 4:57 that afternoon, three minutes before the office closed.

Chapter 53

In spite of the shortage of funds, the county officials went ahead with the Lozier hearing by paying most of the expenses with county warrants at the rate of $2 per witness for each summons to appear in court and five cents per mile in travel expense to and from the courthouse.

On June 1 Judge Shay convened the hearing in the county courtroom, with so large a battery of lawyers, witnesses and officials on hand that the judge had to order the public barred from the small room. The hearing lasted four days, and at its end the judge ordered the Loziers bound over for trial at the October term of District Court. Since no bond was admissible for first degree murder, the two were returned to solitary confinement, one in the Lincoln County jail, one in neighboring Dawson County.

With the "Pappas case" in abeyance pending the decision of the State Supreme Court, and no more to be done in the "Hunter case" until October, little more of interest was to be expected for the summer. For the rest of June the local newspapers' biggest headlines were devoted to the activities of one Adolph Hitler across the ocean and to North Platte's "Best Baby" contest, with 474 babies in the competition.

County officials were not idle, however, and in late July Sheriff Sayman found Tim Glines, night clerk at the Ritner at the time of the assault on Sam Pappas, in Casper, Wyoming, and returned him to North Platte to explain why, as a subpoenaed witness, he had not shown up at the Haynes trial, back in February. Convicted at a brief hearing for "obstruction of justice" for leaving town before the trial, he was sentenced to forty days in the county jail.

At the same time Judge Shay authorized probate of the John Hunter estate, setting the court date for early October and listing assets of $19,000 in cash, 1,600 acres of land in McPherson County and several small parcels of land near North Platte, for a total of nearly $24,000. His widow, Caroline, and his parents were his heirs.

By mid-September Glines had served his forty days and was released from custody, only to be promptly re-arrested and charged with contempt of court for failure to appear at the Haynes trial as a subpoenaed witness. Convicted again, he served a second forty days in jail.

"That's that damn county attorney's work," Haynes growled to

Annie. "He did that just to keep Glines where he can lay his hands on him in case the supreme court grants us a retrial in October."

"If he testifies he can hurt you quite a lot, can't he?" Annie asked.

"Yeah. He saw all the damn blood and gore that night. But we still got a few tricks we haven't used yet. You wait and see. I'll get off."

By the month's end the Hunter murder was in the headlines again. Forty-four jurors had been empaneled and twenty-three more names added to the list of state witnesses, making forty-eight in all. On October 4 the District Court convened to select the jury, a chore that took slightly more than five hours, as compared to the three days it had taken to pick a jury from among the sixty-five veniremen examined in the McKenzie trial the previous year. Neither was this jury locked up at night, as the other had been.

The trial got under way that same afternoon in the district courtroom before a small audience of only forty people, three of them women. One was Annie, one was John Hunter's sister, the third was his good looking widow, who did not thereafter attend the trial, except on the day she was called to the witness stand.

The setting was dramatic. The accused murderer and his wife, a handsome couple, though noticeably pale after five months in solitary confinement, sat quietly at their table with their attorneys, the dignified and prosperous Dale Duncan, Jr., and William Shuman, head of the old Tax Payers League. District Judge J. L. Tewell, a large, imposing man in his black robes, imparted a Thespian air to the scene. Even the room itself, its great size and its heavy dark wood paneling, lent an atmosphere of drama and suspense. John Hunter's grinning skull and bleached bones on the consul table drew the eyes of all, making some to shiver and still others to turn away.

In a forty-minute opening address, assistant special attorney Milton Murphy demanded the death penalty for the defendants, after which court recessed for the day.

The public, expecting the selection of the jury to take at least a day, and disappointed at missing the opening of the trial, was on hand in full force the second day. The big room, built to hold two hundred people, was crowded to the walls.

Caroline Hunter, called to the stand that morning, testified that the skeleton was that of her husband. She was able to identify it, she said, by the teeth and by an old break in one of the leg bones, a break he had suffered as a boy on his father's McPherson County ranch. John's sister verified her testimony.

Ferd Sirek, one of the principal witnesses, was on the stand for a long three hours, visibly sweating at times as he answered, or parried, the barrage of questions hurled at him by the attorneys of both sides.

His story was virtually the same as the one he had told the county attorney and his barn audience the day the bones were unearthed.

Harold Lozier, also questioned for three hours, seemed at ease and quite unflustered as he told a straightforward story of his association with John Hunter. A young married man trying to get a start, he said, he had been asked by Hunter, the bootleg king, to rent the Sirek place and set up a farming operation as a front for the stills John planned to operate. He told how Hunter had furnished the $1,000 he had paid Sirek for a year's rent on the place, and had put up another $1,800 to buy cattle and stock the farm. The partnership, he explained, of his labor and Hunter's money constituted a blind for their bootlegging operation.

Hunter, he said, had left for Omaha on the evening of August 5, driving his roadster, and he had not seen him since. Lozier and his wife had then left the farm for a day or two to visit her aunt near Lexington. He knew nothing of the murder, nor of the burial in the still room under the barn. Yes, on Sirek's orders he had filled in the still room before August 5. There had been no dead man in it then.

In its questioning of the many witnesses, the defense several times attempted to develop the concept that Hunter had had trouble with an unknown "higher up" who had killed him, or had him killed, to get him out of the lucrative illegal liquor business. Then why, the state wanted to know, if there had been no body in the cave when Lozier filled it in, did the murderers dig the grave out again, *all the way to the bottom*, to bury Hunter's body? That point had been stressed by the farmer neighbors who had helped dig up the bones—the skeleton had been found on the very bottom of the six feet deep cave. The question was never answered.

After seven full days the case was given to the jury at 5:17 on the afternoon of Tuesday, October 11. A crowd of more than 300 jammed the courtroom that last day, listening intently to the impassioned closing statements of the attorneys, and to the judge's stern instructions to the jury. Sixteen hours and twenty minutes later, at 9:45 on Wednesday morning, Judge Tewell delivered the "not guilty" verdict. The Loziers were not present in the courtroom, and only twenty-three spectators made it there in time to hear the expected decision, followed by the order to release Harold Lozier and his wife.

The Loziers' departure for California the next day went unnoticed in the stir caused by the headline in that day's *Telegraph*.

U. S. Sues Hunter For $55,000 Back Liquor Taxes

According to the paper, the tax had been levied on 36,000 gallons of liquor made and sold by Hunter.

It had been the court's intention to probate the Hunter estate the day following the close of the murder trial, but now, with the government's claim pending, there was no knowing when the estate could be settled, probably not until the June term of court in 1939.

Having failed to convict the Loziers, the county, due to its chronic lack of funds, could do no more toward finding and prosecuting another suspect and, very likely, it would never be known who had killed the bootleg king. But there were many Lincoln County citizens who were of the opinion that the real murderer still walked among them.

Over coffee and huge slices of Lela Comstock's angel cake, Annie and Art discussed the trial and its outcome. "Who do *you* think killed John Hunter?" the old woman asked, her eyes mere slits in her sagging face.

"Whoever it was, they'll never find out now," Haynes replied confidently.

Annie wanted to ask him why, then decided not to. Better to let it drop; for there was still the possibility of Haynes' retrial on the Pappas business, and maybe McKenzie and Baxter, too. They had been lucky so far, but would their luck hold? In the meantime they had better get back to business. In spite of County Attorney Diedrich and his dedication to the enforcement of bluenose laws, prostitution and gambling still paid well in North Platte.

On October 14, 1938, at a brief graveside service attended only by his sister and a handful of old friends from the Sandhills, the bones of the King of Nebraska Bootleggers were buried in the North Platte cemetery. His funeral, including the price of the lot where he was finally to rest undisturbed, cost $135.

Chapter 54

May of 1939 was unusually hot on the plains. By June the torrid heat had spread across the nation, and in July temperatures climbed yet higher. In North Platte's three theaters the ceiling fans merely stirred the fetid, sultry air; in its churches on Sundays the swish of hand-held cardboard fans, distributed by W. R. Munson's undertaking parlor, made it difficult to hear the sermons. In the city's homes table fans buzzed day and night.

With rural power lines still in the future, country residents and their livestock could find little relief and pigs and poultry died, overcome by the smothering heat.

On July 6 the news that Sheriff Charlie Sayman had been killed in an automobile wreck in Utah fell like a bomb into the heat dulled community. It was hard to believe! Except for the four years that Al Benton had held the office, 1922-1926, Charlie had been sheriff of Lincoln County for twenty-seven years.

He had represented the law during a rough period in the county's history; through the bootlegging years when he had raided stills all up and down the valley; through a period of cattle rustling and horse stealing; and through the Hunter murder affair. And never, to anyone's knowledge, had he shown the white feather or a yellow streak. Now it had all come to an end in scrunching, crashing metal on a highway nearly seven hundred miles from home.

Because of the heat the family held his funeral in the evening. Even so, with the temperature still at 103 at seven p.m. the big First Presbyterian Church, packed to the walls, was suffocatingly hot. The banks of flowers that filled the chancel had wilted even before the service began.

Annie, plying her fan vigorously, listened intently to the eulogistic sermon—and thought of the deed she had made out in Charlie Sayman's name nearly a quarter century ago. That deed had won her many favors and saved her a good deal of money, and that morning she had taken it from the pile in her desk drawer, torn it to bits and dropped the pieces into the kitchen range.

Mary, reading the account of the funeral in the next days paper under the headline, "Hundreds Pay Tribute To Sheriff Sayman," remembered the times she had run away from Annie and her whip, only to be taken back to servitude by the man whose praises everyone was now repeating. He had not been unkind to her, he had simply treated her as if she had been a dumb animal, another of Annie Cook's possessions.

Chapter 55

Due to demurrers, delays, postponements, and change of venue pleas, further action in the now famous "Pappas Case" did not come on until 1940. In the more than two years that had passed since the earlier trials there had been some changes. In December of 1938 Carl McKenzie's father had withdrawn his bond and the ex-policeman, unable to raise another, had finally gone to jail. Collis Bell, Haynes' attorney, had been appointed Assistant Attorney General of Nebraska and, as such, had disqualified himself to represent him, should he go to trial again.

In April the supreme court finally got around to reversing McKenzie's conviction and ordering that a new trial be held. Welcome news for the ex-officer who had now been in the county jail for fourteen months. In June the same court denied David Baxter a new trial. As a city councilman and chairman of the police committee, he was McKenzie's superior, the court ruled, and should have commanded him to stop the beating. He was ordered to Lincoln immediately, to begin serving his two-year sentence in the penitentiary.

Arthur Haynes was granted a new trial, to be held at the fall term of court.

With the Pappas case again on dead center for the summer, county attorney Diedrich turned his attention to another long festering sore in his community. For years he had complained vigorously against the dice tables, slot machines and punch boards that flourished in almost every business establishment in the city. The last two were especially detrimental, he charged, because juveniles were their best customers. All such devices were illegal in the county and all under the age of eighteen were expressly forbidden to play them, yet few owners prohibited minors at the machines, or seemed even to notice that they were there. Such practices, Diedrich said, were making gamblers out of the county's young citizens and should be stopped. When neither city nor county officials would take any action, the county attorney took the matter into his own hands.

On the morning of August 2, 1940, four crews of husky young men, manning four large trucks, made a series of lightning raids across the town, seizing more than three hundred slot machines and pinball games, and dozens of punch boards, from sixty different locations. So well had Diedrich planned his raids, city officials and police knew nothing about them until they were well under way.

The county attorney stored his haul in the two jury rooms on the top (fourth) floor of the court house and announced, by means of a head-lined news item in the *Telegraph*, that all machines would be smashed as soon as the money they contained had been removed. The cash, he said, would be applied against the costs of the raid.

The number of citizens who blessed Diedrich for rounding up and incarcerating the one-armed bandits was about matched by those who cursed him for it. Though the machines had played but a small part in the Cook-Haynes combination, Annie and Art had not been pleased by the raid. Who knew where the ambitious county attorney would go snooping next?

There were many red faces in the town a little later, when Diedrich put one of the slot machines in a downtown shop window, showing how it had been "fixed" so that it could *never* pay off with a "jack pot." Very few of the confiscated machines were "honest," he stated, and very likely most of the owners had been aware of that fact.

The "smashing" was accomplished later that fall by merely opening the jury room windows and heaving the machines through them, to crash on the cement below. The few that escaped serious damage were finished with a sledge hammer, wielded by the angry county attorney himself. The remains were hauled to the landfill south of the city—where the big American Legion club house stands today.

Samuel Diedrich, the Lincoln County Attorney who finally ended the long reign of gambling and prostitution in North Platte. (Courtesy NP Telegraph.*)*

When the Pappas trials came on again in the fall, District Judge Tewell dismissed the charge of kidnapping that had hung over McKenzie for so long, but ordered him to stand trial again on the remaining charge of assault and battery. Haynes, too, was ordered to appear for a new trial, in the same court and on the same charge.

The October trials were virtually a replay of those of 1938; the same packed courtroom, the same witnesses telling the same stories—except for Charlie Sayman, now more than a year in his grave (his testimony was read into the record) — even the same verdict, "guilty as charged."

On December 3, three years and ten days after the bloody episode in Room 25 of the old Ritner, Judge J. L. Tewell pronounced sentence upon Arthur Haynes and Carl McKenzie for assault and battery upon the person of Sam I. Pappas. Each was to be fined "*$25.00 and costs.*"

According to the convoluted reasoning of the judge, inept handling of the case by the state had greatly and unnecessarily increased the expenses of the trial, therefore the defendants, *who had already been put to considerable expense to defend themselves*, could not be expected to pay the court costs in full. Accordingly, he was assessing Arthur Haynes only $215, and Carl McKenzie $197. The county must bear the remainder of the costs.

Then, looking sternly at the unfortunate McKenzie, he stated, "This whole affair seems to be all your fault, and if you had not already served nineteen months in jail I would have passed a much heavier sentence upon you. Case dismissed."

At the beginning of the trial Defense Attorney Charles Baxter had declared, "Art Haynes said nothing, did nothing, and didn't even know anything about what was going on in this transaction (the beating of Sam Pappas)." It seemed that the judge believed him.

At any rate, while McKenzie and David Baxter paid dearly for the "favors" Haynes had once accorded them, the gang lord himself was the only one of the three who did not spend so much as a day in jail.

Chapter 56

By the spring of 1940 Hitler's armies were marching in Europe and America was "edgy." Many government officials were promoting a "peace-time draft," in case the U. S. went to war. By September Congress had passed the Selective Service bill, requiring the registration of all U. S. males aged twenty-one through thirty-five, and President Roosevelt had signed it into law. A month later America's young men were registering in their country's first peace-time draft.

Annie had rented the north Eighty to a young farmer classed 4F because of an old knee injury and poor eyesight, and the cropland on the home place to old August Johnson. Prices for all farm produce were going up and she had seen to it that Joe, Liz and Henry put in the big gardens and set out the cabbage plants, purchased now from the Henry Field nursery.

When Joe turned twenty-one that July, Annie began to worry. Joe, she declared, was not to be drafted. She needed him right where he was and she would see to it that he stayed there.

Since the age of six Joe had planned to run away from Annie's cruelty as soon as he was old enough to take care of himself. In his early teens he had thought about it often—and only one thing had stood in his way—his affection for old Frank Cook. Young as he was, he believed that his presence at the farm was a help to the old man and that he should stay as long as he was needed.

When Frank is gone, he promised himself, I'll leave.

He was seventeen when Frank died, old enough to make it on his own, but a curious process of reasoning prevented his going right away. For all of his growing up years Annie Cook had controlled his life, ordering his every move, never permitting him to think for himself or make the simplest decision on his own. He knew almost nothing of life off the farm, never even having been allowed to go into a store and make a purchase for himself. It would be difficult, learning to be a part of the outside world.

And there was another thing, the strange and reluctant loyalty he felt toward the slit-eyed, loose-lipped old woman. In spite of the years of cruelty and abuse, she represented the only mother-figure he could remember. She had provided him the only home he had ever known—and she needed him now. He could see that.

Joseph Martin Cook, Age 24.

She still had Liz and old Henry, but the big gardens and the farm chores were more than they could handle without him. And so, although he thought about it a good deal, he put off leaving. In the spring he told himself that he would go in the fall, after the summer's work was done. In the fall he decided that winter was not a good time to start making it on his own, he would wait until spring.

Occasionally, after Clara's death, Annie had told him that someday "all this," with a wave of her broad hand indicating the farm and its buildings, "will be yours." But Joe, knowing of the pile of deeds in the desk drawer, put no stock in the promises. He didn't know who would get the farm but he was sure it would not be Joseph Martin Cook.

All that summer of 1940 Joe watched Annie fume and fret about the draft and the immediacy of war, and listened to her plans for keeping him from having any part in it. When the draft board for their district was set up and the first numbers drawn, she began visiting the members of the board. With Joe driving and the back of the car loaded with farm produce, potatoes, apples, squash, cream, butter and eggs, she made the rounds. As he carried in the bags and baskets, and listened to her telling each board member that she didn't know how she'd ever make a living or pay her taxes if Joe was drafted, he could see the men's embarrassment. By law they were to administer the draft without fear or favor and the old woman's offerings looked suspiciously like bribes.

After each drawing the newspapers reported the names and numbers drawn, and each time it looked as if Joe might be in the next drawing Annie renewed her efforts to keep him out of the draft—until the board came to dread her coming, and Joe to feel more ashamed and embarrassed each time he had to carry her gifts to the harassed men.

By the spring of 1941 the numbers of most of the farm boys in the valley had been called and many of the lads Joe had gone to school with were already in the service of their country. He knew that he should be among them, and he didn't know if Annie's exertions on his part had anything to do with the fact that he wasn't.

Early in May he settled the matter for himself by running away. As Liz, and then Mary, had done so long ago, he walked to town.

The ticket office of the old North Platte Greyhound bus depot occupied one corner of the waiting room, a large restaurant filled the remainder of the big building. In mid-afternoon, a slow time of the day at the depot-restaurant, Ting Adams, the manager, watched a thin, shabby, shaggy-haired young man come uncertainly through the door, and recognized him as "the Cook boy from the old Poor Farm." It was seldom that anyone saw the lad apart from the old woman and Ting, surprised, said "Hello Joe, what are you doing in town?"

"I'm leaving."

"Fine. Where you headed?"

"I want to go to Kansas City."

"Good idea. Here, will this help?"

Adams didn't know what prompted him to pull the $20 bill from his pocket and hand it to the boy, enough to buy a ticket to Kansas City and have some eating money left over, but the look of relief that came over the thin, scared face was its own reward.

When he left the farm that day, Joe knew only that he had to get to Kansas City and Lester McConnell. Lester's ailing wife had died, three or four years back, and he had married her young sister, Roberta, a little later. Soon afterward he gave up farming and moved to Kansas City.

Before he left, McConnell told Joe that, whenever he decided to leave Annie, he would be welcome at his home and that he would help him in any way he could.

The McConnells, pleased that he had finally made the break, took him in and attended to his needs. Roberta fed him all he could hold and urged him to eat more. Lester loaned him money for a haircut and decent clothes, then got him a job with the Wilson Packing Company where he was employed, and where he could help him learn to work for someone other than a scowling woman with a whip in her hand.

Joe did not write to Annie, nor to anyone else at home. So far as he knew there was no one in the valley who would care that he was gone, or expect to hear from him. With the passing weeks life seemed better and better to the skinny boy from the Poor Farm. With plenty to eat, he was filling out, actually growing. He made friends, enjoyed his work, and knew the satisfaction of earning, and spending, his own money.

And then one day at work a blinding headache tormented him. By morning it was gone, only to return again a few days later. When the headaches came on him almost daily, Lester took him to a doctor.

"Maybe it's from all the times Annie walloped you on the head," his friend said, "and we'd better tell the doctor about it."

The doctor thought a shot would correct the matter, but as he pulled the needle from Joe's arm his patient collapsed, unconscious.

Ten days later Joe woke up in the hospital. Curious, and somewhat alarmed, he sat up in his bed and looked about him as a nurse came into his room with a thermometer in her hand. Her face turning pale, she said, "Here, you can't sit up in bed like this. We just got through pumping your spine and you're not supposed to be sitting up at all. Doesn't your back hurt like everything?"

"No, I don't have any pain anywhere. What am I doing here?"

"I'll go get the doctor. You lay down now, and don't you get out of that bed, or move, until he gets here."

A few minutes later the nurse came back. "The doctor will be here in a minute," she said.

"Nurse," Joe said, "I want to ask you something. I'm right beside a baby ward, ain't I?"

"Why yes, but how did you know?"

"When I first woke up I could hear a baby crying. But it's not crying now because it's dead."

"Have you been out of this room? After I told you not to get out of bed?"

When Joe assured her he hadn't been out of the bed, she told him to wait a minute and she'd go see about the baby.

When she came back her face was as white as the sheet on his bed.

"Yes," she said dazedly, "that baby died a few minutes ago. *How did you know?*"

Joe did not know how he knew. It was like the Hand that had appeared at the window before Clara's death, but he was always to believe that God took the sick baby just as he, Joe, woke up that morning, after his strange ten-days-long sleep. For some reason he was the one chosen to live, and he made up his mind that day that he would try to be worthy of the gift of life so newly bestowed upon him, and to do whatever it was he had been spared to do.

Before he left the hospital the next day the nurse told him that, if he didn't already know it, he had a great friend in Lester McConnell. "He came to see you every evening and stayed over an hour. He must think a lot of you."

Shortly after Joe went back to work, a Kansas City Postal Inspector came to see him at his station in the Wilson plant. "You'd better be picking up your mail at the general delivery window at the main post office," he said. "There are several Selective Service letters there for you, and you can get in trouble for not answering that kind of mail."

The government letters notified him that he was to report for induction into the United States Army at Fort Warren, Wyoming. The deadline was four days away. The other letters were brief notes from Annie, urging him to come home. He had been foolish to leave, she wrote, since the whole farm was to have been his someday, but she would forgive all if he would come home right away. The last note, written a month ago, informed him that she was through with him, ungrateful bastard that he was, and that she had gone to the draft board, told them to put him in class 1A, and to send the notice to Kansas City.

Chapter 57

Joe resigned from the plant, collected his pay and caught a bus for Cheyenne. With a sizable group of men, he reported for his physical at Fort Warren. There, he wrote to the McConnells that evening, "they made a 4Fer out of me in a hurry because of a hernia I got a year or so ago." The next day he bought a bus ticket to North Platte.

He wasn't quite sure why he went back to North Platte, for he had liked Kansas City and his life there. Perhaps it was a touch of homesickness, a desire to see the farm and the valley again.

Near noon on a sunny November day he dropped off the east bound bus and walked again into the old Greyhound depot. Adams did not recognize the young man until he said, "I just came in to thank you again for that twenty you gave me, six months ago." Then he pumped his hand warmly and asked him to tell him all about it over a square meal in the dining room.

"I sure didn't know you," Ting said as they sat down. "You've changed a lot from that runty kid you were when you left here last spring."

"What do you plan to do now?" Joe's host asked him as they finished their meal.

"Oh, I'm going out to see how old Annie and Liz are getting along, and then maybe I'll get a job here and see how it goes."

He called Annie from the bus station. "This is Joe," he said in answer to the old woman's rasping "Hello."

"Joe? Oh *Joe*! Where the hell are you?"

He told her and she said, "It's high time you showed up again. I'll be right in to get you."

Joe grinned as he hung up the phone. Old Annie hadn't changed. Already she figured she had him back again, to order around as she pleased.

She came in the old Dodge, with skinny old Henry at the wheel. Her driver after Joe left, on their first trip to town he had stopped for the stop sign when they came to Highway 30, only to be ordered by Annie to "drive on. You don't need to stop for those damn signs. Nobody in this county would make me pay a fine."

Joe watched them pull up to the curb, then went out as the old woman heaved herself out of the car and plodded toward him. Wearing her shapeless old crochet cap and felt slippers, she was heavier than she had been in the spring and her neck was dirtier.

Staring at him accusingly, she growled, "You've changed a hell of a lot."

Joe had wondered how he would feel at seeing the woman again, hoping that he would no longer want to cringe before her slit-eyed gaze. To his disappointment the old fear was still there.

When she added, grudgingly, "You've grown, Joe, and you're damn good looking," he wanted to say, "That's because I've had enough to eat for the last six months." Instead, he said, "Hello Annie, how are you?"

Ordering old Henry into the back seat, Annie told Joe to drive, then heaved her bulk back into the front passenger seat, onto old cushions long flattened by her weight. As they drove back to the farm, past autumn-bare fields, the old woman plied him with questions, and was pleased to hear that he was now in 4F. "Good," she said. "We need you on the farm. Liz and Henry couldn't handle the gardens after you left and things have gone all to hell."

She was right, Joe thought, as he turned into the lane and came to a stop at the end of the broken old board walk. It was hard to believe that the place had gone down so much, so soon. Frost-whitened weeds covered the garden plots and clogged the ragged fence rows. The orchard looked tattered and untended, a barn door hung by a broken hinge. Frank had kept the farmstead neat and thrifty looking. Joe had managed to do almost as well, and it pained him to see it now, the weeds, and the general air of neglect. And it would get worse, he thought sadly, for Annie would never hire an extra man to help keep things up. What Liz and old Henry couldn't do would not get done.

Liz looked just as she had the day he left, as bent and skinny and shabby, but peering up at him from beneath her mat of tangled hair, she had recognized him instantly, and was glad to see him.

In the old kitchen Annie, to Joe's surprise, invited him to sit down at the table while she set out coffee and cake. For the first time in his life she was treating him as a person, but he did not enjoy it, for he saw the hungry glances old Liz and Henry cast at the table as she ordered them back to their work outside.

While they ate Annie outlined her plans for the work they would do, now that Joe was home. The Johnsons and Ev Elwood were doing fine with the farm land, though good help was hard to find, what with all the local boys in camps and some already overseas. But what they needed to do was get the orchard cleaned up and sprayed, the big gardens in and tended, and the place neatened up and running right again.

When he could get a word in edgewise, Joe asked about the boys he'd gone to school with, where they were stationed, what branch of the service they were in; and finally he asked about Art Haynes. Was he still coming to the farm?

"He's to be here today, any time now," Annie told him. "I'm buying his Ford V8. It's a fancy car, Joe, and you'll be driving it for me. What the hell do you think of that?"

"How come?" Joe asked.

"Well," Annie narrowed her eyes even more as she explained. "Things went kind of sour for Art after they settled that damn Pappas case. A hell of a lot of people didn't like it that they only fined him a measly $25 for helping beat up that old Greek bastard. It cost the county thousands of dollars for all those damn trials. And then Art had a run-in with a bitchy young fellow up at Sutherland right after you left and got himself shot at. I guess those gun shots blasting past his ear kind of put the fear of God into him. After that people didn't seem much scared of him.

Annie bit angrily into a piece of cake, then went on. "That damned new county attorney is still hell-bent on cleaning up on gambling and closing up the houses, and Art's real estate business is beginning to fall off, so he's decided to clear out. He's going to Idaho. He has a relative there that's got a good thing going in real estate and needs some help. Art's selling everything he has here, raising all the cash he can, and I'm paying him $500 for his damned car." Annie licked her loose lips and rubbed her mole.

After all the years that old Annie and the gang lord had been such close friends, she did not seem very sorry to see him go, Joe thought. Actually, she seemed relieved. Well, Art knew a lot about her, things she wouldn't want told — things Art Haynes might tell if ever he got in a tight enough place.

Haynes came a little later, stared at Joe and had to be introduced. "I sure wouldn't have known you," he said as they shook hands.

The gambler *had* lost considerable of his old cocky confidence, Joe decided, as he watched him turn the V8's title, bill of sale and ignition keys over to Annie in return for the five one hundred dollar bills she peeled from the roll she fished from her apron pocket. The deal finished, Haynes shook hands with Annie and Joe and went out to the yard, where a companion waited in another car to take him back to town.

"That's a damned classy car I just bought," Annie said. "Art bought it to celebrate getting off so easy on the Pappas thing. It's got a heater and a radio. You'll be somebody, Joe, driving around in that."

"I'm afraid not, Annie. I'm not staying, not very long, anyway. I'm going back to town now. Maybe I'll get a job tomorrow, or maybe I'll head on back to Kansas City. I don't know yet, but thanks for the cake and coffee."

Annie hit the ceiling, as he had known she would. Following him out to the yard, she cursed and coaxed by turns, but Joe kept on walking. He had thought of asking Haynes for a ride back to town but, knowing the storm his decision would bring down on his head, his old fear of the woman had kept him silent. Even now, as he walked down the lane, it was hard to keep from cringing, hard to keep his shoulders straight, his head high and his step unhurried.

Half a mile from the farm he caught a ride to town, where he went to the old Manor House and got a room. The next morning he hired out to Elmer Casebolt at the Dodge garage.

Anna Cook, 1943 age 70. This picture was taken in the farmyard in front of two of her poultry houses.

Chapter 58

That winter of 1942-1943 would have been pleasant enough for Joe if it had not been for Annie. He made friends easily, girls noticed his dark good looks, and he soon had a pretty girl of his own to take to the movies and to dances at the old Jeffers Pavillion, where Lawrence Welk and other big name bands sometimes played.

But he never knew when or where Annie might show up — she came to see him at his work, she called him at the hotel, always insisting that he come back to the farm. Her persistence finally became intolerable, and one day in late winter he put an end to her badgering by walking into the draft board office and enlisting under the limited service provision.

He knew that he looked "able-bodied," and all winter he had shrunk from having to explain his 4F status to those who asked, or wondered. By enlisting he had taken care of both his problems.

Annie was furious when she read Joe's name among the new enlistees and draftees in the paper that week. She came storming into the hotel as he was checking out. There in the lobby she berated him for his foolishness and demanded that he cancel his enlistment and get back to the farm where he belonged. Joe told her it was too late, that he was in the service now and there was nothing that she or anyone else could do about it.

"To hell with that talk. I'll get you out," the old woman swore, and stomped away to see the draft board. For weeks thereafter she made life miserable for the board, and for every other government official she could reach. She wrote dozens of letters, cajoling, begging, threatening. Nothing worked. Joe was in the army, beyond her reach, and she hated him.

Soon after his arrival at camp Joe was transferred to the army hospital at St. Louis for surgery to repair his hernia and fit him for regular army service. Then something went wrong, complications developed and the situation became life threatening. In his office Joe's surgeon told him how it was and asked if there was a family member he would like to have present for the surgical ordeal ahead.

"There is only my—mother," Joe said slowly, "and I don't think she'd come."

"Call her anyway," the doctor urged.

Joe put the call through and explained the impending surgery to Annie. As he had expected, she profanely refused to be bothered.

"She says she's too busy to come," he reported.

"Did you tell her you only have about one chance in a thousand of making it through this operation?" the surgeon demanded. Joe nodded.

"That's hard to believe! Well, young fellow. I'm going to call her myself. I don't believe she understands how serious this is."

The doctor placed his call and earnestly explained the gravity of the situation. From the other side of the desk Joe watched the changing expressions that crossed his face as he listened to the woman's refusal—shock, pity, then cold anger.

"But I have no doubt," he said finally, his voice icy, "that you'll be there, with your hand out, to claim his $10,000 Army life insurance payment."

Several weeks later Joe received a letter from Annie. As his next of kin, she had not received notice of his death, she wrote, so she took it that he was still alive. And maybe now, if things had been as bad as that damned doctor claimed, he could get a medical discharge and come home.

In his brief reply Joe told her he was about to be discharged from the hospital but that he didn't yet know where he was to report for duty. Annie then sent off another barrage of letters demanding that Joseph Cook be discharged from the army as unfit for service and sent home.

In the meantime, as the war slowly ground its way toward V-Day, Annie continued to do her part to conserve food (skinny old Liz and Henry were proof of that) and regularly bought more than her quota of war bonds. She could well afford to, for business was very good. Farm crops brought premium prices, her houses in town were thriving and she visited them weekly to collect her money. The county warrant business was good, too. Although a few school districts (with war time prices for crops bringing in more taxes) had gone back to paying their teachers by check, the irrigation company still paid with warrants.

As for tax foreclosures, that business was invariably good. There would always be the poor manager, the risk taker, the property owner struck down by death or a long, expensive illness. And Annie, with her bulging money sack, could go on buying up the best properties and turning them into still more cash.

Even so, Annie thought, as she sat at her desk on a rainy October evening, copying some figures into her worn account book; even so, she wasn't making as much now as she had when Art Haynes was running North Platte's underworld. The son-of-a-bitch had cost her plenty, but she had still made money and she still missed him and their sessions at her kitchen table.

She missed the Reverend Tester, too, gone these five years to a pastorate in South Dakota; and Sheriff Sayman, dead for nearly as long. Old Harley Costin still dropped in once in a while, but the busy parade of Sunday visitors to the farm had faded into the past. There was nothing to come for now, no fruit or melons, or thrifty garden largesse, and the seedy old farmyard was depressing.

If only Joe would come home she could get things going again. At the thought of Joe anger boiled up within her and she cursed him aloud. He had turned into a good-looking young fellow and he belonged to her. She had fed and housed him when he had no home and no one to look after him—and he had repaid her by running off and leaving her just when she needed him most.

Annie could see herself, driving to her business appointments in a fine new car with handsome young Joe at the wheel. She had money and she was a power in Lincoln County, where officials took her orders and did her bidding, mostly, she knew, on the strength of the deeds she kept in her desk drawer.

Thoughtfully, she took the deeds from the drawer and looked through them one by one: Judge Shay, Thaddeaus Long, old Dr. Duncan and W. R. Munson, the Comstocks, Collis Bell, and some later county officials.

Though Bell was now Attorney General of Nebraska he still called on her once or twice a year, to listen to her assurances that the Eighty would be his when she was through with it, and that she still appreciated the favors he had done for her when he was county attorney. Thad Long, too, had long been out of office but he still brought her a loaf of good homemade bread every week, and did other good turns for her.

To each of the yellowing old papers there was now attached a new agreement, a slip of paper stating that the recipient agreed to take in and care for old Liz as long as she lived. She was pleased she had thought of that, a year or so ago, and that she had it all taken care of. Since she was fourteen years older than Liz, it was quite likely that she would pass on before her sister did. And it did not seem inconsistent to the old woman that, although she had starved, beaten and abused her sister for forty years, she should want someone to house and care for her when she, Annie Cook, was no longer on hand to do it.

All her donees had readily agreed to the condition. After all, frail old Liz, a bent little shadow hobbling about in heavy, run over shoes, wasn't likely to long outlast her sister.

Annie slid the deeds back into the drawer and locked it. "Damn that bastard Joe," she muttered as she pulled a tablet to her and began a letter to him. Only a few lines to tell him she planned to buy a fine new car as soon as the war was over, and that she expected him to come home and drive it for her. Art's old V8, she added, didn't look very damn good anymore since old Henry drove it into Elwood's gate post and bent the right front fender all to hell. Henry was getting doddery and didn't see too good any more and she sure needed Joe to drive for her.

That ought to bring the bastard back, she thought as she stamped the envelope and got up to rouse Liz, dozing in her rocker, and plod across the muddy yard to their beds in the bungalow.

Chapter 59

With his honorable discharge tucked into his duffle bag, Joe got off the train in North Platte on a hazy September morning in 1945. Upstairs in the hiring office in the big Union Pacific depot he hired on as a fireman trainee, then went across the street and rented a comfortable room in the old Keith Hotel. After his noon meal at the bus depot-restaurant on the corner, he borrowed a car and drove out to the farm to see Annie.

In the dooryard the chained dogs set up their usual clamor and the old woman came to the door. Her loose lips stretched into a wide smile as she stared at the young soldier. Gawd, but he was handsome in that uniform. "Come in, Joe, come in. Karl Schmidt is here and he'll want to see you."

Annie had hardly changed at all in the two years he had been gone, a little heavier perhaps, a little dirtier, and limping a little more on her felt-slippered feet.

"Just a minute, Annie, I want to look around first."

It was the farmstead that showed the passage of time: in the dead trees, in the weed-grown orchard, unsprayed and untended in the five years he had been gone, in the almost paintless buildings and the grass-grown fence rows. A few old hens, scratching and fluffing their feathers in dust holes in the yard, and one old milk cow, grazing in the weedy little pasture beyond the barn, only pointed up the general air of neglect and decay that hung over the once spruce and well-kept Cook farm, the show place of the valley.

Her slit eyes on Joe's face, reading his thoughts, Annie said, "But you're home now, Joe. You stay and help me and we'll soon have the old place in good shape. And as soon as the new cars are on the market again, I'm going to buy you one of the best. Stay with me, Joe, and you'll be somebody in this valley." The vanilla voice had never been smoother or more promising.

Yes, and you'll be right there in the front seat of that new car with me, Joe told himself. You'll be giving the orders and running things, just like you've always done. Aloud he said, "No, Annie, I can't do that. I've already got a job on the railroad, and a room at the Keith. I'll be living in town, but I'll come out to see you as often as I can."

To his surprise, she took his refusal quietly. Her eyes narrowing a little more but her voice still smooth, she said, "Well, come on in, anyway, and have some cake and coffee with Karl and me."

Old Karl Schmidt was her pudgy German neighbor from up the road a little way. His wife had died a year or so ago, but he had several daughters to care for him and his house, and sons to farm his land, while he visited around. Joe remembered him as a habitual gossip and a non-stop talker. Between the two of them he would soon know all the latest news, gossip, and scandal of the community.

Over their cake and coffee Annie studied Joe, her mind busy with her schemes to get him back on the farm. Her experience over the years had proved to her that anyone could be bought — if the price was right. Most of the few commissioners and other county officials who had resisted her bribes had done so only because she had not offered enough. Joe, she was convinced, would come back to the farm if she made her price high enough.

The next week Annie began visiting the town's garages and talking with their owners: Elmer Casebolt of the Dodge; Frank Hahler at the Buick; York Hinman at the Hudson; Frank Cooksley at the Studebaker; and half a dozen others. She put her name on every waiting list. The lists were long, she was told, but by spring new cars should be coming in and the long empty showrooms filling up again. In any case, the dealers assured her, she would be among the first to be taken care of.

With the coming of spring the dealers began calling her. They had cars to show her if she wanted to come in and have a look. Annie looked at them all but none of them suited her, too plain, too small, not what she was looking for.

Then, on a pleasant day in May, as Henry drove the old V8 down Willow Street, taking Annie to look at a tax delinquent property, she saw a handsome new car at the curb in front of a neat brick house. "Quick, pull in behind that new car," she ordered. The car was a beauty, a shining black Dodge sedan with bright red leather upholstering, and she knew at once that she must have one exactly like it.

As she climbed out of her own car, a young woman came out of the house to get her mail from the box beside the door. Annie recognized her, a girl who had grown up on a farm in the Nichols neighborhood. "H'lo Ethel," she called across the small lawn, "I just want to take a look at your new car."

Ethel Hood stared coldly at the old woman. She and her husband had been among those who had invested their savings in irrigation warrants — up until Annie cornered the market. Now she said shortly, "You may look at it, but don't get in it."

"I'd never want to ride in that car again if that dirty old woman had gotten in it," she told her husband that evening.

Annie plodded all the way around the handsome vehicle, inspecting its every feature, then drove to the Dodge garage. "How come you didn't let me know when that Hood car came in?" she demanded of the dealer. "Because she didn't buy it here," Casebolt told her. "She bought it in Ogallala."

So Annie ordered one exactly like it, and that evening she called Joe to tell him what she had done. "You come home, Joe, and you can have that car."

"I've got a car that's good enough for me," he told her. Annie swore and hung up. It looked as if she'd have to raise her price to get Joe back.

Casebolt sent the new car out to the farm by his head salesman, Charles (Chuck) Corley. In the dilapidated farmyard Corley eyed the snarling dogs, lunging on their chains, then leaned on the horn. He stared curiously at the heavy old woman who came to the door and cursed the dogs into silence, then stepped out. Annie plodded to the car and looked it over with painstaking care, her sharp eyes glinting through their slitted lids. At her side Corley explained the Dodge's "improvements" over pre-war models and answered her questions.

Her inspection finished, she invited the salesman in for a cup of coffee. Corley accepted readily. He had heard much about this strange old woman.

As she poured the coffee and cut the cake, Annie eyed her guest, who would have been surprised at how much she saw through those heavy-lidded eyes. In his mid-thirties, he was slender, good-looking, well groomed, brown hair, blue eyes, well dressed—and greedy. A young man who could be bought. And while she visited with him at her old oil-cloth covered kitchen table she felt the stirring of emotions long buried and thought dead, emotions she had not felt since her visits to Omaha, now nearly forty years in the past.

An hour later Corley drove away in the old V8, his head in a whirl. The old woman was ugly and dirty, her conversation filled with four letter words and profanity. Her slit eyes bothered him and he could understand why people feared her. But he knew she liked him—and she had money, lots of it, so people said—and the $20 bill she had tucked in his pocket as he left the kitchen seemed to prove it. He meant to see more of her.

Annie called the garage the next day to demand that Corley be sent out again, right away. Henry, her driver, said the engine didn't sound right and she wanted it checked. Corley lost no time getting out to the farm. The engine sounded fine, but he fiddled with a spark plug and a wire or two, assured her that everything was all right now, and followed her into the kitchen for more cake and coffee.

Even though Chuck Corley came often to the farm all that summer, Annie did not let up in her efforts to get Joe to come home; for it pleased her to have two good-looking young men visiting her at the farm. As often as she could she found excuses to have Joe drive her on errands in the new car, and stood hurling curses after him each time he drove cheerfully away in his own third-hand little coupe.

It was old Liz who told Joe, on one of his visits, that Chuck Corley came to the farm a lot, and that Annie "just falls all over him and gives him money when he leaves." From then on he managed a few minutes alone with Liz whenever he could, and was not surprised when she told him that Annie had made out a deed to the farm in Corley's name.

"That young fella is sure daft about money," Liz said, her faded eyes sparkling. "He just pats old Annie all over and tells her what a nice lady she is."

Chapter 60

Old Karl Schmidt sat at Annie's table, running on and on, until she broke into his monologue to say, "Karl, come in here with me," and led the way into the old parlor, seldom used any more. Crossing the room, she patted the closed lid of Clara's piano, silent now for more than a dozen years.

"This belonged to Clara," she told him. "You remember Clara? Well, I've been thinking. You have three girls, not married yet, and I have a foster son. A good boy, my Joe. I'd like to see him and your Freida make a match. If they get married I'll give Freida this piano and set 'em up on the north Eighty. You tell Freida what I said."

Annie was pleased with the expression of calculating greed that gleamed in the old German's pale eyes.

Not long afterward one of Joe's fellow workers at the railroad yards, a former schoolmate, said, "I hear Freida Schmidt has her cap set for you, Joe. Old Karl is telling it all over the neighborhood. Says Annie is giving you and Freida Clara's piano for a wedding present, and that you're going to live across the road on the old Lay place. Anything to it?"

Joe stared at him for a long moment. He knew old Karl spent a good deal of time at the farm, and he didn't doubt that Annie had made him the proposition. He remembered Freida from school days—a plump girl with a pale yellow braid of hair down her back, pale blue eyes, and a complexion that reminded him of the skin side of a slab of bacon, "sow belly" as Annie called it.

"Well, how about it?" His friend was half in earnest, half in jest.

"Not if I know it," Joe said. "I haven't seen Freida in months. Old Karl and Annie are crazy."

But the bit of gossip was disturbing, for the old fear of Annie was still strong in him. The old woman had an uncanny way of getting what she wanted, and with him living on her north Eighty she would have him back again. Yes, she might somehow get him married to Freida—unless he was already married to someone else.

For the past two months he had been keeping fairly steady company with pretty, blonde Elena Leech, who already knew about Annie and her campaign to get him back on the farm. That evening he told her of the plan to marry him off to the pale German girl.

"The old girl might pull it off, too," he told Elena, "unless I leave the country—or get married to somebody else. Would you mind driving up to Julesburg with me and getting married?"

They were married the following week, and Annie was livid with fury when she heard the news. She could not abide losing anything that belonged to her.

Joe's marriage almost convinced the woman that she had lost her last chance to get him back. He had gotten away from her back in 1940 and she had tried to get even by turning him in to the draft board the next year, but that had backfired when he was classed 4F. He had escaped her the second time when he enlisted; and now he seemed to have escaped her for the third time by marrying a girl of his own choosing. If she could, she meant to make him regret it.

With a good idea of what awaited him, Joe, compelled by an urge he could not explain, went alone to see Annie soon after his marriage. The tall cottonwoods, newly leafed out cast their pleasant shade over the paintless old buildings; the huge, clumpy old lilac bushes, in full bloom, shed their delicate fragrance across the dreary yard.

From her kitchen window Annie saw Joe stop at the end of the old board walk, and came plowing out to meet him as he stepped from his car. For minutes she cursed him with every vile epithet she could lay her tongue to. The shade of the cottonwoods did not quite reach to the spot where they stood and the afternoon sun was hot. Joe marveled that its heat, combined with the scorching fury that consumed the woman, did not cause her to melt down into her old felt slippers.

After awhile she paused for breath, and then began to tell him about her friend, Chuck Corley. "*There's* a young man who appreciates what I do for him, and it looks like *he* might wind up with everything I own," she waved a thick hand, indicating all her possessions.

"You could've had it all," she went on accusingly. "I meant for you to have every damn thing, but no, you couldn't do the decent thing and come home where you belong, so now I'm through with you, damn your lazy, ungrateful hide. Now Chuck will look after me and Liz, and you can just damn well go to hell." She did not ask him in for cake and coffee.

Even though she was through with him, Annie still called Joe whenever she needed something fixed, a new leather on her pump, or some repair that would cost her if she had to hire a man to make it.

On a pleasant day in the spring of 1948 Joe drove out to the farm in answer to a call from Annie. The damned light switch in the bungalow kitchen had come to pieces and she needed him to come out and fix it.

Electric power had come to the valley before the second World War and Annie had hired the cheapest electrician she could find to wire the bungalow and the old house—and the system had been giving her trouble, off and on, ever since.

At the turn into the lane Joe waited while a man and woman in a Ford drove out onto the highway. "Who was your company?" he asked Annie in the kitchen.

"Harvey and Eileen Moore, from town. They came out to borrow $200. They're behind on their house payments, so I let 'em have the money. Took their I.O.U. for one year."

Joe automatically felt sorry for the Moores. He knew that Annie often loaned money to people who couldn't, or wouldn't, borrow it from a bank. And that she seldom, if ever, lost on her loans, even though she charged a considerably higher rate of interest than the banks. If her debtor could not pay in cash when the loan came due, she had other ways of collecting. One way or another she always got her money's worth—and often more.

He remembered the ranchman from the western end of the state who, a decade or more ago, had borrowed $3,000 to close a quick deal that he didn't want his banker to know about. He could still see Annie, pulling at her mole and saying, "Sure, I'll let you have the damned money, but what do I get for security?"

"How about this?" the cattleman had asked, pulling a Bull Durham tobacco sack from his pocket and handing it to her. "It's diamonds," he explained. "I sold a car load of cattle to a speculator last week and that's what he paid me with. He'd just taken 'em in on another deal.

"They're genuine," he said, as Annie hefted the little sack. "I took 'em in to Dixon's (a local jeweler) and he said they're good, but I'll have to take 'em to Omaha or Denver to get my money out of them." Annie dropped the sack into her desk drawer and made out the note.

"For how long?" she asked.

"Not long," the man grinned. "Not at the interest you charge. Thirty days will be long enough." Annie filled in the date, watched the ranchman sign the paper, then dropped it into the drawer with the diamonds, and counted out the money. "Remember, I want this back in cash," she told him. "I don't trust banks."

The rancher paid off his note on a sweltering July day, counting out the money in $100 bills and handing it to her. Annie recounted it while the man fanned his sweating face with his wide-brimmed Stetson. Taking his note from the drawer, she scrawled "paid" across it, handed it to him and pushed the drawer shut.

"Wait a minute. What about my diamonds?" The cattleman reminded her. And the woman, rubbing her mole, had looked him straight in the eye and asked, "What diamonds?"

Joe would never forget the way the tall, sunburned man had looked at Annie, then clamped his hat on his head, turned on his booted heel and walked out.

Joe had coffee and cake with Annie, listened to her many complaints, then went on over to the bungalow to put in the new light switch he had brought with him. Presently old Liz came hobbling in. "Joe," she said, peering up at him from under her tangled mat of hair. "I got something to tell you. You ain't going to believe this, but Chuck Corley's been sleeping with Annie."

"No," Joe's shocked voice sounded loud in his own ears. "Liz, you gotta be kidding."

"I'm not," she denied earnestly. "I see him go in her room. Sometimes he stays *all night*. Annie always has me make up her bed with clean sheets before he comes."

Joe left, still shaking his head in disbelief. He remembered old Frank's story of Annie's trips to Omaha, and the neighbor boys' tales of Annie and the Greeks from the railroad section cars on the sidetrack, long ago. He had supposed that part of her life long past and not to be repeated. After all, she was seventy-five years old now, maybe more. But Annie was Annie. Nothing she did *should* really surprise him.

It was Chuck Corley's part in the sordid affair that shocked him. Chuck was less than half the old woman's age, a good-looking young man with a nice home, a good wife and two young daughters. Respected, so far as Joe knew, by his associates, and a successful car salesman in one of the town's leading garages. He belonged to the First Methodist Church, to the Junior Chamber of Commerce, the Elks and the Lions. He had everything going for him the way it was, Joe thought. But that deed to one, or maybe both, of Annie's Eighties must have proved too tempting.

It *had* to be greed on Corley's part—but Joe could not imagine a greed so consuming as to lead a fastidious man like Chuck to go to bed with an ugly, dirty old woman like Annie—and the knowledge sickened him.

Chapter 61

Over the years sporadic attempts to rid the town of gambling and prostitution had had little success until County Attorney S. S. Diedrich had cleaned out the gambling establishments at the beginning of the 1940s. Art Haynes' departure in 1941 had helped there. Now many of the town's leading citizens were demanding that prostitution go, too. The several "establishments" on downtown Main Street, the flock of seedy hotels on Front Street, and the houses on the north side were a disgrace to the town, they said.

It had flourished too well, they charged, and far too long, especially under Mayor Duncan, on whose desk a plain envelope had allegedly appeared every Monday morning. Annie knew all about that envelope — stuffed with one thousand dollars in bills — to which she had regularly contributed. Except for occasional token raids on the sleaziest Front Street hotels when no one of importance was likely to be involved, it had guaranteed non-interference from the law.

By the middle of the decade Annie had seen the direction of the winds of change and had begun to divest herself of her own houses while she could still get a good price for the businesses they harbored. She was none too soon. In 1949 the citizens voted into office a mayor and a city council pledged to divest the town of prostitution.

The sale of her houses cut her off-the-farm business down considerably. However the irrigation company still paid its bills with county warrants, whose holders came to her house to cash them, and she was still active in her private loan business.

So Annie, now well past seventy-five and grown heavy and short of breath, was finally content to take life a little easier, to favor her aching feet a little more, and to give more time to her friend, Chuck Corley, who came almost every evening to the farm these days.

When, late in the fall of 1950, she lost her driver it proved only a minor inconvenience. Old Henry, tripping on a broken step as he came down the stairs in the old barn, had fallen on a carelessly discarded cultivator shovel at the bottom and cut a deep gash in his knee. One of his daughters came to get him and, after the doctor sewed up the wound, took him home to live with her.

From then on Annie called Corley, Joe, Judge Shay, Thad Long or the Moores to bring her whatever she needed from the stores, or to come after her when she needed a ride to town. Occasionally, when the weather was pleasant, she shuffled down the lane to the road and sat on a box she kept there for the purpose, to wait until a neighbor came along and offered her a ride.

In town she got out on the west side of the courthouse and plodded up the walk to the Jeffers Street door, then turned in at the first office on the right, that of the new county clerk, Andrew Dale. She enjoyed walking into his front office and telling him to call Judge Shay, on the floor above, then shuffling on into his private office and settling herself in his desk chair to wait for the judge.

Even though Dale was not one of her inner circle of county friends—there were few of those any more—using his office in which to meet the judge saved her the difficult climb up the stairs, and gave her the feeling of still being in control. The judge usually came down right away. Bidding him shut the inner office door, she talked with him awhile, then had him take her home.

On the Friday afternoon of March 30, 1951, the judge drove her home and was having cake and coffee with her when Eileen Moore came to the farm to deliver Annie's laundry and pick up her soiled things. For the past two years Eileen had been making weekly laundry trips—ever since the day she and Harvey had driven out to tell the old woman they could not pay their note, and would she please grant them some extra time.

To their surprise and relief Annie had been quite willing to extend the note. She and her sister had been doing their own washing on their old Maytag, she said, but they were getting too old to do it any longer. But if Eileen would do it for her, at a $1.25 or $1.50 a week, with everything ironed, she could pay off the note that way. As the Moores drove out the lane they congratulated themselves again on dealing with such a nice old lady. She wasn't at all like some people said she was.

In the old kitchen Annie smiled and rubbed her mole. When the Moore's had paid off their note she would make out a deed to the north Eighty in their name—and get her laundry done for free for as long as she lived.

When Eileen and the judge had gone, the old woman remembered that she hadn't given her rifle a good cleaning for quite awhile. Sending Liz to the bungalow for the gun, she got out her tools and spent the evening cleaning, polishing and reassembling the weapon.

As she worked she smiled, thinking of all the people who, over the past thirty-five years, had warned her that keeping her money at home was an open invitation to thieves, and that one of these days she was bound to be robbed. Well, she had sure proved them wrong. What if everyone did know that she kept her money at home? They also knew that she had free roaming killer dogs protecting the place at night, and that she slept with a high-powered rifle at her hand. In addition she now had the young Spitz that Chuck had brought her a year or so ago, a fierce little dog trained to go to the throat on command. Any man, planning to rob Annie Cook would be taking his life in his hands.

That night, as usual, Annie and Liz turned the outside dogs loose at dark. With Annie carrying the newly cleaned rifle in one hand and her money bag in the other, they left for the bungalow a little later. Sending Liz ahead to turn on the porch light, and then the kitchen light, Annie set the rifle down by the kitchen door and dropped the heavy canvas money bag that had replaced the paper sacks of Clara's time on the table.

Locking up for the night by hooking the screen door on the inside and wedging a dining room chair under the kitchen door knob (she had lost the key long ago) she picked up the money bag and took it to bed with her as she always did.

The barking of the outside dogs wakened her. The barking was urgent, not the kind that warned coyotes, coons and skunks away. "Liz," Annie yelled, "get up and turn on the porch light. See what's making those damn dogs tear around like that." As she spoke the dogs fell suddenly silent.

She heard Liz pad across the kitchen floor, move the chair away from the door and click on the porch light — and then a strangled cry of fright. At that Annie froze, remembering her rifle, still leaning against the wall by the kitchen door.

Heavy footsteps crossed the kitchen floor behind the gleam of a flashlight, and then the kitchen light came on. From her bed she could see two masked men in the kitchen. The shorter of the pair came straight to her door, reached inside, switched on her bedroom light and came to her bedside. He wore a knitted cap, pulled down over his ears, and a woman's stocking, with holes cut out for eyes, masking his face. Wordlessly, he held out his hand to the old woman and, just as silently, she pulled the money sack from beneath the quilts and handed it to him. She knew he would take it from her in any case, and if she resisted he might get rough.

The man snatched the heavy bag, turned on his heel and went out. As he passed the light bulb, hanging from the ceiling in the center of the kitchen, he smashed it with his flashlight, then smashed the porch light as he and his companion went out into the night.

As soon as they were gone Annie scrambled out of bed and plowed into the kitchen. "Quick," she yelled, "the telephone." Feeling her way to the wall, she found the instrument and yanked the receiver from its hook.

"Dammit," she swore, "it's dead. The bastards cut the wires."

Fumbling her way to the dining room door, she found the switch and turned on the light there. "Liz, where the hell are you?"

"Here," Liz whispered from the far side of the kitchen table.

"Get your coat on and get over to Elwoods. Have Ev call the sheriff and tell him to get his damned butt out here as fast as he can."

When Liz had pattered away into the darkness, she put on her own coat and sat down to think. Two things bothered her. One, she had heard no car. Two, the dogs behavior. There could be only one explanation.

The outside dogs had barked a furious warning—and then suddenly fallen silent, indicating that the thieves, frequent visitors to the farm, had left their vehicle some distance away, walked on to the house and spoken to the raging dogs. The same was true of the house dog. He not only had not made a sound but had wagged his tail a time or two as the thief made off with the money bag. Furthermore, throughout the perpetration of the robbery neither of the men had said a word, which could only mean that she would have recognized their voices.

There was no doubt about it, Annie concluded, she had been robbed by men who came often enough to the farm to know their way around, and to be recognized by the dogs. She knew, too, that there was little she could do about it.

They could have been any of half a dozen men she knew, but she wasn't sure enough of their identity to bring charges against any two. And then another thought intruded—she might get some satisfaction out of this yet, *What if she could pin the robbery on Joe?*

There seemed no chance now that she would ever get him back, and a little stretch in the pen might teach him a lesson. In the time left to her before Liz, her teeth chattering from her run through the chilly night to the Elwoods, came back to the bungalow, and before Sheriff Discoe's car turned into the lane, she settled on the information she would give out.

The sheriff and his deputy looked over the scene of the crime and questioned the two women. That done, Annie took them to the old house, stirred up the fire in the kitchen range and made coffee. When it was light enough to see, the officers went out to look for tracks.

A short time later an eager reporter from the *Telegraph* drove in. Over more cake and coffee Annie told her story again. When the reporter had gone she called Joe, told him she had been robbed and that she wanted him to come out as quick as he could.

"It was about time," Joe bluntly told the angry old woman as he came into the kitchen. "The whole country knew you kept a lot of money here. It's a wonder it didn't happen a long time ago. Now, what is it you want to see me about?"

"I told the damned sheriff and that nosey reporter that I had about $14,000 in that bag. Well, it was a damned sight more than that and you know it. They'll be asking you a lot of—questions, too, and I want you to tell 'em the same thing I did."

Joe told her he would, and then asked her what she intended to do with her money from now on, put it in the bank as she should have done all along, or what?

No, not a damned bank, she swore, but she'd figure out something.

Joe left her then. He didn't like the malicious glint in her little eyes as she almost smiled at him, but he couldn't help feeling a little sorry for her. He knew her loss had been heavy, the proceeds of many years of scheming and saving, and he didn't wonder that she looked angry, old and tired—her putty colored jowls sagging into the folds of her dirty neck.

Chapter 62

The *Telegraph* for March 31, 1951, carried the story.

Big Robbery At Farm Home

"The work and savings of a lifetime gone and I don't even have enough money to pay my taxes. Through occasional tears, 77-year-old Mrs. Anna Cook told a *Telegraph* representative of her shattering experience of being robbed of $14,000 by two masked men."

In reply to his question "What did the robbers look like?" the reporter wrote, "Frightened and nervous, neither of the women recognized the men or were able to give a very complete description. Mrs. Cook said the shorter of the two wore a yellowish cap and a jacket that looked like an army jacket.

"Mrs. Cook, who has lived on the farm since 1893, said she had last counted her money in February. She had $10,000 then, she said. She and her son, Joe, both estimate that she had taken in at least $4,000 since then, for farm products, crops, rentals, etc.

"The former keeper of the county poor farm is puzzled about the reaction of her dogs. Though they barked a warning, one is considered a pretty fair guard dog and ordinarily gives strangers a rough time, but did not seem to frighten the masked robbers.

"Mrs. Cook said the masks seemed to be rags or old stockings pulled over the men's heads, with holes made for the eyes. Car tracks indicated the thieves opened a gate from a field east of the house, drove their car across it and then walked across a small alfalfa patch to the house. Mrs. Cook's gritty little sister, Lizzie, padded barefoot the quarter-mile to the Everett Elwood home and Elwood notified the authorities. Lizzie reached the Elwood home just about midnight.

"Sheriff Discoe said today that investigation of the crime is continuing but there are no new developments to report."

The authorities were not long in coming to question Joe. He knew Annie kept a goodly sum of money at the house, he knew how to get into the farmyard by "opening a gate into a field east of the house," and driving across it. He knew the dogs well and they would not have attacked him, he had been in the army and might well have a "jacket that looked like an army jacket."

Everything fit—except that Joe had been at work in the Union Pacific yards from eight o'clock that night until four in the morning. He not only had punched the company time clock but had fellow workers to swear that he was on the job that night.

Reluctant to give up so promising a lead, the officials gave Joe a polygraph test. When the instrument confirmed his statements, they called in and tested the fellow workers who had testified to his presence in the yards throughout the night of the robbery. They, too, seemed to be telling the truth—and there the matter rested, mostly because Annie did not push the investigation any farther. To do so might well uncover secrets in her past that would not only damage Annie Cook but various prominent and respectable people in the county.

In the parade of cars to the Cook farm in the days immediately following the robbery there may have been a few individuals who came only to sympathize with an elderly woman in the loss of her "savings of a lifetime," but there were undoubtedly others who came to advise her of the wisdom of dropping the whole thing. There may even have been some who were willing to make it worth her while to do so. The sizable roll of bills that Annie turned over to Judge Shay in County Clerk Dale's private office a little later would have bolstered any such suspicions.

Still firmly opposed to banks, she had the judge buy a good "strong box" and hide it in his home. From now on, she said, she would bring him her money and he would be responsible for it.

Chapter 63

Chuck Corley hurried into the old kitchen late on the afternoon following the robbery. He had gone to Omaha on Friday, he told Annie, to pick up a special-order car and drive it home for a client and had just now heard about the robbery. "I came as quick as I could. Now tell me all about it."

Annie told her story again, biting off her words angrily. "Dammit, Chuck, I'm damned sure I know the bastards that robbed me but I can't prove it. It could've been Joe. The skunk that took the money was about his size, or yours. It was somebody that knows this place and the bungalow—but there's half a dozen men knows that.

"Dammit, Chuck, I meant for you to have that money. I only meant to keep it and use it as long as I needed it, then turn it all over to you, along with the land, so you could take care of Liz."

Corley was properly comforting and sympathetic, and when he had calmed the angry old woman down somewhat, he brought the talk back to the land. All these many months he had worked toward that one end—the land, and now seemed the right time to make it sure.

"About that land, Annie, until you have those deeds made out by an attorney and signed before a notary public, they're worthless to me. Why don't you let me bring a lawyer out here and get them made out right, signed, notarized, and everything?"

"I suppose you're right. I should see to it, and I will. I'll set a day soon and you can bring your man out and we'll take care of it."

"Why not name your day now, tonight, and have it done?"

"No, not tonight. I'm too damned upset, but soon. And now, you're staying the night, ain't you? I'm so ____ mad I got to have somebody to talk to."

Following the robbery Annie had difficulty sleeping. On the nights that Corley did not stay with her she sat at her desk while old Liz dozed in her chair. Going over her books again and again, she tried to figure out ways to squeeze a little more from this account or that one, or to cut down a bit more here or there. And when she finally wakened her sister and plodded with her across the yard to the bungalow, it was only to lie awake until dawn, trying to decide which one of her associates had robbed her—and what she could do about it.

Joe had been eliminated (she had never believed him guilty anyway) but there were several other good possibilities, even Chuck, though she firmly closed her mind to him as a suspect. Her thoughts kept going back to his employer, Melvin Arnold.

Corley had told her, a year ago, that his new boss, Arnold, had bought the Dodge agency and garage from Casebolt with money borrowed from his brother, a well-to-do Omaha businessman. Shortly before the robbery he had mentioned that affairs at the garage seemed a little shaky, that Arnold's brother wanted his money and "old Mel is pretty worried. He's trying to float a loan at the First National but prospects don't look too good."

A few days after the masked men's visit, Annie asked Chuck, with a side-long glance from her slitted eyes, if Arnold had been able to pay his brother off yet. "Oh yes," he replied easily, "he got his loan and everything's fine now."

"I wonder," Annie said grimly to herself, "if he got that loan from the First National, or from me?" Arnold had been to the place with Corley often enough for the dogs to learn that he was a friend and not to be bothered, and to have learned the layout of the farm. But even if she was right there was nothing she could do about it, and so she laid awake at night and fumed in silence.

A month or so after the robbery a renter stopped in to give her a roll of bills, her share of some stored corn he had sold, and that night again she sat late at her desk, going over her books. She'd have to get that money in to Judge Shay right away, she thought. Any cash at the farm now made her nervous, she'd have to catch a ride to town tomorrow. And then a new thought struck her. Why wait until tomorrow?

A sudden rumble of thunder rattled the old house and a gust of rain splattered against the window. All the better, she decided as she got up and plodded to the telephone. In Hershey the operator, wakened by the shrilling of the night bell on her switchboard, hurried to the board and put on her headphones. "Number please," she said.

"Get me 4506 in North Platte, quick." The girl, recognizing Annie Cook's coarse voice, inserted the proper plug and pressed the key. A man's voice answered and the woman said, "Morgan, I want you to come out here right away."

"Not now, Annie," there was a pleading note in the man's voice. "Millie is very low tonight. The doctor says she may not live until morning, but I'll come as soon as I can."

"You come right now." Even the operator shivered at the menace in the woman's voice.

"All right, Annie," the man said slowly, tiredly. "I'll be right out."

Annie hung up the phone and turned away as another gust of rain hit the window. She knew the judge's wife had been an invalid for many years, and that he was devoted to her, but bending him to her will had momentarily relieved her own pain and anger over losing the money. Tonight, once she had turned the money over to the judge, maybe she could sleep.

She felt better the next morning, and when old Karl Schmidt ambled into her kitchen she sat down with him, over coffee and cake, prepared to enjoy a long session of neighborhood gossip. When he asked if there was anything new on the robbery her face darkened and she replied grimly, "Not a damn thing. They're all a bunch of lazy bastards at the courthouse, pulling down their pay checks just for sitting on their damn butts—and me without even enough money to pay my ____ taxes."

A sudden calculating gleam came into her hooded eyes as she looked at the paunchy old German. "Karl," she demanded, "what am I going to do about those damn taxes anyway? For fifty years I've paid 'em right on time, never a day late. But this year I don't have the money, and they're due next week."

Schmidt spread his pudgy hands helplessly, and the old woman went on, "Karl, do you suppose you could go in and pay 'em for me by May 1. Everybody knows you've got the money in the bank, that you wouldn't even miss it. Before the summer's over I'll be able to pay you back. It's less than $500, Karl, and it would sure be a hell of a lot of help to me, right now." Before he left old Karl had promised to pay the taxes.

When Corley came out that evening he found the old woman in high spirits, and when, as on other evenings during the past month, he mentioned the deeds she agreed readily that it was time they set a date to take care of the matter. How about Thursday, May 10. But only for the north Eighty, she stipulated. "I'd better hang on to this Eighty where I live for a while longer."

"But why? The deed gives you the right to a 'life estate' in the place. As long as you *live* it's still yours."

"I know, but I'm not ready to sign this one away yet. But don't worry, I'll take care of it in plenty of time."

On the appointed day Corley brought his attorney, Charles Baxter, his secretary and her typewriter to the old kitchen, where the deed to the West Half of the Southeast Quarter of Section Thirteen, Township 14, North Range 32, was soon drawn in Charles Corley's favor, duly signed and attested by Baxter, a notary public.

As Annie dropped the paper into her desk drawer and locked it, Corley patted her approvingly on the shoulder. "Now I've got to get these people back to town," he said, "but I'll see you soon."

On the way down the lane, Baxter said, "That was quite a bargain you made, Chuck. One of the best Eightys in the valley for 'one dollar and other valuable consideration.' How'd you swing that?"

"Oh, the poor old lady needs a friend," Corley answered easily. "She thought that foster son of hers, Joe, would come home and look after her, but he won't. Hardly gives her the time of day anymore, her and that poor old half-witted sister of hers. But she has to have somebody, so it looks like I'm elected. She's a grateful old soul, though, and insisted on deeding me that north Eighty for helping her out."

"Lucky you."

When next Joe came to the farm, Liz told him of the signing and notarizing of the deed. Back in town he went around to the Dodge garage. As sales manager, Corley had his own office and Joe stood in the doorway for some time before the dapper salesman looked up.

"Oh. Hi, Joe. Something I can do for you?" His manner was patronizing, condescending, his expression contemptuous, almost sneering.

"Not a thing, Chuck. I just wanted to take a good look at a man who will do what you're doing, just for a hunk of land."

Corley's face turned a dead, sickly white as Joe grinned and walked away. Annie's boyfriend would never sneer at him again.

Chapter 64

Annie was not well, that winter of 1951 and '52. In the fall she caught a heavy cold that hung on and on. Chuck Corley was full of sympathy and concern, and gentle urges to make out the deed to her home Eighty. Early in the new year she consented, and on January 7, 1952, Corley again took Baxter, his secretary and her typewriter to the farm.

With the second deed signed, witnessed and locked in the old desk, Corley breathed a sigh of relief. Afterward he still drove out to the farm two or three times a week but never stayed long. "He's always in a big hurry to get back to town," Liz told Joe on a cold day in late January when he drove out to see how the old women were getting along. "But he always tells her some bad things about you. He don't like you at all."

"No, I guess he don't," Joe agreed cheerfully.

Annie had stayed in her bed, that day, and the bungalow was cold and dank. She would not have the oil heater in the living room lighted, and the fire in the old kitchen range could not overcome the winter-long chill in the big house.

"No wonder you can't get over that cold," Joe told her. "Why don't you sleep in the old house, where it's warm, or else heat this one up?"

But the old woman said she knew what she was doing and she'd be all right as soon as the weather warmed up. Anyway Doc Reardon was looking after her. She'd had him out just last week and he'd left some medicine that was helping.

The winter merged into spring, but Annie still coughed and complained that her lungs hurt. On a pleasant May morning Earl Comstock drove out from Hershey to bring her the can of coffee she had ordered, and a fresh butterscotch cake. "Set down a minute," she invited.

Earl had paid for the coffee himself and Annie went to her desk, but instead of money she took from the drawer the deed she had made out to him and Lela so many years before. "Read it," she commanded, after a spasm of coughing, as she handed it to him. He knew the document by heart but, obediently, he read it over again, including the agreement that he and his wife were to care for old Liz as long as she lived.

"See," the old woman wheezed, "this is your future home. You and Lela have been good to me and you are to have this Eighty and the bungalow. Eileen and Harvey are to have the north place. I keep both deeds right here in my desk," she went on, dropping the paper back in the drawer and locking it, "and I keep the key in my apron pocket, right here, and if I drop dead some day that's where you'll find it."

Earl was smiling when he came out into the yard, where a few scraggly lilac bushes still bloomed, and got into his old pickup and drove away.

A week later, early in the morning, Annie fell in the kitchen of the old house and could not get up again. Cursing her bad luck, she told Liz to call Chuck Corley and tell him to come out as quick as he could, and to bring the ambulance and the doctor with him. "He says he'll be right out," Liz reported.

Whatever was wrong, there was little pain as long as she didn't try to move. Liz had brought a pillow for her head and, except for her coughing, she was fairly comfortable. So she lay as still as she could and made her plans.

"Liz, call Lela and tell her to come over right away," she said presently. "Tell her I'll want her to stay a few days to look after you and the place."

Corley came, just ahead of the Comstocks, and Annie handed him the key to her desk drawer. "Get your papers," she told him. "The Comstocks will be here any minute." He folded the deeds, slipped them into his inside coat pocket and knelt down beside Annie just as Earl and Lela hurried in, followed by the doctor and the ambulance men with their stretcher.

All was hurry and confusion then, with the doctor quickly checking his patient, informing her that she had a broken hip and getting her onto the stretcher. "Just a minute," Annie said, halting the dash to the ambulance. "Lela, you'll be in charge here while I'm gone. Just don't let anyone but Mr. Corley in, and don't let anybody take anything away. I want everything exactly the same here when I come back. Now, let's get the hell out of here."

At home that noon, Elena and Joe listened to the noon news from the local radio station, KGNF, as they ate their meal. Startled to hear Anna Cook's name in the list of daily hospital admissions, Joe got to his feet. "I'd better get over there and see what's happened," he told his wife.

At the hospital he was told by the nurse on Annie's floor that Mrs. Cook was in private room 203 but that she was to have no visitors.

"Why? Who said so?" Joe demanded.

"Those are Mr. Corley's instructions. He says he is in charge."

"We'll see about that. I'm her foster son and I'm going in." Stepping around the nurse, he pushed the door open and went in. At the beside he was startled at the old woman's appearance. He hadn't seen her in the past two weeks and was surprised at how much she had failed.

"Annie, what happened?"

"I fell and broke my damned hip."

"How did you get here?"

"Chuck brought me. He took care of every damn thing. If I had to depend on you I'd prob'ly be out there on the floor yet." Her slit eyes gleamed with satisfaction. Ignoring her malice, Joe asked her what the doctor said.

"He says he'll have to put me in a damn cast, and that I'll be laid up in this ___ hospital for a long spell. But you won't have to bother yourself about me. Chuck's looking after things and every damn thing I've got will be his someday. It could've been yours, Joe, if you'd just showed a little gratitude for all I did for you. But no, *you* had to run out on me. Now get out and let me rest."

Joe went back the next morning. The door to Annie's room was still closed and when a different nurse tried to tell him that Mrs. Cook was to have no visitors, he ignored her and went on in. He could see by her eyes that she recognized him, and that she was worse. Her breathing was more labored, her color bad. "Hi Annie," he said, and patted her hand and went away.

By afternoon she was irrational, bawling over and over, "Oh gawd, help me take care of my money, Oh gawd, help me take care of my money, Oh gawd...."

From the first she had been a difficult patient, giving profane orders, complaining, refusing to take her medicine. Her nurses had encountered such crotchety behavior in patients before, but seldom had they had to deal with one so filthy. The two young nurses assigned to undress and bathe her had been appalled at what they found, clothing so soiled and odorous that they could scarcely breathe as they cut it off her, uncovering a flabby heap of rolls of fat engulfing ridges of oily dirt. The unfortunate nurses soaked and scrubbed until the old woman began screaming curses and ordered them to get the hell out and leave her alone.

When Joe went back that evening, on his way to work, she was much weaker, though she still seemed to recognize him. Her eyes were dull and sunken, her mouth hung slackly open. As he stood looking down at the flabby old face he remembered what Frank had told him, long ago, about a "sickness of the mind," and that they should feel sorry for Annie.

Frank had been right, he thought. Poor old woman. All she had to show for nearly eighty years of living was her farm, a little money and the questionable loyalty of a dozen people she had "bought." Not a friend in the lot. Not a real friend anywhere. On his way out he stopped at the nurses' station to ask them to let him know when the end came.

The call came shortly before dawn, with a request for instructions as to where they should send the body. "We were told that you are in charge of arrangements." the nurse said.

"Call W. R. Munson's," Joe told her. Old W. R. had been dead for years now, but Annie would probably have wanted his old firm in charge of her final arrangements. "Was anybody with her when she died?" he asked "No one," the nurse replied.

Joe had not been the only one alerted to action by the news of Annie's hospitalization. Over on the north side of town, Mary's neighbor, Abbie Wonka, heard the radio hospital report and ran across the street to the Cauffmans. "Mary," she exclaimed, hurrying into the kitchen, "you should've been listening to your radio. They just said Annie Cook's in the hospital."

Mary and her husband, Lewis Cauffman, and their two young children, Lewis and Pearl, were at the dinner table. Mary froze in her chair and the others stared at her. They all knew about Annie Cook—and how Mary feared her.

"Are you sure?" she finally asked.

"That's what they said. 'Mrs. Anna Cook, admitted this morning'."

"I must go tell Irene. Abbie, you come with me." With her friend in tow, she ran across the yard to the small building that housed Irene's beauty shop. The younger woman was shampooing a customer when her mother burst in with the news. She, too, was speechless for a long moment. Then she whirled on her mother and said, "Oh, Mom, let's go right out and get Grandma."

"But you have appointments," Mary objected practically. "You'll have to stay here and take care of them."

"I'll go with you," Abbie Wonka offered.

With her husband at the wheel of their car, Mary and her friend were soon on the way to the farm. Mary was silent on the drive, her emotions too chaotic for words. It was hard to believe. After twenty-eight years she was finally to see her mother again! Hard to believe it had been nearly half a lifetime since the night she had run away from Annie and the farm, and that, for most of those years she had lived within ten miles of her mother, yet had not seen her, nor heard her voice.

What would her mother be like now? Was she still sane, or had all the years of starvation and abuse driven her mad? Would her mother know her? Would she actually be able to bring her home with her? The questions whirled in her head.

In her excitement and anxiety she did not notice the weedy, dilapidated appearance of the yard, nor pay any attention to the snarling of the chained dogs as she hurried to the door, where Lela Comstock stood, her kindly face worried and anxious.

"Hello, Lela, I've come for my mother."

"But I can't let her go. The last thing Annie said was that everything must be the same here when she comes back as it was when she left this morning."

"I don't care what Annie said. I've come for my mother." Mary was surprised at her own firmness and determination as she gently pushed the older woman aside and went into the kitchen. Across the room she saw an old woman, terribly bent, skinny and shabby, a pitiable creature.

For a little space the two peered at each other, then suddenly the old one sang out, "Why, there's my Mary," and came as fast as her lame back and legs would let her to meet her daughter.

"I've come to take you home with me, Mom, so let's get your things and get out of here," Mary said. Even with Annie gone, the place felt menacing, dangerous to her.

"Let me get my clock and Mama's picture." Liz spoke as if she had been expecting Mary, then hobbled into the old store room to get the clock and the picture of her mother she had brought with her from her Denver home half a century ago.

"I'm ready now," she said, a toothless smile lighting her wizened little face. Then, "Good-bye, Lela," to her still protesting caretaker as Mary and her friend helped her out to the car.

Chapter 65

Back in town, Irene Dauphin watched the driveway from the window of her shop as she shampooed and combed and curled. She was twenty-three years old and she had never seen either of her grandmothers, a circumstance that left her feeling cheated. But today, in just a little while, she hoped to meet her only living grandparent.

As she worked her mind went back over many things: her pleasant childhood on the Bignell Flat farm with her grandfather, her mother's weekly visits to do the laundry and bake and sew for them, and then her mother's marriage to Lewis Cauffman in 1937 when she was nine.

The following year her grandfather had sold the farm and they had moved to town to live with Mary and Lewis. She hadn't wanted to leave the farm where she had felt safe and secure, and where almost every animal was her special pet. But even more compelling than her homesickness for the farm had been her dread of living in town; for Mary, who was never to lose her fear of Annie, had passed it on to her children.

She remembered the winter she was eight and had the measles. Her mother had taken her to town to care for her and, due to deep snow in the country, had kept her in town to go to school after she recovered. Daily she had warned her to watch out for old Annie and her car. If ever a car stopped beside her on the street, Mary told her, and an old woman spoke to her, she was to run for home as fast as she could.

"No matter what you are doing, you run for home. That old woman will get you if she can, and if she ever gets you out to her place she will starve and beat you, and no one can get you away from her, not the sheriff, not anyone."

To the little girl the ominous words had meant endless terror, causing her to play only in her own yard, and to run most of the six blocks to school and back, looking often behind her for an old black Dodge with an ugly old woman in the passenger seat.

Once, on the way home from the neighborhood grocery with a bottle of milk, she thought she saw the car, coming slowly up behind her. With a gasp of pure terror, she began to run. The bottle slipped from her fingers to shatter on the cement walk, but she ran on, driven by her sickening fear. When she dashed into the kitchen and gasped out her story, her mother's face turned white and she took the trembling child into her arms. A day or two later she had taken her back to the safety of the Bignell Flat farm.

After she and her grandfather came to town to live, she often asked about her grandmother Lizzie, and as her mother talked she had come to love the gentle little woman, and to hate more fiercely the mean old witch who had beaten and starved her for so long.

Her grandfather had died in 1940. She had become a teenager and gone on to high school, and then to the local beauty school. By the time she graduated her kindly stepfather was ill with cancer and could no longer work. In order to be near to help her mother, she had set up her beauty parlor in the little two-room building on the back of the lot, from where she now watched the driveway for the return of the car that would be bringing her legendary Grandma Lizzie home.

When the car turned into the driveway and stopped, Irene watched while her mother, Abbie and Lewis helped a small, bent old woman from the vehicle and into the house. A few minutes later she put her last customer under the dryer, then ran across the yard to her mother's living room. After one quick, searching look at the little woman in the chair, her eyes met her mother's above her grandmother's head. Mary's eyes were filled with despair.

Easter Sunday, 1942. Irene Dauphin age 14.

Old Liz was unbelievably dirty—from the matted mop of hair on the top of her head to the heavy, cracked old shoes on her feet, she reeked of her long unwashed existence. "Never mind, Mom, we'll get everything taken care of," the younger woman said as she dropped to her knees beside the chair and put her arms around the frail, filthy old woman. "Hello, Grandma, I'm so glad to see you," she said.

While Mary heated soup and fed her toothless mother, Irene finished her customer and closed her shop. Together they helped old Liz out to Mary's neat little backyard wash house, cut her filthy clothes off her skinny body and helped her into a wash tub full of warm suds.

"I've been wanting to get out of those old long johns," Liz said, making a face at the garment Mary had thrown across the room, "but Annie wouldn't let me. She said we had to wear 'em 'til the fourth of July."

"But why?" Irene demanded.

"Oh, I guess Annie was cold. But I wasn't. I've been steaming in 'em for a week."

As the two women gently scrubbed the encrusted filth from old Liz's skeletal body, ancient scars appeared, a criss-cross of thin white lines across her back and shoulders, arms and legs, souvenirs of the cutting whip lash Annie had once wielded so vigorously. Other puckered scars on her arms and legs Mary recognized as mementos of the sharp teeth of Annie's succession of savage dogs.

The sight of the old lesions set Mary's own scars to stinging in sympathy, the old burn on her cheek, the welts on her own arms and legs, still faintly visible after thirty years; and her hip bone, nicked by Annie's butcher knife, still hurting her when she was overtired.

Mary lifted her mother's left foot and began to wash the thin leg above it. "Ouch, be careful, that hurts," Liz exclaimed.

"Mom, whatever happened? This looks like a new scar, a bad one."

"It is. One day last winter Annie got mad and sicced old Bruno on me. He knocked me down and chewed my leg. Annie had to take me to Dr. Reardon and get it sewed up. Then it got worse and she had to take me back again. But it finally got well. It still hurts sometimes."

With tears in her eyes, Mary tenderly sponged the limb with its angry, puckered scars. No wonder the wound had gotten infected, living in such filth. And why hadn't Dr. Reardon done something about it, notified somebody? But no doubt Annie had some hold on him, too, and he didn't dare talk.

The bath finished, they dressed the little old lady in some of Irene's things and put her in a chair to see what to do about her hair. "It will have to come off, close to her head," Irene said of the filthy mat. As she gently clipped the tangled wad away both women gasped at sight of the fat-bellied wood ticks embedded in the scarred, dirty scalp.

With the ratted tangle of hair gone, the ticks removed and her head thoroughly shampooed, the seventy-six-year-old woman seemed to lose some of her years. The gamin spirit of her long-ago girlhood almost glowed again in her faded dark eyes and in the toothless smile on her pixie-like little face.

That night, with the weary old woman safely in bed and asleep in the small bedroom next to her own room, Mary went out and burned every stitch of the rags she had cut off her mother that afternoon. The next day she went down town and bought new clothes for her, and shoes that fit her small feet and a lacy cap to cover her shorn head.

Chapter 66

On the morning that Annie died Charles Corley was standing on the courthouse steps when the custodian unlocked the big front doors. Striding confidently into the office of the Register of Deeds, he recorded both his deeds, returned to his car and headed for the Cook farm, now the "Corley farm."

He had paid a high price for that farm, he admitted to himself, and ownership had come none too soon. For the past year his marriage had been in trouble. His wife had grown increasingly resentful of his frequent absences from home and he knew she suspected he was seeing another woman, and that she would have been horrified if she had known the woman was Annie Cook. But, now that it was over and he was a wealthy man, he hoped that he could make her understand.

Anticipating the sure events of the morning, Joe said to his wife as they finished breakfast, "Come with me, Elena, let's drive out to the farm. It will be pretty lively out there today."

They found the farmyard full of cars and the old kitchen crowded. Beside the Comstocks, Judge Shay was there, and Thad Long, the Moores, old Karl Schmidt and several former county commissioners. The drawer of Annie's old desk was open and papers scattered about. Everyone was asking questions, and no one seemed to have any answers.

Then the door opened again and Chuck Corley came in. Smiling triumphantly, the dapper Corley waved some papers at the suddenly silent crowd. "You folks had just as well go home," he told them. "I have my deeds to both farms right here, all signed, notarized, *and recorded*. Yours aren't worth a plugged nickel."

The stunned silence held while Corley's car roared out of the yard and down the road. Joe was disappointed that Corley had not noticed him in the back of the crowd, he would have enjoyed watching him wilt. Then one of the old county commissioners began to curse softly as he put on his hat and went out to his car. "She sure had me fooled," another said, with a sickly grin, and left. "My wife's going to feel bad about this. All those loaves of bread she baked," Long said as he and Judge Shay turned to go.

Joe and Elena stayed to sympathize with the Comstocks and the Moores, good people who had worked hard for old Annie for more years than they cared to remember.

"I never thought she'd do *this* to us," grey-haired Lela Comstock said, despair in her eyes and voice. "That's right," her husband said. "Why, just a week ago...." He went on to tell Joe of his visit to the farm, and that Annie had told him the key to the desk drawer would be in her apron pocket. "But when we got here that Corley was already here, and the doctor and the ambulance," Lela said. "We never had a chance to get the key."

"Corley prob'ly already had it, damn him," said her husband, who was not a swearing man.

"And look at all the washing and ironing I did for her," Eileen Moore lamented. "She had to have *everything* ironed, even the towels and underwear, and everything was so dirty. They must've worn their clothes to bed, and they never took a bath. And they wore those heavy old long-legged under drawers right up to the Fourth of July. They really did."

"Well, don't feel too bad yet," Joe counciled them. "I'm betting this whole thing will wind up in court and you can turn in your claims then. Just hang in there and see what happens."

From the farm Joe went directly to the mortuary. Since the arrangements seemed to have been left to him he did the best he could, selecting the casket (not the best, but a good one), the minister and the hymns. At his request, Elena bought the burial gown at O'Connor's Department Store, "something quiet and pretty."

To Joe's knowledge, Annie hadn't darkened the door of a church in the last ten years, so he asked the minister of the church he and Elena attended, the First Lutheran, to officiate. For the hymns he chose three of Frank's old favorites.

Friday morning, Memorial Day, the mortician called Joe to let him know Annie was ready for viewing and that he would like him to come in and see if everything was all right.

Joe stood a long time beside the coffin. For Annie, she looked very nice. Death and the mortician had done away with most of her wrinkles, her slack mouth seemed smaller, neater, and with her eyes closed she seemed less menacing. Elena had chosen a plain blue gown, "quiet and pretty" as Joe had specified, and a light blue, lace-edged cap covered the mat of dirty grey hair that had defied the beauty operator. But then, she had worn caps for years anyway.

Looking down at her, Joe tried to remember the good things about her, the few times she had been kind to him, or that she had spoken to him in her vanilla voice. The times—he could count them on the fingers of one hand—when she had made the peach cobbler that he loved.

In spite of his desire to remember only the good, he recalled all the deeds she had made out to people who could be of service to her. She had outlived so many of them: Sheriff Sayman, the banker, two or three of the county commissioners, and W. R Munson. With the death of each one she had torn up his deed, smiling her loose, humorless smile as she did so. She had destroyed Munson's in 1945. Of them all she probably owed him the most—for all the death certificates that, like Clara's, he had signed the way she told him to.

Then another memory came back to him, something he hadn't thought of in a long, long time. It had happened the summer after his mother died, when they had had a patient at the farm, an elderly man, still able to work a little.

Annie didn't think he worked fast enough and, at whatever he was doing, hoeing in the garden, carrying in cobs or wood, she often ordered the little boy to "shove 'im, Joe, shove 'im. Make 'im work faster."

To Joe it was a game and he ran and shoved the old man with enthusiasm. Not until he was older did he realize how cruel his "play" had been—and then he had forgotten about it. Regretting that he had remembered it now, he turned and hurried away.

When Joe had gone the Munson hearse carried Annie back to the farm where, as the valley custom decreed, she was to "lie in state" in the parlor of the old bungalow until the funeral in the Hershey Methodist church the next day.

Many came to look at her; for the mysterious old Cook farm and the strange old woman who had run it for more than half a century, still attracted visitors. Lela Comstock, her friendly face lined and careworn, greeted all callers and welcomed them into the parlor. In spite of her betrayal at Annie's hands, the kindly woman had still felt obligated to perform this last service for her.

All day long, and into the evening, the callers came, to stand for a minute or two beside the open coffin. "She looks so nice, doesn't she?" most of them said, a faint surprise in their voices.

The little church was well filled the next afternoon, and the chancel banked with flowers. As Annie had had him do at Frank's and Clara's funeral, Joe counted the wreaths and bouquets, thirty-five in all. Mr. and Mrs. Charles Corley were there, sitting well toward the front, and Judge Shay. The Longs were there, and the Carl Schmidt family, including the pale skinned Freida and her sisters. Mrs. Augst Johnson was there, doubtless remembering the night, eighteen years ago, when Annie had insisted she sit with her at Clara's wake. Most of the neighbors were there, concealing their relief that the old woman and her rifle were no longer a threat to them or their livestock.

The Comstocks and the Moores sat together, sharing their disappointment in the loss of the farms they had so confidently expected to inherit on the day that Annie died. In the pews reserved for the family Mary Cauffman sat with her mother, old Lizzie Knox, and her husband, her older son, Will Dauphin, and his family, her daughter, Irene, and her two youngest children.

For Joe and his wife there seemed no special place. He was not "family," like Lizzie and Mary, neither was he an "inheritor," like Corley. Yet he was surely more than just a neighbor or an interested spectator, like most of the others. So they sat well to the back, and paused only a moment as they filed by the casket in the mourners' line.

When only the family remained in the church, the mortician bowed to Mary and went out, leaving them alone to bid farewell to their dead. Holding her mother's arm, Mary stopped briefly at the coffin, then turned away. The sight of her aunt's face brought only painful memories. But perhaps now, at long last, she could be free of the terror she had lived with for so many years.

Irene looked long at the face of the woman she had feared for as long as she could remember. She had never seen the woman before and she looked harmless enough now, but the fear had been so real, so deep that, even now, it threatened to rise again and choke her as it had when she was a little girl. She could only be glad, wholly glad, that the old woman was dead.

At the cemetery Joe was surprised to see a metal urn filled with wilting carnations in front of the Cook monument. Who had put them there, he wondered, and why? Otherwise the lot looked just as it had at Frank's burial, fifteen years ago. The marker at the head of Clara's grave was the only one there. Annie had never bothered to place one for Frank, and there would probably be none for her. There was no one left who cared enough to put one there.

Chapter 67

Taking her mother into her home was a privilege Mary could ill afford. Her husband's worsening illness had forced him to quit his work and, with no pay check coming in and steadily mounting doctor's bills, their savings were soon gone. Mary had gone back to work, cleaning homes, motels, beauty shops, serving as a part time waitress and helping cater parties at the country club.

No one could stretch a dollar farther than Mary Cauffman, but with old Lizzie's need of vitamins, special foods and extra care it was difficult. "Don't worry, Mom," optimistic young Irene told her. "I'll help all I can and we'll get along. The big thing is that we've got Grandma."

Then, a few days after the funeral, Mary's friend and benefactor, Mrs. Sharpley Thompson, owner of the town's leading dress shop, advised her to put in a claim against the estate. The whole town was talking, she said, about what was to be done with old Annie's fortune. No will had been found and Chuck Corley was claiming everything on the strength of the deeds he had and a bill of sale to everything else she owned.

But, said Mrs. Thompson, her good friends, Judge Shay and Nate Elsen, had told her Corley could not execute his deeds until the estate had gone through probate. "Everybody's filing claims, Dr. Reardon and the funeral home, all the people that Annie owes. You should put in a claim, too, Mary, for your mother for all those years Annie worked her so hard. You could get a lot of money out of it. Get yourself a lawyer. He'll tell you what to do."

"But I don't know any lawyers, and I don't have any money to hire one."

"Nate Elsen's a good lawyer, and he would take your case on a percentage deal, to be paid out of the money you get from the estate. If you want me to, I'll tell him to see you about it."

Mary agreed, and then, nodding toward old Liz, dozing in an overstuffed chair much too large for her, Mrs. Thompson asked how she was doing.

"She's so thin," Mary worried, "and she's afraid to eat all she wants. She's afraid I'll stop her, like Annie did. I have to coax her to eat more, even when she's still hungry. And she misses her little rocker. It was a chair she brought with her from Denver. It just fit her."

"Then why don't we go out there and get it?" asked the efficient Mrs. Sharpley Thompson.

"Do you suppose we could? Would they let us have it?"

"I don't see why not. Let's go as soon as you get this other business set up."

Elsen came to see Mary the next morning, agreed to take the case on a percentage, or contingency, basis, and advised her to have herself appointed her mother's guardian and put in a claim for $75,000. The attorney then offered to apply for the office of administrator of the estate if Mary requested that he do so.

Accompanied by Nate Elsen, Mary applied for guardianship that afternoon before the greying old county judge, Morgan Shay. Appointed and bonded, Mary was unhappy with the wording of her guardianship paper – "...Lizzie Knox, who is of the age of seventy-six years and is enfeebled by age and ill health.... Wherefore petitioner prays that the court make and enter its order determining that said Lizzie Knox is a person mentally incompetent."

Lizzie was not "mentally incompetent." It was only that she had been kept in hiding and told what to do for so long that she was no longer able to meet and talk with strangers nor to make decisions for herself.

On Elsen's advice, Mary also filed a petition to have the Corley deeds set aside, and "to see if there is an estate to be probated and, if so, that an administrator be appointed to protect the rights of the claimant, Mrs. Lizzie Knox, a mentally incompetent."

Judge Shay appointed Elsen administrator, ordered him to see to his bond for the office, and set June 30 for the court hearing to approve the appointment. And so began the long trail of "the Annie Cook estate" through the courts.

That afternoon, with a small trailer hooked on behind their car, Mary, her husband, Liz, Mrs. Thompson and Abbie Wonka drove out to the farm. Chuck Corley met them in the yard. With the help of the Comstocks, he said, he was very busy getting the place cleaned up and ready for the sale of Mrs. Cook's personal property. Was there something he could do for them?

"Yes," said Mrs. Sharpley Thompson. "There are a few things here that belong to Mrs. Knox. She would like to go in and get them."

Mrs. Thompson bought her cars from the Dodge agency and the company's head salesman was anxious to cooperate. "Of course," he said, "come right in and look around."

They drove away a little later with Lizzie's small rocker, a patented platform chair that rocked on little wheels, in their trailer. "I'm sure glad that's over," Abbie Wonka said when they were out of the lane. "That dirty old place gives me the creeps."

Chapter 68

Corley was a busy man, that June. Confident that his deeds and bill of sale would stand up in court against any claim crazy old Liz and her daughter could bring against the estate, he went ahead with his plans to claim and enjoy his wealth. Although he didn't yet know how much the estate was worth, he guessed it to be in the neighborhood of $50,000, a very satisfactory sum—as long as he didn't think about how he came by it.

Fixing on June 25 for his sale date, he put the Comstocks to work readying the personal property for the sale. While Lela washed, cleaned and dusted the contents of the two houses, Earl repaired the barnyard fences, cleaned up the long-time accumulation of weeds and trash, and put the contents of the old barn, chicken and brooder houses in shape to be sold.

Evenings and Sundays Corley drove out to the farm to go through drawers, cupboards and closets. Annie, it seemed, had never thrown anything away and the accumulation of more than half a century was overwhelming. The trash fires Earl tended smouldered day and night.

In the wide upstairs hallway of the bungalow they found five large trunks, each filled with bulky bundles wrapped in brown paper and tied with twine string, after the fashion of the 1920s and '30s. The bundles yielded sheets, towels and pillow slips, dozens of them, stacks of them, bought and charged to the county, back in the days of the poor farm when Annie regularly made all the January white sales.

In one of the upstairs closets they found Clara's many fine gowns, hanging limp and dusty from their supporting rod. Crepe de Chines, taffetas, satins, voiles and foulards, heavy with beads and braids, still flaunting their aged elegance.

And behind the row of dresses, pushed back under the sloping roof, they found dozens of pairs of women's shoes: high-topped lace and button shoes, oxfords, slippers with buckles and bows at their pointed toes. Each pair was still tied together, just as it came from the bargain table where Annie had picked it up for .98¢ or so.

"Poor old Annie," Lela said, holding up a pair of soft kid shoes with high tops and pointed toes. "Eighteen eyelets high, and she never wore them, never even had any of them on. What do you want me to do with 'em?"

"We'll put 'em out on a table," Corley decided. "Some of them will bring a dime or a quarter a pair, just for a curiosity. Stores haven't carried those high-topped things for years." From another of the long closets under the eaves they dragged more than a dozen forty-eight pound sacks of flour, paid for by the county and stored there since Annie had bought them for bread for the county poor. Mouldy now, and full of worms, the foul stuff was difficult to handle and dispose of.

The week before the sale Corley ran his sale bill in the *Telegraph*.

Public Auction
Wednesday, June 25th, 7:30 p.m.

9 miles west on Hi-way 30, 1 mile north, quarter mile west. Davenport and chairs, occasional chairs, 9 large rugs, throw rugs, two 3-piece bedroom suites, springs and mattresses, end tables, rockers, upright piano, china closet, two 8-piece dining room sets, drop-leaf table, library table, 5 large trunks, 12 dining room chairs, dressers, high boy chest, lamps, clothes dryer, radio, cooking utensils, pressure cookers, 6 ft. refrigerator, square tub Maytag washer, double burner oil heater, coal and wood range, Singer sewing machine, brooder equipment nests, feeders, etc., oil drums, garden tools, and lots of other items.

The personal effects of the late Mrs. Anna Cook.

L. E. Sage, Auctioneer.

It was all there, the fine furniture Annie and Clara, with Munson's help, had selected more than thirty years ago: the elegant plush davenport and chairs, the two 8-piece sets of expensive china, the imposing double burner oil heater for the parlor, Mary's prized old Maytag (Earl Comstock had kept it running until Annie turned her laundry over to Eileen Moore), Clara's piano, the handsome blue enamel and nickel-trim Windsor kitchen range.

When Corley drove into the farmyard on the evening before the sale, Comstock told him that Nate Elsen had sent a man out to get Annie's Dodge that day. "He had a court order for it, so I had to let it go."

"Never mind. I'll take care of that later," Corley said, berating himself for not having taken possession of the car sooner. He doubted if he could do anything about it now.

June 25th was a clear and pleasant day and "the personal effects of the late Mrs. Anna Cook" quite filled the cleaned and neatened farmyard that evening. By 7:30, when Joe arrived, cars lined the lane and overflowed onto both sides of the county road for a quarter mile in either direction, while a huge crowd milled and eddied among the furniture and "other effects."

There was nothing at the farm that Joe wanted. In the scars he carried on his person he had quite enough mementos of the old farm to last him the rest of his life. But he was curious to see what went on, and he wanted to watch Chuck Corley swaggering about as the new owner of the best farm in the valley.

It was a satisfaction to Joe to know how Corley had become the owner, and to imagine what would happen if he were to share his knowledge with the crowd here tonight. And it further gratified him to know that Corley feared that very thing.

Potential buyers were thickest around the long dining room table, heaped high with stacks of new bed linens and towels, and around the kitchen table from the old house, piled high with the bargain shoes that Annie had never worn. Joe remembered her so often coming home from town with a pair of new shoes, tied together by their strings, hanging over her arm. He had wondered why she bought them, or what she did with them, for he had never seen her wear anything but the felt slippers.

Inside the old kitchen he saw fortune hunters pulling up the last of the old linoleum, soggy as wet cardboard with age and wear, until the ancient board floor was bare. So far as he knew, no one had found so much as a thin dime.

The sale promptly got under way. The first items offered, the parlor furniture, rugs and rockers, sold quickly; for they were old and out of date and there were few bidders. The tables, cupboards and dressers, anything with a drawer in it, took longer, for there were many bidders, raising each other's bid a dollar a round at first, then fifty cents or a quarter as the totals mounted.

The lucky bidders, eager to learn exactly what they had bought, quickly paid for their purchases, then pulled out the drawers and examined them carefully, each hoping to find a secret compartment or hidden crevice that might still hold a forgotten cache of bills. Some of the furniture was almost destroyed before the new owners gave up the fruitless search. The mattresses fared even worse, being literally torn apart by their buyers, and the wreckage left to litter the yard.

By dark everything but the handsome Windsor range was sold. The auctioneer had been unable to coax a single bid for the big cook stove from the crowd; for the whole community had long since converted to gas, oil or electric cookery. The old range was left where it stood, at the far side of the yard, gradually to lose its elegance to the ravages of time and weather.

Adding up the proceeds of the sale in the old kitchen that night, Corley was well enough pleased with the total, $977.35, plus the $14.82 he had received for the 114 pounds of live chickens (the last of Annie's old laying hens) sold earlier to the Swift Produce Company.

He was doing all right, Corley told himself, except for the trouble at home, where his wife complained bitterly that he no longer talked to her about his business. But how could he? Except for the fortune that he now considered his, he would like to forget it himself.

Chapter 69

The day following the sale Corley had a long talk with his employer, Melvin Arnold. With Nate Elsen already in possession of Annie's car, and sure to be appointed administrator of her estate when the court convened on Monday, it was beginning to look as if the battle over the estate might be long and difficult.

"Get yourself a good lawyer," Arnold advised. "You can't do any better than Charlie Baxter. We'd better talk to him today."

The next day Arnold also filed a claim against the estate – for $5.60 for changing the oil in Annie's Dodge.

Although she seldom went anywhere in the red upholstered car after old Henry left, two weeks before her death Corley had offered to take her in to see her doctor, and to have the car serviced while he waited for her. Now he and Arnold congratulated themselves. The incident, so unimportant at the time, now proved invaluable in that it gave Arnold a legal right to have a part in the probate.

On June 30 Judge Shay confirmed the appointment of Nate Elsen as administrator of the Cook estate and ordered that all claims against it must be filed by October 23, or be forever barred.

In the weeks that followed the claims piled up. Most were routine, a few were surprising. Munson's Undertaking Parlor filed it's claim for the funeral in the amount of $897; St. Mary's Hospital submitted it's bill of $53.55 for two days in a private room, including x-ray, dressings, medicine and laboratory fees. Dr. Reardon's claim for his services came to $147.

The Comstock's filed a claim for $12,000 for work done for Anna Cook over a period of eighteen years. Then came old Karl Schmidt with his bill for $439.44 for the taxes he had paid for Annie in 1950, and Joe with a claim for $1,342.50, money he had sent home to Annie for the purchase of war bonds while he was in the army.

The North Platte Floral Company's claim for $3 for a pot of flowers, ordered by Annie the day before she broke her hip, explained the wilting carnations at the foot of the Cook gravestone on the day of her funeral. She had never before bothered to put flowers on Clara's or Frank's graves. Why had she done so this Memorial Day? Joe wondered.

On September 26 Arnold, "a creditor of the estate," through attorney Baxter filed an objection to Joe's claim on the grounds that it was outlawed, and asked that Administrator Elsen be instructed to file an inventory of the estate. Joe promptly filed another claim, for $30,000, for his "years of labor and services" performed for Annie on the farm.

With the approach of October the action speeded up. Elsen requested the court to set aside both Joe's claim for $1,342.50 and Corley's deeds. He also reported that he had on hand $955 from the sale of Annie's Dodge, and the sum of $1,375.63, received from Judge Shay—the contents of the strong box he had kept for Annie after the robbery. The Judge also reported that he had found in the strong box an unpaid note for $200, money loaned to Harvey and Eileen Moore in 1948.

The next day Arnold, "creditor of the estate," filed his objection to Joe's $30,000 claim and the Comstock's $12,000 claim on the grounds that paying them would leave the estate insolvent.

On October 10 Mary filed her claim for Lizzie Knox, a mentally incompetent, in the amount of $75,000. The following day Eileen Moore filed a modest claim for $817 for five hours of labor per week, at .50 an hour, from April, 1949, to April, 1952.

The probate opened on October 23 in the small county court room, to a standing room only crowd that overflowed into the hall. Interest in the case had run high all summer. There were many questions: How much was old Annie Cook really worth? Would Chuck Corley get it all? If he didn't, who would? Would the poor old sister Annie had worked so hard she went crazy get anything?

In the courtroom Mary and her mother sat at their table. Lizzie was neatly dressed; her dark, glossy hair, grown out to form a curly cap for her small head, had a striking narrow white streak from her right temple to the nape of her neck—a natural marking such as many women paid high prices to acquire in beauty parlors. She sat quietly in her chair, her back so bent that she had to tip her head far back to look directly at the court scene.

Joe was there with his attorney, Don Lowe; the Comstocks and the Moores with theirs. Corley, his usual trim, freshly barbered self, sat at another table with Mel Arnold and their attorney, Charles Baxter. Judge Morgan Shay presided and the probate got under way.

As if the case were not already murky enough, Arnold further muddied it by objecting to the claims of both Lizzie Knox and Eileen Moore on the grounds that all the claims now filed amounted to more than twice the value of the entire estate. Demanding that Elsen, as administrator, be instructed by the court to file objections to the claims, he went on to file an objection of his own to Elsen as administrator because he was also Mary's attorney and had advised with both Joe Cook and Mary in the pursuit of their claims, while at the same time petitioning the court to set aside the Corley deeds. As administrator, Baxter argued, Elsen could not represent both the estate and a claimant and should, therefore, be removed as administrator.

To the casual spectator it looked as if Melvin Arnold, a creditor of the estate, was very much afraid he would not be paid his $5.60.

The second day of the probate began with Elsen's objection to Mary Cauffman's $75,000 claim on behalf of her mother, and to the claims of Eileen Moore and the Comstocks. All other claims, he allowed, should be admitted and considered.

By the end of the day the hospital bill had been allowed in full, as was Arnold's $5.60 claim for the oil change. Also allowed was the Munson funeral bill for $879.90 and Karl Schmidt's claim for the $439.44 in taxes he had paid for Annie. The doctor's claim was allowed, except for $27 for treating Lizzie Knox's dog bites, which was deferred. North Platte Floral's claim for $3 was also deferred. And with that the tangled skein of the Anna Cook estate probate was continued until December 1, when a further attempt to unravel it would be essayed.

Up to this point attorney Elsen had "represented himself," as the *Telegraph* termed it, but after Arnold's strong objection to his representing Mary as well, he at once engaged the firm of Beatty, Clarke, Murphy and Morgan to represent him in setting aside the Corley deeds. At the same time he advised Mary to retain the firm as her attorneys, permitting him to step aside. Mary agreed, and the newest member of the firm, young Earl Morgan, thereafter spoke for her and her mother.

On December 1 Elsen replied to Arnold's demand that he be removed as administrator by showing that Lizzie Knox's claim to the estate had been filed by the firm of attorneys and that he, Elsen, in no way represented Mary and her mother. He then vigorously assailed Arnold's right to attack him as administrator of the estate because he, Arnold, was not a real "party in interest" in the proceedings.

Arnold was, Elsen charged, merely a "nominal party, lending his aid by reason of having a small and technical claim against the estate allowed in order to enable him to represent his employee, Corley, and help him deprive the estate of the land. Arnold's attorney, he said, was actually defending Corley's right to the deeds, as well as his own minuscule claim. He went on to accuse Arnold of having "gratuitously interfered and intermeddled therein, far beyond any financial interest which he has.

"You," the young attorney stated, glaring at Arnold, "are being used by Corley and his attorney for the purpose of embarrassing the litigation of this estate." The case was then continued until the spring term of court.

In March, 1953, Judge Shay dismissed Arnold's petition for Elsen's removal as administrator, whereupon Arnold and Baxter promptly filed an appeal to the District Court of Lincoln County. In May Joe's attorney, Don Lowe, brought his claim before the court. Arnold, with his attorney, was there to show that, if even Joe's first claim were allowed, it, with all the other claims so far approved by the court, would make the estate insolvent since, exclusive of the land, it amounted to only $2,330.63. There seemed grave danger that Arnold would not be able to collect all of his $5.60—until the court obligingly dismissed Joe's smaller claim on the grounds of no substantiating evidence and the statute of limitations.

In an accounting before the court on July 1, Elsen reported that Corley had sold Anna Cook's personal effects for a sum unknown to him, and that he had found thirteen heirs, the children of Annie's brothers and an older sister. He also requested that the estate (land) be appraised. The court appointed an appraiser, satisfactory to both sides, and then adjourned.

Chapter 70

It had now been well over a year since Annie's death and times were hard at Mary's house. The previous summer, when she had filed her mother's claim for $75,000 she had hoped for an early settlement of the estate and better times for herself and her family. There might even, she told her mother, be enough money to build a new house, one with a nice, large bedroom for Liz, in place of the very small one she had now. And old Liz, smiling and rocking contentedly in her little rocker, nodded agreement.

Liz was happy, these days. Mary's care and attention to her diet had put a little flesh on her bones, but not much. Good food and the privilege of eating all she wanted had come too late, as had the opportunity to be fitted with a set of teeth to replace those Annie had knocked out. Her gums were much too shrunken, the dentist said. There was nothing left to hold the teeth in place.

So Mary chopped and pureed her mother's food, bathed her daily and dressed her in clean garments. Irene shampooed and "styled" her cap of dark curls, highlighted by the silver streak running through it; and delighted her with little gifts of sparkling earrings for her small ears.

Lewis, unfailingly kind to her, visited with her and took her for rides in the car as long as he was able. Young Lewis, an ardent fisherman, caught catfish in the river north of town and brought them home to his beloved granny, and little Pearl played paper dolls for hours on end with the child-like old woman.

In April Lewis Cauffman died. His small insurance policy paid for his simple funeral—and not much else. Mary continued to work at her many jobs. She had two children to support and put through school and a mortgage to pay off. If ever her mother should get her money maybe she would not have to work so hard. Maybe she could stay home and give the enfeebled old woman the care and attention she needed and deserved.

In late July both Elsen, administrator, and Arnold, creditor, appeared in county court to oppose Joe's $30,000 claim against the estate. When, in August, the court dismissed the claim and a flurry of other court activity followed, Mary's hopes rose. The appraiser's report was heard and filed, showing that the land was worth approximately $41,000, making a total of more than $43,000, plus some rentals and crop sales, to be probated.

Then Eileen Moore, with her attorneys, came before the court to protect her claim for $817 for three years of washing and ironing done for Annie. Each week she had made the eighteen mile round trip from her home to the farm and she figured $1.26 per trip a fair charge.

Elsen, representing the estate, and Arnold, creditor, objected to the mileage. Through his attorney, Arnold showed that there had never been a written contract between Annie and Eileen Moore and, anyway, Mrs. Cook had given Mrs. Moore enough garden produce to pay for her gasoline, he claimed. Cut to $490.50, the claim was allowed.

The Comstocks, accompanied by their attorney, also came to court that August to hear their claim considered. The claim listed "cooking, sewing dresses for Annie and Liz, driving Annie to town, working in the gardens, orchard and fields, and carpentering, among the tasks performed for Mrs. Cook during the eighteen years preceding her death. The worth of their labors, they estimated, came to $12,000.

With Arnold and Charles Baxter present to argue and object on the grounds that the Comstocks had no written contract with Anna Cook, and that their claim was vague and not sufficiently specific, the court reduced it from $12,000 to $7,140, "a fair sum for the services performed."

The Comstocks immediately appealed the decision to the District Court, as did Joe the summary dismissal of his claim, thus pushing any settlement date well into the future. Once more Mary went home to carry on as best she could. Even yet, it seemed, old Annie's punishing hand was reaching out from the grave to make things hard for her.

In the summer of 1954 Virginia Corley filed for divorce from Charles Corley. He had once been a kind and loving husband and father, she stated in her appeal, but in the last five years he had become violent and abusive and was seldom at home. As head salesman for the Arnold Dodge Agency, she understood that he drew a good salary, and that he had since come into some extensive land holdings from which he enjoyed rents and profits. Therefore she was asking a substantial sum in alimony, and that he be restrained from entering her home in the future.

In October Virginia Corley was granted her divorce, custody of their two daughters and generous alimony and child support. In the loss of his home and family, after twenty years of marriage, Charles Corley made another large payment on his alliance with Annie Cook.

On June 21, 1955, more than three years after Annie's death, Liz and Mary's claim finally came on for trial in the county court. The long delay had served to whip up the fervor of interest inherent in the case. Perhaps now, after all the years, some answers to the mysteries surrounding Annie Cook and the old Poor Farm would be revealed. Once again the small courtroom and the wide hallway were packed with an absorbed audience.

Old Judge Shay had finally disqualified himself on the grounds that he was "too familiar with some of the personalities involved in the case and would not have been able to act without prejudice." M. M. Maupin, a long-time North Platte attorney and judge, took over the bench and the hearing got under way.

Nate Elsen was in his place; Mary and old Liz, with their attorney, were in theirs. Arnold, sided by Attorney Baxter was on hand to defend his claim of $5.60.

Witness Tells Of Whip
Brutality Charged In Claim For $75,000 Against Estate

were the headlines in the *Telegraph* following the first day's evidence.

"The late Anna Cook, who operated a Lincoln County Poor Farm at Nichols, regularly used a buggy whip on her sister and niece and once stabbed her niece in the side with a butcher knife, the niece charged...today as a hearing began on a $75,000 claim.

"The claim was filed against the estate by Mary Cauffman who alleges she is the duly appointed guardian of Lizzie Knox, a person mentally ill and an heir at law of the estate of Anna Cook, who died May 27, 1952.

"Mrs. Cauffman took the stand and testified that she went to the Cook farm when she was five years old and stayed until 1923. She said her mother went to the farm about 1905 and was there continuously until the death of Mrs. Cook. During that time, she testified, she and her mother worked from morning until night and received no compensation for their work.

"We did the daily housework, the farm chores, worked out in the fields, picked the fruit, took care of 150 ducks, 150 geese, 400 chickens, and never less than ten cows. We had to clean the manure out of the barn and clean the chicken pens. Lizzie and I did everything and all Anna did was give orders."

Mary testified that in numerous conversations with Anna the latter promised to make compensation for their work but never did. In 1923 she got the poor farm and the work mounted. "Whenever the work wasn't done just when she wanted it done, or if it wasn't just right, Anna would use the buggy whip on mom and I." Mrs. Cauffman told the court.

"I don't think a day passed that we didn't get whipped. Mom and I were really scared," she said.

In 1923 she said she left the farm for North Platte, following an argument with Anna. "She stabbed me in the side with a butcher knife. I still have the scar," she said.

She also testified that Frank Cook, husband of Anna, did the field work on the eighty-acre farm. He never slept in the house and never ate meals with Anna, she said. He slept in a beet shack in the winter and in the haymow in the summer.

"Joe Cook of North Platte testified that Mrs. Knox was never given any clothes except 'stuff outsiders gave to Anna.' He confirmed the testimony that Lizzie and Mary were forced to clean the barn and chicken houses, and had to work from 4 a.m. to 10 p.m. 'For a long time I thought Lizzie was a patient,' Joe Cook said. 'She was treated worse than some of the patients.'

"I saw Anna 'sic' the dogs onto Lizzie many times," he continued, "and it was strictly against the rules for Lizzie to eat with Anna. Company got fried chicken and we got the leftovers or took what Anna gave us."

On the second day of the hearing Eileen Moore, who testified that she did laundry for Mrs. Cook after 1946, said that "Lizzie was terribly mistreated, and that no family relationship existed between the sisters. Nobody would treat a sister like that," she said, and went on to tell that "Mrs. Cook had two dogs that were not house-broken. The dogs dirtied sacks and Mrs. Cook made her sister wash the sacks every day in cold water without soap."

Ed Kovanda, a neighboring farmer, told how he had once stopped Mrs. Cook from striking her sister with a stove poker. He had rented acreage from Mrs. Cook one year, he said, and on the basis of his observation of Mrs. Knox's work, he believed that a fair and reasonable salary would have been $1 an hour for an eight-hour day.

Joe Cook, called to the stand again that afternoon, gave the additional testimony that Mrs. Cook became "more and more worried about taking care of Lizzie Knox," and that she executed as many as fifteen property deeds and special agreements to provide for the care of her sister. "Every paper I ever saw mentioned Lizzie, and she was provided for in each of them." She made the deeds to different people, he explained, and her main concern seemed to be to provide for her sister. The last of such deeds, he testified, was made in favor of Charles Corley.

The next witness, Dr. S. A. Reardon, stated that he treated Mrs. Knox for dog bites at various times, and that "the last dog bite was quite severe." He said he had seen Mrs. Knox without shoes and shabbily clad, but that Mrs. Cook had definitely asked him, "two or three times," for suggestions about financially taking care of Lizzie in the future.

The final witness for the plaintiff was Nate Elsen, who testified that Judge Shay had given him certain papers relevant to the case, papers found when he opened Mrs. Cook's strong box. Explaining that the papers were copies of income tax returns filed by Mrs. Cook in 1948, 1949, 1950 and 1951, each listing Lizzie Knox as a dependent, he entered them as exhibits for the *defense*.

His next exhibit was a quit claim deed from Mrs. Cook to Judge Shay, signed by the deceased on July 17, 1948, covering both her farms. His last two exhibits were wills, made by Mrs. Cook and designating Judge Shay as beneficiary. One was dated September 7, 1948, and witnessed by Earl Brownfield (banker) and H. Van Doran, of Hershey. The second was dated April 3, 1951, and witnessed by a Dale Moore and a Bell Carpenter. Both left everything Mrs. Cook owned to the judge.

Elsen explained that he had entered the papers as exhibits because Joe Cook had testified that all the wills and deeds made by Mrs. Cook were accompanied by "agreements." There were no "agreements" with the wills made to Judge Shay, he stated emphatically.

During the entire hearing Baxter, on behalf of his client, Melvin Arnold, had repeatedly entered objections to the testimony of the witnesses for the plaintiff, thereby delaying and prolonging the proceedings. At one point Attorney Morgan, his patience wearing thin, objected to Baxter being present at all, citing as grounds that he had no valid interest in the claim being heard.

To prove his point he pulled $5.60 in bills and change from his pocket and offered it to the court "to pay Mr. Arnold's bill in full and thereby eliminate Mr. Baxter from the case." Judge Maupin, hiding a smile, disqualified the motion and the hearing limped on.

On Thursday Baxter argued for the defense of Arnold and his $5.60 claim. He called the only witness for the defense, Everett Elwood, who had farmed Anna Cook's north farm since 1946. Elwood stated that he had seen no abuse during the time he had known the sisters. He testified to making daily visits to the Cook home and to eating lunch with the two women. He had cleaned the chicken houses two or three times a year, he said, and no one else had cleaned them. He had picked the fruit for one-half of the crop, helped feed the chickens, and had done other chores about the place.

Baxter then took the floor to state the case for the defendant. His manner was both easy and contemptuous. He intended to make it plain to all that the claim of Lizzie Knox and her daughter was ridiculous and baseless.

"The $75,000 claim is for services rendered by Mrs. Knox during forty-six years with Mrs. Cook," he began smoothly, toying with his gold watch fob. "The petition claims that Mrs. Cook did not pay her sister for hard work on the farm. *Why should she pay her?* The relationship was a family matter, and Mrs. Knox was living with her sister, Anna Cook, because she was mentally retarded, and because she could not get out in the world and make a living for herself.

"As to Mrs. Knox doing drudgery work, as testified by witnesses for the plaintiff, that is pure bunk. The evidence hasn't proved that there was abuse by anybody. If there was brutality, why didn't the county officials take Lizzie Knox away from Anna? Let's get down to the *facts*. We know that Anna kept her sister for forty-seven years, and the witnesses have testified to only five or six instances of what they call brutality, and some of those were only inferences. The truth is that Mrs. Cook didn't have to keep her sister. But she did, and because she did her sister did not become a public charge.

"The doctor testified here that Mrs. Knox is mentally retarded. And the truth is that none of the other relatives — except Anna — would touch her," he concluded, with a dismissing gesture toward the bent little figure at the plaintiff's table.

Baxter then strongly criticized Attorney Morgan, the reporter for the *Telegraph* and the witnesses who had testified to "brutality" in the treatment of Mrs. Knox by Anna Cook. In his view they had all been extremely biased and unfair.

The hearing had been scheduled to end on Thursday afternoon with Attorney Morgan's closing statement for the plaintiff. But when Baxter finished his oration and, with a confident smile and nod to the judge, sat down, Morgan sprang to his feet, his face flushed with anger, and stated, "Your Honor, Attorney Charles Baxter's statement that there has been no evidence of brutal treatment of Mrs. Knox by Mrs. Cook must be answered."

"Very well. This hearing will continue tomorrow morning at ten o'clock for the purpose of hearing Attorney Earl Morgan's answer to Attorney Charles Baxter," the Judge said.

Still angry when court convened the next morning, Morgan demanded what more evidence of brutality the court needed than Joe Cook's evidence that he had *seen* Mrs. Cook sic savage dogs onto her sister, once even tearing off her clothes, or Dr. Reardon's testimony that he had *several times* treated Mrs. Knox for dog bites, "the last time quite severe?" And what about Ed Kovanda's testimony that he had once stopped Mrs. Cook from beating Mrs. Knox with a stove poker, or Mrs. Cauffman's testimony concerning daily lashings with a buggy whip? Didn't the court believe the neighbors when they testified to the hard work, shabby clothes and poor food, *leftovers*, that had been Lizzie's lot?

"Charles Baxter asks why, if such brutality prevailed, the neighbors and the county officials didn't take Lizzie Knox away from Anna? The reason was that the neighbors were *afraid* of Mrs. Cook. As for the county officials—Mrs. Cook was a scheming old woman. All of the deeds and wills she had made out to them, and to other people, were a part of her plan to get people to do favors for her on the promise that she would deed her property to them."

At the conclusion of Attorney Morgan's "reply" to Attorney Baxter, the hearing ended and the judge stated that he would take the case under advisement until September 28, 1955.

Chapter 71

Through the rest of that long, hard summer Mary worked many hours away from home and, with the help of Irene and eleven-year-old Pearl, cared for old Lizzie. Between appointments in her shop, Irene hurried across the yard to check on her grandmother, but it was the little girl who filled the gap, cheerfully waiting on the frail old woman, talking and giggling with her until she nodded off in a contented nap.

September 28 was the date of their next day in court, but Mary knew that it meant no relief for her. Even if her mother were awarded the balance of the estate, there would still be the matter of the Corley deeds to settle. With two children and a failing old mother to support, she wondered if she would be able to hang on until that day should come? If it ever did. Corley might still win the case.

Mary and Liz were in their places in the county courtroom, on that sunny September morning. Judge Maupin was on the bench and Nate Elsen at his table, smiling and kindly looking as always. At ten o'clock the judge began his memorandum opinion and Mary listened carefully. So much depended on what the court should decide today.

"In the beginning," the judge intoned, "this claim appeared to present difficult legal problems. However, after receipt of excellent memoranda furnished by all counsel involved, and some independent research on the part of the court in connection therewith, the difficulties of decision originally appearing to the court, with one exception, largely vanished. The court therefore makes the following finding of fact and legal conclusions therefrom.

"1. Lizzie Knox took up her residence with Anna Cook and her family about 1905 and remained on the Cook place until the death of Anna Cook on May 27, 1952.

"2. Lizzie Knox worked throughout the period of her stay there at difficult manual tasks common to farm labor, many of which are considered in the community as exclusively within the province of male labor. In later years, preceding the death of Anna Cook, these tasks were not as onerous as in earlier years, but to the extent that work remained to be done as directed by Anna Cook, such tasks were carried out by Lizzie Knox. These services rendered over the years by Lizzie Knox were of monetary value to Anna Cook throughout the years.

"3. The record contains no evidence of value of such services as were performed by Lizzie Knox prior to the early 1920s though there is reliable evidence of the extent and nature of Lizzie Knox's labors as early as 1910 and there is credible evidence concerning the value of these services from the year 1926 forward.

"The court being duly advised in the premises and upon consideration of the record and the evidence finds generally for the claimant and against the administrator and finds that the administrator of said estate is indebted to the claimant, Lizzie Knox, for services rendered by said Lizzie Knox to said Anna Cook in the amount of $32,450, no part of which has been paid and that claimant is entitled to recover said amount from the administrator of said estate.

"WHEREFORE IT IS HEREBY ORDERED, ADJUDGED AND DECREED BY THE COURT that the claimant's claim be and the same is hereby allowed."

Mary let out her breath in a long sigh of relief. A figure had finally been named and, to her, $32,000 was a goodly sum of money. It would certainly make things easier for her and provide a few luxuries for old Liz.

The "one exception," she learned, had been determining the amount to be paid Lizzie Knox for her years of hard labor for her sister. It had finally been settled by allowing $700 per year for the 46 years, 4 months and 26 days Lizzie had worked for Anna.

The following week Administrator Elsen filed his appeal from Judge Maupin's decision with "objections thereto of the administrator and of Melvin Arnold, claimant." Mary found it hard to believe. Three years ago Nate Elsen had been *her* attorney, determined to help her gain control of Anna Cook's estate in her mother's name and for her use. Now he seemed to have gone over to the other side and to be just as determined to cut her down to a pittance if he could. It could be years before the estate was settled and *anyone got any money.*

Mary looked sadly at her mother. In spite of nutritious food, vitamins and loving care, the old woman had grown frailer, nearer to the point of needing round-the-clock care. If the money didn't come soon it would be too late for Liz.

Near the 2nd of December the hearing to set aside the Corley deeds came on. Mary and her attorney were present but old Liz's chair was empty. She was no longer able to leave the house. Administrator Elsen was at his table and a Lexington attorney was on hand to represent the thirteen absent heirs. Charles Corley, trim and confident, sat beside his new attorney, a highly reputable criminal lawyer from Ogallala and, of course, the ubiquitous Mel Arnold and Charles Baxter were there.

The plaintiffs, Mary Cauffman on behalf of Lizzie Knox, and Administrator Nate Elsen, charged that Charles Corley had, "by the practice of undue influence over the mind and person of Anna Cook," induced her to deed him the property, and that, for two or three years previous to Anna Cook's death he had "commenced a course of visitation to her home," and that he had so ingratiated himself with the old woman that she had been willing to deed him all her property. He did this, Elsen declared, "after telling Annie he would care for her property and hold it in trust for her mentally incompetent sister, Lizzie Knox."

The plaintiffs further charged that Corley had collected all rents and profits from the land since the death of Anna Cook and had spent and dissipated the same, and that he had further complicated the case by mortgaging a portion of the land. Without the land the remainder of the estate would not be nearly enough to cover the claims which the court had already allowed.

Finally, the claimants asked that a receiver be appointed to take charge of the land and its future receipts until settlement of the case was accomplished, and that Corley be requested to repay all monies he had so far received from the estate.

In reply to the charges, defendant Corley asked the court to require the plaintiffs to set forth "the specific acts of undue influence, fraud and coercion alleged to have been performed by him which had induced Anna Cook to execute the warranty deeds" which he now held. The fact was, he testified, Mrs. Cook had deeded her property to him only in "consideration of past services and kind acts" performed by him.

The court took the matter under advisement until a later date.

On a cold January forenoon, two weeks after the hearing, Mary came home from cleaning motel rooms to find her mother in tears. She had tried to get to the bathroom in time, the little old woman sobbed, but she hadn't made it and everything was a mess. Irene, wrapping a permanent that morning, hadn't been able to leave the shop, and Pearl was in school.

Mary spent the afternoon on the telephone, resigning from all her tasks away from home, and soliciting laundry customers. By evening she was back to "taking in washing," and had all the work she could handle. She could do the laundry in her little wash house a few steps from her back door, and the ironing in her kitchen or living room, and so be with her mother day and night.

In her bed that night Mary had the overpowering feeling that Annie's cruel hand was even yet reaching out from the grave to prevent her money from ever being of any help to her or Liz.

Times had been hard for a long while. They would be even leaner now. Her children didn't ask for much, but now she would have to refuse them even that. Poor old Liz asked for nothing, but a little extra money would have made it possible for her to buy the out-of-season fruit the frail old woman loved, or the electric heating pad that would have made her nights more comfortable.

Early in April Nate Elsen came to Mary with an offer to settle her claim for $12,000. If she would accept his offer, he said, he would dismiss his appeal to District Court for the purpose of reducing the $32,450 awarded her in County Court, back in September. There was a good chance, he told her, that she might have the $12,000 right away.

The estate had now been in litigation for four years and Mary, desperate for money to care for her family, agreed to accept his offer. Two weeks later the court approved the agreement and ordered that "Lizzie Knox recover from the estate of Anna Cook, deceased, the sum of $12,000 with interest at six percent from this date."

Chapter 72

That first day in court was rough on Charles Corley. Interest in the case ran high and the big room was well filled with spectators, curious citizens who had waited a long time to see how "the Annie Cook case" came out.

Following the conclusion of the probate hearing in June, Joe left for Oklahoma. His marriage to Elena seemed to be breaking up and home life was no longer pleasant. He had long wanted to see the Sooner state and now seemed a good time to do it. However, there was still the matter of Chuck Corley and his deeds.

According to the docket the case would not come to trial in District Court until June of 1956, time enough to explore Oklahoma and consider what to do about his marriage. To insure that he would be back in North Platte in time for the Corley trial, he arranged with his friend, Dan Sanchez, the court reporter, to let him know when to return.

A year later, on receipt of notification that the trial would begin on June 24, Joe headed home. Back in North Platte Sanchez told him the first day of the trial would be taken up with the charges and with testimony before a jury, and that the case was scheduled to go to the jury on the morning of the 25th. Joe planned to be on hand for that part of the proceedings.

Up front Judge John Kuns was on the bench; Nate Elsen, plaintiff, veteran of many appearances in the long-running litigation, with his attorney, Earl Morgan, was there.

Opposing him was Corley, with his council, the commanding John McGinley of Ogallala. Virginia Corley, a defendant and cross-petitioner, was represented by Attorney Horace Crosby of North Platte. Mary Cauffman, though she had no part in the proceedings that day, was present to see how it turned out.

The charge, as set forth at length by Morgan, stated that the conveyances (deeds) to the land in question were procured by Charles Corley from Anna Cook by the exercise of fraud, coercion and undue influence. Furthermore, Morgan charged, Corley's filing of his deeds at the courthouse within hours of Anna Cook's death suggested "that they were made in contemplation of her death," and that they should be set aside and all of the property of the deceased be subject to the payment of just debts against the estate.

The defendant, spruce and confident at the beginning of the session, lost much of his assurance and visibly wilted as the day wore on. The barrage of questions hurled at him by Morgan were searching and embarrassing. The court wanted to know, in intimate detail, a great deal about the years of his association with Anna Cook.

But, all in all, at the end of the day Corley thought he had done well, parrying the most pointed questions, answering others with protestations of his sympathy for the old lady, who had no one else to turn to. His overall desire, he insisted, had been to assist her and set her mind at rest in regard to the care of her feeble-minded sister, should she outlive her.

When questioned as to what he had done for the sister, Mrs. Knox, with the funds he had appropriated from the sale of the personal property, and the rents he had collected, he admitted that he had done nothing. "I saw no reason to do anything," he declared. "Her daughter had taken her from Annie's home into her own home and I saw no reason to interfere."

At 4:30 Judge Kuns dismissed the court and the jury for the day, to reconvene at ten o'clock the next morning.

Wearing a well-fitting, expensive new suit, Corley strode into the courtroom, his confidence fully restored. The jury, the administrator and all the attorneys were in their places. Mary, after ironing far into the night, was also present. The judge made his entrance and took his seat. The case was ready to continue to its anticipated speedy end, when the judge would make his charge to the jury and send it out to make its decision.

With the scene all set, Joe stepped into the courtroom, stopped in full view of the dapper defendant, and looked steadily across the room at him. Corley's face paled and his eyes bugged. Then, his shoulders suddenly sagging, he leaned slowly to his attorney and whispered something to him. While utter quiet settled over the big room, McGinley sat for a moment, his face a puzzled study, before asking if he might approach the bench.

After a brief, low-voiced conference the judge, also looking puzzled, dismissed the jury and called for a conference of Corley, Elsen and their attorneys in his chambers. Corley, it seemed, had changed his mind. He no longer wished to press his case; instead, he said, he was willing to settle out of court. The sum agreed upon was $2,500, for which Corley would sign away all claims to the land.

Joe was well satisfied with the outcome of his plan. It had turned out exactly as he had hoped. By showing up at the right moment in time he had forced Corley to withdraw his claim. He had counted on the fact that, greedy though the man was, he would not dare face the testimony Joe could have brought against him in proof of "coercion and undue influence." The little decency and pride Corley had left dictated that he owed his young daughters and their mother, who bore his name, the right not to be thoroughly ashamed of that name.

The deeds voided and set aside, Elsen immediately petitioned the court for permission to sell the Cook farm and settle the estate. Mary braced herself to wait a while longer.

Early in September the district courtroom filled again as Administrator Elsen prepared to make his report on the sale of the home Eighty and the distribution of the receipts. Present were Mary and Corley, with their attorneys, and Horace Crosby, representing Virginia Corley. Joe was there as an interested spectator and, of course, Melvin Arnold with Baxter at his elbow.

The genial Nate Elsen reported that he had sold the original Eighty for $25,800 but that there was still corn on the land from the crop of 1955, title to which was in dispute between the estate and others; and that, in an action pending in the court, judgement had been entered in favor of defendant Corley against Mary Cauffman, guardian of Lizzie Knox, plaintiff, in the sum of $2,500 in the form of a lien against the land. The administrator's request that he be authorized to discharge the lien by payment of that amount was granted by the judge and the court dismissed.

As the room emptied into the hall, Joe held a brief conversation with John McGinley and Robert Crosby. Their answers to his questions pleased him. Of the $2,500 awarded Charles Corley that day, $1,000 would go to McGinley for his services, the other $1,500 to Virginia Corley.

"I don't know just what you did, but you sure fixed Chuck Corley's clock," Crosby told Joe, patting him on the arm. On his way to the stairs Joe passed Corley, Arnold and Baxter. Grinning, he gave them an airy wave of his hand. None of the three returned his salute.

Chapter 73

Had Annie Cook actually spent the last winter of her life planning, in the dark recesses of her twisted mind (and there were some who suspected that she had), to leave behind her confusion, perplexity, chaos, turmoil and endless delays, she could have done no better than the actual state of affairs that had confronted all those involved since the day of her death. In the more than four years that had passed, not a cent had been paid by the court to anyone, and not a move could be made without first petitioning the court, a status quo designed to drive the litigants mad with frustration.

Following the appointment of the receiver, the neighbor-renters farming the Cook place had not been able to apply fertilizer to the land, nor make needed repairs, without first petitioning the court. And, after the crop was harvested, it could not be sold until the court permitted and approved the sale.

The Monday following the settlement with Corley, Mary, worn to the breaking point, went to Nate Elsen's office. She could go on no longer without help, she told him. She reminded him that she had agreed, months ago, to settle for a pittance of the amount for which he had advised her to sue in 1952, and to which she believed her mother was entitled; and that, though $12,000 had been awarded her mother by the court six months ago, not a dime had yet been paid to her for the support and care of Lizzie Knox. Unless something was done soon, she concluded wearily, she would lose her home to the mortgage and she, her mother and her two young children would have to "go on the county."

Elsen reduced her plea to legalese and summed it up in an application to the court that read, "Comes now Mary Cauffman and shows to the court as follows: That on June 2, 1952, she was appointed guardian of Lizzie Knox, her mother, and duly qualified to act as such guardian. That Lizzie Knox is now seventy-nine years of age; that more than forty years prior to May 28, 1952 Lizzie Knox had been residing with Anna Cook; that by virtue of hard physical labor, mistreatment, abuse, and lack of necessaries (food), the physical and mental well-being of Lizzie Knox was practically destroyed. That on May 27, 1952 Anna Cook died and Mary Cauffman immediately took Lizzie Knox into her home; that at that time she (Mary Cauffman) was not and is not now financially able to properly care for her wants and needs and supply her with necessary medicines and drugs; that at the time Lizzie Knox came into the home of the petitioner she was wholly without any clothing and shoes whatsoever; that she was debilitated, suffering from malnutrition and in a very weakened condition; that your petitioner expended for the benefits of Lizzie Knox the sum of $50 for vitamins, medicines and drugs; that in addition it was necessary to purchase underclothing, dresses, shoes and the like in the sum of $100, all of which are items properly chargeable to the assets of the estate of Lizzie Knox.

"Your petitioner further shows to the court that Lizzie Knox does not have full and complete control over her bodily functions; that her condition is such that she is required to have constant care and supervision; and that your petitioner, the daughter of Lizzie Knox and her sole and only heir at law, is interested in her happiness and welfare, but that she is not financially able to supply all the wants and needs of Lizzie Knox out of her own limited income; and has been required to support herself and family, in addition to Lizzie Knox, by taking in washing.

"WHEREFORE petitioner prays the court to enter an order authorizing the guardian of Lizzie Knox (Mary) to pay to Mary Cauffman (herself) the sum of $150 for expenses heretofore incurred on behalf of Lizzie Knox and further that the court enter an order directing an allowance be made for the care, support and maintenance of Lizzie Knox in the amount of $150 per month."

Chapter 74

With the Corley deeds safely set aside it seemed that the Cook estate might now be settled. Elsen reported the sale of the north Eighty and the court authorized the payment of all duly considered claims against the estate. Four years and four months after the first appearance of the murky case in the county court Annie's bills were paid: The sum of $439.44 to old Karl Schmidt, and $147 to Dr. S. A. Reardon, including the $27 he had charged for treating old Lizzie's dog bites; $879.34 to the Munson Funeral Home; and $3 to North Platte Floral for the pot of flowers that had wilted at the Cook graves years ago.

For all her hours of washing and ironing, for all her trips to the Cook farm, for the $200 note she had paid twice, Eileen Moore received $285.23. The Comstocks, after fighting their $12,000 claim all the way through the State Supreme Court, were paid a total of $6,130. As for Melvin Arnold and his $5.60 claim; it had served him well through a dozen or more court sessions and he now generously assigned it to Charles Corley, "to be used as he sees fit." Corley claimed it from the estate. It was all he was to receive of the fortune he had once expected to own.

Old Liz's claim, too, was paid and the sum of $12,000, with interest, but less $4,147.33, the attorney's share, was deposited in the name of Mary Cauffman, guardian—to be expended as needed, *and as approved by the court*, for the care of Lizzie Knox, a mentally incompetent.

There now remained some $16,000 in the estate. From this sum the administrator would be paid for his four years on the case and the remaining court costs and fees would be settled. The remainder was to be divided among the heirs, old Liz and the thirteen nieces and nephews.

And then, on September 21, 1956 Joseph Martin Cook, as the grandson of Anna Cook, filed his claim to the entire sum. Joe felt that his action was justified. Old Liz had gotten almost all she was to have from the estate and he would not be hurting her; the other debtors and the various lawyers had all been paid. Only he, Joe Cook, who had, through no fault of his own, been compelled to give Annie Cook sixteen years of his life, had received almost nothing including enough to eat, decent clothing and an adequate education.

He had little hope of proving his claim as Anna Cook's heir, and in his own mind he did not believe he was her grandson. But there was always the possibility that, by getting his case in court and made public, he might find out who he really was. To Joe that knowledge would be worth far more than $16,000.

The case came on for hearing on October 15, 1956 with Joe and his attorney, Don Lowe; and Elsen and his attorney, Earl Morgan, on opposing sides. Joe had five witnesses, neighbors, men and women who had known him as far back as he could remember and who believed that he was Annie Cook's grandson.

They testified that Joe had grown up on the Cook farm, that Anna Cook had always claimed that he was Clara's son, that he had been enrolled in school and listed on census returns as such, and that Annie had always claimed him as her dependent grandson on her income tax returns.

As he had expected, the court denied his claim, but offered, on behalf of the legitimate heirs, to pay him $2,200 to withdraw all claim to the estate and sign an affidavit to that effect. Satisfied, Joe accepted the offer and was disappointed only in the fact that no one had come forward to claim him, or to tell him anything about his roots or where he came from.

With the regular payment of her allowance from the estate, Mary was able to give up a few of her laundry customers and spend more time with old Liz and her children. For a little while every afternoon she visited with her mother. Not at her ironing board, with her iron in her hand, and not with a pile of patching and mending (which she hated) in her lap, but just sitting and visiting.

While Liz rocked contentedly, the little wheels of her rocker clacking softly on their platform, the two women talked of many things. Mostly of the years they had lived apart, sometimes of the old days on the farm when Mary was growing up and they lived in fear of Annie and her whip. "Remember," Liz said one day, "remember how you used to have to rub Annie's feet of an evening, and how you learned to crochet just by watching her?"

"I remember. And how long it was before I got hold of a crochet hook, and then I sneaked a ball of twine string out of the kitchen to learn with, but there was hardly ever any time to crochet. And there hasn't been much time since. I've always been too busy taking care of kids and sick folks, working for other people."

Mary fell silent for a moment, while old Liz rocked and smiled, and then she said, "Mom, I could be crocheting right now. I'll get a hook and thread and I'll crochet while we talk."

On a later afternoon, when her mother did not feel well enough to get up, Mary sat beside her bed, her crochet hook flying over the lace edging in her fingers. Breaking a brief silence, Liz said suddenly, "Mary, you remember how it is out at the graveyard? Annie always said there's room for four graves in her place there. She buried Clara in one, and Frank in one, and she's buried in one. There is one more place. She always told me that one was for me, but Mary, I don't want to be buried there. Please, Mary, not beside Annie."

Mary dropped her crocheting and reached for her mother's hand. "Don't you worry, Mom. You won't have to be buried beside Annie. We'll get you another place, and that is a promise."

In the spring of 1957, five years after Annie's death, the court made its final settlement of her estate, the once fabled fortune on which so many dreams had been built. Mary was in court, that 20th day of May, and Nate Elsen and a Lexington attorney, representing the other thirteen heirs.

The Comstocks, the Moores, Judge Shay, Thad Long, Charles Corley, the county officials, none of the people who had trusted in the old woman's promises and in the deeds made out in their names, were there to hear that final settlement, or witness the apportionment of the remainder of the estate.

First to be paid was the administrator's fee, $4,000, then all remaining fees and court costs. Old Liz's share was $2,798.96, of which the court directed that one-third be paid to her attorney before the residue could be placed in Mary's guardianship account. The baker's dozen of other heirs received a few hundred dollars apiece, and when that was done Nate Elsen declared his duties as administrator ended and asked that he be discharged from his post.

Studying the final figures, Mary at last understood why Elsen had fought so hard to cut down the claims of those who had done the really hard labor on Annie Cook's behalf. Had the original claims of Lizzie Knox, Joe Cook, the Comstocks and the Moores been allowed there would have been little money left for the fat fee of the administrator.

Old Lizzie died quietly in her sleep on September 9, 1958. Her hold on life had been tenuous, those last few months, and several times she had reminded Mary of her promise not to bury her in the vacant place beside Annie.

Mary's eldest son, Will Dauphin, helped his mother keep her promise. He owned a four-place plot in the North Platte cemetery and was willing to have his grandmother laid to rest in one of them.

Back in court again to settle her mother's affairs, Mary found that she must now exchange her guardianship of the person of Lizzie Knox, mentally incompetent, for that of administratrix of the estate of Lizzie Knox, deceased. From now on she would not again see those detested words, "mentally incompetent," following her mother's name.

In January, 1959 Mary completed her duties and reported all bills incurred in the name of Lizzie Knox paid. In return the court placed in her hands a check for the sum of $2,867.98, free and clear. All that she was ever to receive in payment for her own hard years of servitude.

With her weary, tear-filled eyes on the check, Mary thought of all the dreams and plans that had been built on Annie Cook's wealth. The Comstocks and the Moores, good people, had planned to live out their lives on their respective Eighties. Numerous county officials had dreamed of what they could do when they came into possession of those same Eighties. Charles Corley had confidently expected to use them as a springboard to wealth and prominence. She, herself, had once drawn plans for a new house, with a special room for old Liz.

Not a single plan or dream had come to be. All had shrunk to this, the paltry sum of the check she held in her worn old fingers, the scanty remains of an evil obsession.

Epilogue

After her mother's death in 1958, Mary lived on in the home she had shared with her second husband, Lewis Cauffman, paid off the mortgage and put her youngest daughter, Pearl, through high school. In 1961 she married for the third time. This marriage, to a kindly German widower, lasted twenty-five years and was a relatively easy time for Mary. In addition to caring for her husband and her home, she continued to work, turning out snow white gowns, sheets and towels for the doctors, dentists and motel owners who depended on her expert work.

Finally, in her seventieth year, her family prevailed upon her to give up her laundry business and "take it easy." It was then that the Gypsy fortune teller's long ago prediction of a "nice, easy life" for Mary began to come true. At last, after all the years of caring for children, and for the sick and aged, all the years of labor to keep food on the table and pay off the mortgage, she had time to read and crochet as much as she wanted to.

During the next fifteen years she crocheted scores of gay, colorful wool afghans and hundreds of fancy hot pan holders for her family and friends. And when her flying fingers tired she turned to her beloved books and magazines.

Then, one afternoon, a woman came to her door, introduced herself and asked if she might talk to her about Annie Cook. "Oh no, *no*," she cried as all the old paralyzing fear and pain surged up within her. "I can't talk about it. *I don't even want to think about it*."

"I'm sorry," the woman said, "I'm really sorry I bothered you. I need to know about it and I hoped you would tell me. Forgive me." She turned away and walked toward her car. Mary watched her until she reached the end of the walk, then suddenly called out, "Come back. I'll tell you what you want to know."

All that afternoon Mary talked. All the old fear and pain and despair poured out of her in a flood of words, a veritable catharsis of long pent up emotions. When her visitor left she felt cleansed, relieved, serene.

Upon the death of her husband in 1986, Mary's children decided she should live with Pearl in her pleasant home in Omaha. Pearl, who fancied antiques, moved her grandmother Lizzie's little platform rocker and the treasured old clock that had come from Russia with her great grandmother, to Omaha with Mary. A year later Mary, too, passed quietly away. Her family brought her back to North Platte and buried her beside Lewis Cauffman.

After the ending of his first marriage, Joe Cook married a second time and raised a family of five children. Two of his daughters became foreign missionaries; a circumstance that caused him to wonder if, that long ago day in Kansas City when the baby in the hospital room next to his had died, his own life had been preserved for that very reason — that he might rear two daughters who would carry on the Lord's work in needy fields.

After their children were grown, Joe and his wife dissolved their marriage and he, too, married a third time, the widow of his old friend and mentor, Lester McConnell. The couple are now living out their retirement years in a pleasant home in Independence, Missouri.

Of Anna Cook's family, the only other living person intimately associated with this story is Irene Dauphine, Mary's older daughter. She and her husband, O. J. Cotton, are retired on a small acreage where they indulge their love of landscaping and gardening. Irene, who inherited her grandmother Lizzie's love for animals, lavishes her affections on her goats, turkeys and "banty hens." Even yet, after all the years, her fear of her great-aunt Annie shows in her voice and eyes when she speaks of her. A fear, she admits that will be with her always.